GOD AND GOVERNMENT

McGILL-QUEEN'S STUDIES IN THE HISTORY OF IDEAS
Series Editor: Philip J. Cercone

1 Problems of Cartesianism
Edited by Thomas M. Lennon, John M. Nicholas, and John W. Davis

2 The Development of the Idea of History in Antiquity
Gerald A. Press

3 Claude Buffier and Thomas Reid: Two Common-Sense Philosophers
Louise Marcil-Lacoste

4 Schiller, Hegel, and Marx: State, Society, and the Aesthetic Ideal of Ancient Greece
Philip J. Kain

5 John Case and Aristotelianism in Renaissance England
Charles B. Schmitt

6 Beyond Liberty and Property: The Process of Self-Recognition in Eighteenth-Century Political Thought
J.A.W. Gunn

7 John Toland: His Methods, Manners, and Mind
Stephen H. Daniel

8 Coleridge and the Inspired Word
Anthony John Harding

9 The Jena System, 1804–5: Logic and Metaphysics
G.W.F. Hegel
Translation edited by John W. Burbidge and George di Giovanni
Introduction and notes by H.S. Harris

10 Consent, Coercion, and Limit: The Medieval Origins of Parliamentary Democracy
Arthur P. Monahan

11 Scottish Common Sense in Germany, 1768–1800: A Contribution to the History of Critical Philosophy
Manfred Kuehn

12 Paine and Cobbett: The Transatlantic Connection
David A. Wilson

13 Descartes and the Enlightenment
Peter A. Schouls

14 Greek Scepticism: Anti-Realist Trends in Ancient Thought
Leo Groarke

15 The Irony of Theology and the Nature of Religious Thought
Donald Wiebe

16 Form and Transformation: A Study in the Philosophy of Plotinus
Frederic M. Schroeder

17 From Personal Duties towards Personal Rights: Late Medieval and Early Modern Political Thought, c. 1300–c. 1650
Arthur P. Monahan

18 The Main Philosophical Writings and the Novel *Allwill*
Friedrich Heinrich Jacobi
Translated and edited by George di Giovanni

38 The Invention of Journalism Ethics: The Path to Objectivity and Beyond, Second Edition
Stephen J.A. Ward

39 The Recovery of Wonder: The New Freedom and the Asceticism of Power
Kenneth L. Schmitz

40 Reason and Self-Enactment in History and Politics: Themes and Voices of Modernity
F.M. Barnard

41 The More Moderate Side of Joseph de Maistre: Views on Political Liberty and Political Economy
Cara Camcastle

42 Democratic Society and Human Needs
Jeff Noonan

43 The Circle of Rights Expands: Modern Political Thought after the Reformation, 1521 (Luther) to 1762 (Rousseau)
Arthur P. Monahan

44 The Canadian Founding: John Locke and Parliament
Janet Ajzenstat

45 Finding Freedom: Hegel's Philosophy and the Emancipation of Women
Sara MacDonald

46 When the French Tried to Be British: Party, Opposition, and the Quest for Civil Disagreement, 1814–1848
J.A.W. Gunn

47 Under Conrad's Eyes: The Novel as Criticism
Michael John DiSanto

48 Media, Memory, and the First World War
David Williams

49 An Aristotelian Account of Induction: Creating Something from Nothing
Louis Groarke

50 Social and Political Bonds: A Mosaic of Contrast and Convergence
F.M. Barnard

51 Archives and the Event of God: The Impact of Michel Foucault on Philosophical Theology
David Galston

52 Between the Queen and the Cabby: Olympe de Gouges's Rights of Women
John R. Cole

53 Nature and Nurture in French Social Sciences, 1859–1914 and Beyond
Martin S. Staum

54 Public Passion: Rethinking the Grounds for Political Justice
Rebecca Kingston

55 Rethinking the Political: The Sacred, Aesthetic Politics, and the Collège de Sociologie
Simonetta Falasca-Zamponi

GOD AND GOVERNMENT

Martin Luther's Political Thought

Jarrett A. Carty

McGill-Queen's University Press
Montreal & Kingston • London • Chicago

ISBN 978-0-7735-5150-3 (cloth)
ISBN 978-0-7735-5151-0 (paper)
ISBN 978-0-7735-5197-8 (ePDF)
ISBN 978-0-7735-5198-5 (ePUB)

Legal deposit fourth quarter 2017
Bibliothèque nationale du Québec

Printed in Canada on acid-free paper that is 100% ancient forest free (100% post-consumer recycled), processed chlorine free

This book has been published with the help of a grant from Concordia University's Aid to Research Related Events (ARRE) Program. Funding was also received from the Liberal Arts College, Faculty of Arts and Science, Concordia University.

McGill-Queen's University Press acknowledges the support of the Canada Council for the Arts for our publishing program. We also acknowledge the financial support of the Government of Canada through the Canada Book Fund for our publishing activities.

Library and Archives Canada Cataloguing in Publication

Carty, Jarrett A., 1975–, author
God and government: Martin Luther's political thought / Jarrett A. Carty.

(McGill-Queen's studies in the history of ideas; 73)
Includes bibliographical references and index.
Issued in print and electronic formats.
ISBN 978-0-7735-5150-3 (cloth). – ISBN 978-0-7735-5151-0 (paper). – ISBN 978-0-7735-5197-8 (ePDF). – ISBN 978-0-7735-5198-5 (ePUB)

1. Luther, Martin, 1483–1546 – Political and social views. 2. Political science – History – 16th century. I. Title. II. Series: McGill-Queen's studies in the history of ideas; 73

BR333.5.P6C37 2017 284.1092 C2017-903626-2
C2017-903627-0

This book was typeset by Marquis Interscript in 10.5/13 New Baskerville.

To my dear wife,
Nikki Alexis

Contents

Acknowledgments

To paraphrase Sir Isaac Newton, if this work has seen further into its subject, it is because I have stood on the shoulders of giants. Although this book is not *The Principia*, and its subject matter is far from being the foundation of classical physics, I am, in a very little way, like the great Newton, for I am heavily indebted to the towering scholars on Luther, the Reformation, the history of political theory, theology, and philosophy that I have relied upon for guidance in my own study and am grateful for the countless hours of intellectual pleasure they have given me.

This book is a natural succession to my previously published anthology of Luther's political writings, *Divine Kingdom, Holy Order*, in that it is a full analysis of the works that I introduce in that volume. The anthology contains most of Luther's works that I focus on in this book; therefore, this book coheres with the anthology as an extension of that same project. Accordingly, I thank Concordia Publishing House (St Louis, Missouri) for helping propel this book by their confidence in the earlier project.

From the first submission of my manuscript, it has been a great pleasure to work with McGill-Queen's University Press. I have been so ably and professionally led by my editor, Jacqueline Mason, and I am very grateful for her help. I wish to also acknowledge Kathleen Kearns, who took the reins when Jacqueline left for maternity leave. I must also thank the anonymous reviewers whom the press secured for my benefit. Their very careful reviews considerably strengthened my arguments and analysis; their astute reading and generous assistance served the manuscript very well.

Two people deserve special thanks in regard to the development of my early drafts: Jeremy Horsefield and Michael Zuckert. Jeremy professionally edited the entire text when I passed it on to him in a fairly rough draft form – and yet still, in keeping with his character, remained my friend. Michael read an early version of the manuscript from start to finish and gave extensive notes and constructive criticisms – all of this generosity coming a decade after I had finished being his graduate student at the University of Notre Dame. He is a model scholar and teacher.

I wish to express my gratitude to all of my friends in academia who have encouraged me and helped in some way to keep this project going, especially Geoff Kellow at Carleton University, Ottawa, and Travis Smith, Paul Allen, and Matthew Anderson at Concordia University in Montreal. Hearty thanks are due to the faculty and staff of the Liberal Arts College at Concordia; I have been blessed to be part of this delightful group of scholars, teachers, and friends. Particular thanks are due to Fred Krantz, the senior mentor of us all. I am happy to say that I have finally followed through on his command to get this manuscript done. The final recognition in this vein is due to the students of the college, who keep my mind fresh with their questions and insights in every class that I teach.

Finally, I thank my family. I have been blessed with great parents, Patrick and Carol, who have always loved and supported me, and my sister Paula and brother-in-law Rob, who are there for me at a moment's notice. My daughters, Hannah and Olivia, are too young to read this acknowledgment, but I should thank them, too, for being the delights of my life (and for, incidentally, teaching me to focus and work when they are either out of the house or sleeping). But, most of all, I thank my lovely wife Nikki, whose partnership I cherish for all the blessings it has brought to my life. This book is dedicated to her.

Abbreviations

MODERN EDITIONS OF LUTHER'S WORKS

LW *Luther's Works*. American Edition. Edited by Jaroslav Pelikan, Hilton C. Oswald, and Helmut T. Lehmann. 79 vols. Saint Louis, Philadelphia, and Minneapolis: Concordia Publishing House and Fortress Press, 1955–.

WA *D. Martin Luthers Werke: Kritische Gesamtausgabe, Schriften.* 85 vols. Weimar: Böhlau, 1883–.

WA BR *D. Martin Luthers Werke: Kritische Gesamtausgabe, Briefwechsel.* 18 vols. Weimar: Böhlau, 1930–1985.

WA DB *D. Martin Luthers Werke: Kritische Gesamtausgabe, Deutsche Bibel.* 12 vols. Weimar: Böhlau, 1930–85.

WA TR *D. Martin Luthers Werke: Kritische Gesamtausgabe, Tischreden.* 6 vols. Weimar: Böhlau, 1912–21.

OTHER SOURCES

BC *The Book of Concord: The Confessions of the Evangelical Lutheran Church.* Edited by Robert Kolb and Timothy Wengert. Minneapolis: Fortress, 2000.

CR *Corpus Reformatorum. Philip Melanthonis opera qua supersunt omnia.* Edited by Karl Gottlief Bretschneider and Heinrich Ernst Bindseil. 28 vols. Halle and Braunschweig: Schwetschke, 1834–60.

GOD AND GOVERNMENT

INTRODUCTION

ON 16 FEBRUARY 1546, AS HE LAY DYING, Martin Luther wrote on a slip of paper, which he then left on his bedside table.[1] He would die only two days later. This is what he wrote:

Nobody can understand Virgil in his Bucolics and Georgics unless he has first been a shepherd or a farmer for five years.

Nobody understands Cicero in his letters unless he has been engaged in public affairs of some consequence for twenty years.

Let nobody suppose that he has tasted the Holy Scriptures sufficiently unless he has ruled over the churches with the prophets for a hundred years. Therefore there is something wonderful, first, about John the Baptist; second, about Christ; third, about the apostles. "Lay not your hand on this divine Aeneid, but bow before it, adore its every trace."

We are beggars. That is true.[2]

Luther's deathbed reflection provides some insight into the theology and biblical interpretation he had held to for much of his life: left to its own devices, human understanding is weak, and yet the Bible is unfathomably deep. A sufficient understanding of scripture

1 Brecht, *Martin Luther: The Preservation of the Church*, 374–5. Johannes Aurifaber (1519–1575), his friend and colleague, copied the note and kept it in his collection of Luther's sayings, while another friend, Justus Jonas (1493–1555), kept the original; some other friend, now unknown, recorded a slightly different version of it. Both copies were in turn added to the *Tischreden*, or *Table Talk*, the collection of Luther's sayings from conversations that he often had at the dinner table (hence the collection's name). The version given is from the anonymous copy.

2 LW 54: 476; WA TR 5: 317–18 (*Table Talk* no. 5677; no. 5468 is not included in *Luther's Works* but is found in WA TR 5: 168). The differences in the text are slight.

required much more than one lifetime. But Luther's observation was not despondent, for his conclusion that "we are beggars" was not a cry of despair concerning human limitations but a thanksgiving for the divine gift of biblical understanding. The gift of the Word is a surpassing and transcendent wonder; nevertheless, through faith, God gives human beings an understanding of the Word they could not otherwise acquire.[3] God gives humanity biblical understanding, and like the beggar receiving alms, Luther was thankful for it. Hence, he paraphrased the first-century Latin poet Statius's praise of Virgil's *Aeneid*: bow before the Bible's majesty and adore its every trace.[4]

In fact, Luther's last written words *affirmed* the ability of human beings to understand their world. With requisite experience and a wise guide, farming could be learned in a reasonable amount of time. Political wisdom, however, was much more difficult: only with twenty years' experience could one begin to understand the letters of Marcus Tullius Cicero, one of Rome's greatest statesmen and thinkers. Just as Luther had preached in his very last sermon only days earlier, and following Aristotle's meditations on the matter, few people are truly qualified to govern even if they consider themselves politically wise.[5] But here, in his last text, Luther believed it was possible to acquire an understanding of politics within a human lifetime, and long experience and classical sources were excellent guides for doing so.

Political wisdom, as well as government in general, was a gift from God, Luther believed, but it was a divine gift known and used by humanity all over the world, in all civilizations. That ubiquity did not mean that government was honoured and cherished the world over; one of God's most precious and important gifts, it was nonetheless often attacked, abused, or neglected. Luther explained: "It is the devil's custom to hate the works of the Lord. He's hostile to whatever God holds dear – the church, marriage, government."[6]

Luther's thoughts on government were not only a subject of these sayings and brief conversations among friends. Rather, they were emblematic of wide-ranging, engaged, and theologically and biblically grounded political thought. In fact, from his early career as a

3 Brecht, *Martin Luther: The Preservation of the Church*, 375.
4 LW 54: 476, n. 41; Publius Papinius Statius, *Thebiad*, XII, 816–17.
5 LW 51: 385–86; WA 51: 189.
6 LW 54: 422; WA TR 5: 151 (no. 5431).

reformer to his last days, Luther had a great deal to say about temporal government: what its purpose was, how it ought to be used, what its limits were, and how it ought to be obeyed and honoured. Moreover, Luther's views on temporal government were consistent and sustained over decades of tumult in one of Europe's most divisive upheavals in the early modern age.

At the core of Luther's political thought was his "two kingdoms" teaching. First elaborated in *Temporal Authority: To What Extent It Should Be Obeyed* (1523), but by no means exclusive to this seminal treatise, this idea taught that humans were ontologically dual beings with both spiritual and worldly natures. As such, they were subjects of two kingdoms: one spiritual, or an inner kingdom, and one temporal, or an outer kingdom. Both kingdoms had governments and means of rule over their subjects. It was the responsibility of temporal government to bring order to the "outer" kingdom by means of laws, good morals, and coercion. The spiritual kingdom was ruled exclusively by the Word and gospel and had no recourse to worldly law or coercion. For Luther, these kingdoms were made to be separate but coeval; neither held authority over the other. God had given them both to rule over the whole of humankind, in body and in spirit. Neither could be jettisoned without jeopardizing God's governance over humanity.

This two kingdoms idea in Luther's seminal treatises was intimately connected to his theology of *sola fides* ("by faith alone"), his interpretation of the Bible through his theology of "law and gospel," and his struggle with seemingly contradictory imperatives from Jesus and the apostolic teachings of Paul and Peter. Thus, the two kingdoms concept, for Luther, was at once theologically and biblically based; helped to further the cause of church reform; and settled vexing questions of conscience about how to be both a good Christian and a good citizen or subject. With this core two kingdoms idea, Luther was able to teach emphatically that temporal government was a most precious gift from God and accordingly had to be praised, honoured, obeyed, and served as such.

Luther developed and applied this core teaching on government in response to a few of the sixteenth century's most difficult conflicts. In the Peasants' War of 1525, he excoriated both peasants and princes for their disregard of the temporal kingdom. His concept of the need to protect the temporal kingdom was also at the heart of his measured endorsement of Protestant resistance against the Holy Roman Empire in the aftermath of the Diet of Augsburg in 1530. It even informed how he saw the anticipated Turkish invasion of Europe and the justification of war and military service.

Luther also considered the Bible rife with teachings on temporal government. Foremost among them were the teachings of the apostles, particularly Peter and Paul, and their injunctions to honour and obey government as a gift from God. But Luther also found political teachings throughout canonical scripture. From the book of Genesis to the prophet Zechariah, Luther found in the Old Testament abundant lessons on ruling and being ruled and on God's purposes for temporal government. In the Psalms, for instance, Luther found wisdom for princes that complemented the wisest teachings of the ancient Greeks and Romans. Luther even considered the Song of Songs to be an encomium – a song of praise – for government.

In short, throughout his famous career, Luther had a great deal to say about political matters. He arrived at a core teaching about temporal government, developed it, applied it, and wrote about it frequently and consistently in a variety of contexts and formats. He believed that his political teachings were of epochal significance, and that the understanding of government that he and evangelical reformers were bringing to light was nearly as significant as the teachings of the apostles or St Augustine. Luther even claimed that his *Temporal Authority* was one of his favourite works. Luther considered himself an important thinker and teacher on temporal authority, and in his astonishingly vast writings a significant amount was devoted to understanding the temporal kingdom and God's purposes for government.

Despite all of the evidence to the contrary, however, Luther's political thought has often been dismissed as inconsistent or even incoherent. Even when Luther has been taken seriously, his political theory has been appropriated in a number of strikingly divergent, and often directly contradictory, ways. His ideas have been considered absolutist, fascist, democratic, reserved, impassioned, rebellious, conservative, modern, medieval, legalistic, antinomian, liberating, and regressive.

There are a number of reasons for this confusing array of interpretations of Luther in the history of political thought. First, confession-based and ideological histories once dominated the field, and these histories often biased their readings and analyses of his political ideas to the point of ignoring or misreading key evidence. Hence, many Protestant historians, for example, emphasized Luther's supposed proto-liberalism and advocacy for freedom of conscience, whereas Catholic historians emphasized his revolt against scholasticism as a rejection of authority, reason, and natural law. Marxists saw Luther as a bourgeois revolutionary, whereas fascists saw him as a forefather of authoritarianism. In all these cases, Luther's political ideas were painted with the same confessional or ideological brush, concealing Luther's true colours. Confessional and ideological biases dictated that Luther be retrofitted and confined to a role in a later version of historical progress; seldom was there an account that attempted to present his political ideas from a perspective that – as much as possible – appreciated Luther's own.

Second, Luther's works are immense. His output was truly astounding; merely *reading* Luther's complete works would be an impressive accomplishment, let alone interpreting them. Not only are his writings voluminous, but aside from his biblical commentaries and lectures, they tend to be episodic – written to address a particular issue or controversy – rather than systematic. Luther wrote no *Summa Theologiae* or *Institutes of the Christian Religion* in the manner of Thomas Aquinas or John Calvin. Thus, an understanding of his theology, not to mention the political thought derived therefrom, has to be acquired from a large number of writings produced over his career. Some texts, such as his *Christian Liberty* (1520), are much more definitive than others, but it requires a deal more work to piece these and other works together in order to see the system of Luther's thought.

Third, Luther's mission in life was foremost as a pastor and preacher of the Word (which is not simply to say a preacher of the Bible), not as a political theorist. Luther's political thinking began not with political philosophy but with theology. This does not mean that his writings on temporal government were an afterthought or of some pale, tertiary importance to his theology. Far from it: Luther's thought on government and the temporal kingdom were made clear by his understanding of the Word. Luther understood government through his relationship to God, in much the same way as he understood the divine purposes of marriage and fatherhood. To assimilate his political thought, there must be a solid understanding of how it was so intimately connected to his evangelical theology and biblical interpretation.

This is where several well-known treatments of Luther's political thought fail: in the effort to understand it, they have often trusted that careful considerations of his theology and biblical interpretation can be safely discarded in favour of an examination of only a small number of his overtly political writings. While certainly some approximation of Luther's thought on government can be formed from these writings, narrowing the textual field in this way leads to misjudgments and errors. For example, despite abundant textual evidence to the contrary (particularly in his biblical commentaries), it has been argued that Luther's political thought made no appeal to natural law, or that temporal power, with regard its own affairs, was unlimited. Moreover, errors like these are compounded when Luther's political thought is then considered to be influential in the rise of absolutism or the modern state.

Fortunately, recent scholarship on Luther, the Reformation, and the history of political thought has produced many notable studies that avoid these errors and pitfalls of the past. Luther and Reformation studies are becoming more holistic in their assessments, and less narrowly confessional in ways that skewed Luther's legacy as either a heroic figure of pure Christianity, or a harbinger of all that is spiritually destructive and evil. Likewise, recent political theory has also become much more aware that too narrow a focus on political ideas and questions can often conceal the context in which these ideas were formed or meant to apply. This book is intended to follow from these scholarly reconsiderations of Luther's political thought, while at the same time holding a critical stance toward what was problematic, unresolved, or unanswered in them.

This book offers a unique, comprehensive account of Luther's political thought. It aims to present Luther's political thought as closely as possible to his own articulation of it, paying close attention, therefore, to his theology and biblical interpretation, to the historical context of the Reformation and its ecclesial and political controversies, and to a wide range of Luther's own writings, some of which have been misread, overlooked, or ignored. This study gives an overall account of Luther's two kingdoms teaching, as well as the theology and ontology behind it and the programmatic reform that accompanied it. It pays particularly close attention to Luther's emphasis on temporal government as a divine gift, as well as his claim that he was restoring the apostolic understanding of its purpose, which had been lost by a corrupted Christian church. Critical assessments on his political ideas are also offered, as well as a general appraisal of their influence and significance.

This book begins with an account of why Luther's theological protest and revolution also necessitated his articulation of his own related political theory (chapter 1). In chapter 2, an overview of Luther's political thought is given, with special attention to his seminal treatise on the matter, *Temporal Authority*. This chapter also accounts for the limitations of this treatise, noting that any interpretation of his political thought will be skewed if this treatise is the only focus of attention. The biblical basis for Luther's political thought is the focus of chapter 3, with due attention to not only the roots of his political thought in early struggles with the Bible but also how the Bible helped expand his political thinking, particularly in several lectures and commentaries in his later career. Luther's political thought during two of the most controversial political affairs of his day, the Peasants' War and the Protestant resistance against the Holy Roman Empire, is examined in chapter 4. Although Luther's political thought did indeed develop and change with these tumults, a basic consistency is apparent at the core of his writings. Chapter 5 examines the problems and challenges in Luther's political thought in the midst of several serious controversies brought about by programmatic reform: education, church oversight, aiding the poor, marriage laws, and policing subjects. In chapter 6, an overview of Reformation political thought across confessions and ecclesial divides is offered. In this comparative account, Luther's unique contribution to the political thought of the Reformation is described. Finally, in chapter 7, the significance of Luther's political thought is assessed, with attention also to how it has been misappropriated in several influential studies of the history of political thought.

Whenever Luther wrote about government – as with other things that he considered to be gifts from God – he wrote with the highest praise and thanksgiving. This fact stood in stark contrast to his notoriously polemical style when speaking or writing about his enemies. As the pre-eminent leader of the Reformation, Luther made *many* enemies, and it is not difficult to find him fulminating against them in his works. Like so many of his age, he considered many of his bitter foes as pawns of the devil, and thus it was common for him to employ scatological and demonological insults against them: "[S]hame on you too, you blasphemous, desperate rogues and crude asses – and should you talk to an emperor and empire like this? Yes, should you malign and desecrate four such high councils with the four greatest Christian emperors, just for the sake of your farts and decretals? Why do you let yourselves imagine that you are better than crass, crude, ignorant asses and fools, who neither know nor wish to know what councils, bishops, churches, emperors – indeed, what God and his word – are? You are a crude ass, you ass-pope, and an ass you will remain!"[7] But – in a telling contrast – Luther's praise for government was fervent and vigorous. Consider, for example, his passage from *The Large Catechism,* a key document meant for teaching the faith: "Through civil rulers, as through our own parents, God gives us food, house and home, protection and security, and he preserves us through them. Therefore, because they bear his name and title with all honour as their chief distinction, it is also our duty to honour and respect them as the most precious treasure and most priceless jewel on earth."[8] Curiously, Luther's ardent praise of government has been overlooked in many treatments of his political thought. In popular history, Luther has sometimes had the unjust reputation of having been a dour preacher, raising suspicion over loving too much the things of the world. One could scarcely get Luther's view of government more wrong: he adored it as God's gift and called it the most precious jewel on earth. This book explains why.

7 LW 41: 281; WA 54: 221.
8 BC 407; WA 30 I: 153.

1

Luther's Protest and the Path to Political Reform

THE MAKING OF A REFORMER

Early in his adult life, Luther began to wrestle with a great spiritual question: how can human beings be justified – made right by God – and so saved upon death, when time and again seemingly everyone falls into sin? This problem preoccupied him during his time as an Augustinian monk in Erfurt and as a professor and biblical exegete at the University of Wittenberg. But, most significantly, his questioning of the doctrine of justification led him to become a pre-eminent leader of the Reformation, for he came to believe that the contemporary church had lost the knowledge of the right relationship of humanity to God and God to humanity.[1] He came to believe that the church had become unmoored from sound theology and that it had set Christians ignorantly adrift with respect to how God justified a sinful humanity. The controversy over the sale of indulgences in 1517 was for him but the first manifestation of this theological crisis. From that time onward, as Luther developed a comprehensive theology, the signs of a gravely corrupted church became increasingly clear to him. His polemical treatise *The Babylonian Captivity of the Church* (1520),[2] for instance, charged the church with a litany of degradations that

1 The history of Luther's fascinating personal struggle with the doctrine of justification is told in its wider context by a number of excellent biographical sources, including Brecht, *Martin Luther: His Road to Reformation*, 51–161; Oberman, *Luther: Man between God and the Devil*, 113–74.

2 LW 36: 3–126; WA 6: 497–573.

included simony, patronage, abuse of papal power, ignorance of scripture, and defilement of the sacraments.

As his theology developed and his criticism of the church sharpened, Luther began to deny the church's sovereign claim over *all* temporal authority as yet another of its corruptions. He began to argue, instead, that all civil government was granted its authority by God, but not through a mediating church; therefore, service and honour to government were as much service and honour to God as were clerical offices. In declaring corrupt *any* spiritual authority that claimed political authority for itself, Luther was also questioning the legitimacy of existing political powers – including that of the Holy Roman Empire, in which he lived – that furthered the ends of a corrupted church by failing to respect the true natures of spiritual and temporal authority.

Thus, Luther's theology of justification led not only to programmatic church reform but also to a political theory for the reformation of temporal authority. This happened in fairly short order. The indulgence controversy began in the fall of 1517; only five years later, in the late fall of 1522, Luther was writing his definitive political treatise, *Temporal Authority: To What Extent It Should Be Obeyed.*[3] In the years that followed its publication, Luther was absorbed in enormously significant political controversies, such as the Peasants' War (during which he wrote *Admonition to Peace: A Reply to the Twelve Articles of the Peasants in Swabia*; *Against the Robbing and Murdering Hordes of Peasants*; and *An Open Letter Against the Harsh Book Against the Peasants* – all in 1525),[4] the perennial issue over the justice of war (*Whether Soldiers Too Can Be Saved,* 1526),[5] the supposedly imminent Turkish invasion of Europe (*On War Against the Turk,* 1529),[6] and the weighty matters of the limits of obedience and the legitimacy of armed resistance (*Dr Martin Luther's Warning to His Dear German People,* 1531).[7]

Luther's political thought developed within a rich political and intellectual context. This chapter offers a broad overview of that context, giving special attention to the paradox of German imperial

3 LW 45: 75–129; WA 11: 245–80.

4 LW 46: 3–43; WA 18: 291–334; LW 46: 45–55; WA 18: 357–61; LW 46, 57–85; WA 18: 384–401.

5 LW 46: 87–137; WA 19 II: 623–62.

6 LW 46: 155–205; WA 30 II: 107–48.

7 LW 47: 3–55; WA 30 III: 276–320.

power and the challenges of the papal monarchy during the sixteenth century. The political insights of two influential but contrasting "mirror of princes" works, Desiderius Erasmus's *Education of a Christian Prince* and Niccolò Machiavelli's *Prince*, are also examined. This chapter also briefly accounts for two broad intellectual influences – humanism and observantism – that contributed to the development of Luther's political thought.

The chapter then examines *how* Luther's political thought developed out of his career as a reformer. Thus, the account begins with his "discovery" of *sola fides* ("by faith alone") and his early struggles with contemporary theologies of justification as he lectured on the Psalms and Paul's Epistle to the Romans. An account of how Luther's discovery led to a major reform movement follows, with a focus on the debates of 1517–19. Finally, this chapter explains Luther's theology of law and gospel and how his political thought first began as a clear and direct teaching founded upon it.

THE POLITICAL WORLD OF EARLY SIXTEENTH-CENTURY EUROPE

The Paradoxical Power of the Holy Roman Emperor

When Charles V became the Holy Roman emperor in 1519 – in the midst of the growing conflict between Luther and the Roman Church – he became, arguably, the most powerful figure in sixteenth-century European politics. His empire covered much of Europe, included a multitude of languages and cultures, and commanded the allegiance of many princes, lords, and nobles. Symbolically, the emperor was the secular head of Christendom and the latter-day inheritor of an imperial authority that claimed its lineage from the ancient Roman Empire. Yet, paradoxically, Charles's *effective* power was remarkably limited.[8]

Although it was widely recognized that the empire was often too weak to function effectively as the supreme European realm that it

8 The gathering of the Worms Reichstag of 1495, the creation of the *Reichsregiment* in 1500, and the division of the empire into *Reichskreise* in 1512 all aimed to resolve the lack of effective and uniform imperial rule. For a general overview of imperial politics in the period, see Ozment, *The Age of Reform*, 245–60.

symbolized, efforts at reform did little to strengthen it. Rather, instead of consolidating effective rule, imperial reforms only revealed its dysfunction.[9] However, instead of consolidating the emperor's control, these reforms gave more power to local authorities over their respective territories. Imperial reform had helped create for Emperor Maximilian I (1459–1519) – Charles's grandfather and a Hapsburg – a worldwide, supranational dynasty (including Austria, Germany, the Netherlands, Burgundy, northern Italy, the Iberian Peninsula, and even New World Spanish colonies), but the particularism of the princes, nobles, and free cities severely constrained his effective power.[10]

In Luther's day, the Holy Roman emperor relied on the cooperation of local authorities under him and had few resources with which to either persuade or coerce them to follow his wishes. Luther's own prince, Frederick the Wise (1465–1525), who was an Imperial Elector,[11] provides an excellent example of this dependence. Merely the fact that Luther remained *alive* in the 1520s attests to the relative weakness of the emperor. Luther had been accused of heresy in 1517 and was excommunicated by Pope Leo X in 1520. However, instead of being subjected to a hearing in Rome, Luther was examined, by Frederick's arrangement, before the imperial diet at Worms the following spring. Frederick even guaranteed him safe passage. After Luther's condemnation by Emperor Charles's Edict of Worms, Frederick managed to keep him hidden at Wartburg Castle, near the town of Eisenach in Thuringia, until the spring of 1522, so that even damnation by both pope and emperor did not harm him. An emperor's edict condemning Luther as a "notorious heretic" was

9 Krieger, *König, Reich und Reichsreform im Spätmittelalter*, 36–54; Angermeier, *Die Reichsreform 1410–1555*, 145–229.

10 For a look at Maximilian's influence and importance, see Benecke, *Maximilian I (1459–1519)*, 175–81. The standard biography remains Wiesflecker's enormous five-volume *Kaiser Maximilian I*. Luther's famous Italian contemporary Machiavelli criticized Maximilian in *The Prince* (chapter 23) for not knowing how to seek good counsel. In Machiavelli's *Discourses on Livy* (2.11) Maximilian serves as Machiavelli's example of a prince who can aid allies not by force but by name only.

11 In addition to Saxony, there were six other electors of the emperor: the margrave of Brandenburg, the king of Bohemia, the Palatinate of the Rhine, and the archbishoprics of Cologne, Trier, and Mainz. These electorships were first instituted in the thirteenth century to solve the problem of imperial succession, and they enjoyed sovereign privileges from the emperor's jurisdiction. See Zophy, "Electors," 31–2.

still no match for the privileges and power Frederick wielded in his own territory.

Moreover, the Holy Roman emperor had to contend with the political objectives of the papacy in the fifteenth and sixteenth centuries. Although the Great Western Schism (1378–1417) had severely weakened the power of the papacy over temporal affairs in the centuries that followed, it had by no means rendered it impotent. In fact, in Luther's lifetime, there was a considerable rebirth in the political stature of the Bishop of Rome. For an emperor such as Charles V, this rebirth was ambiguous, for while popes could sometimes bolster Hapsburg rule over the empire, papal political and ecclesial interests often collided with imperial interests. The famous clash between Charles V and Pope Clement VII (r. 1523–34) illustrates how tenuous the relationship between emperor and pope was and how contentious it could become. Largely to secure the papal lands in Italy, Clement frequently changed the papacy's political and military allegiances in the first half of his pontificate, at times siding with the emperor and seeking his protection, and at other times consorting with imperial enemies. In 1527 – during the crucial years when imperial and papal unity was needed to repel both the Reformation and a feared Turkish invasion – the imperial forces of Charles V invaded Italy, sacked Rome, captured the pontiff, and held him prisoner for over six months.[12] Although the pope eventually had to submit to the emperor, this famous episode showed how far the Holy Roman emperor's symbolic standing as the head of Christendom was from the political reality.

The Quandary of the Papacy

On 31 October 1503, exactly fourteen years before Luther's publication of the "Ninety-Five Theses," Giuliano della Rovere was consecrated as Pope Julius II. Famous for his patronage of artists such as Raphael and Michelangelo, his military exploits on behalf of the Papal States, and his impetuosity,[13] Julius II, or the "Warrior Pope,"

12 For a detailed account of Charles V's interests and the implications for the papacy, see Geoffrey Parker, "The Political World of Charles V," 113–226; and Brandi, *The Emperor Charles V*, 237–91. See also Chastel, *The Sack of Rome*.

13 Machiavelli, *Discourses*, III. 2.3, *Prince*, chapter 25.

would wander far from the saintly papal archetype of Gregory the Great (r. 590–604) to become one of many notorious Renaissance-era popes.[14] For him the papacy was in a daunting quandary. The gap between the papacy's claims of authority and its effective power had grown so glaring that popes, even to exert their authority in church affairs, had to assert their political authority through diplomatic and military allegiances and direct control over the surrounding territory of Romagna. Facing hostile secular powers from outside the church and a conciliar movement from within it, as well as disasters such as the Great Western Schism, the papacy's authority was curtailed and resisted by enemies all over Europe. By the mid-fifteenth century, the papal monarchy had retreated from its high-water mark in the High Middle Ages. Unless it recovered some of its former political standing, the papacy would be threatened with oblivion.

One papal strategy was to return Rome, the seat of the church's power, to pre-eminence in the Western world. By the early fifteenth century, the Avignon papacy and conciliar conflict had nearly destroyed Rome as a seat of power, and its culture and economy were in steep decline. Yet by the beginning of the sixteenth century, owing in large part to the papacy's efforts, Rome was restored to some portion of its ancient glory. Coordinating civic and cultural movements into a Roman revival, the papacy restored itself as it restored the city: it sponsored great Renaissance artists and architects for the rebuilding of both church and civic sites,[15] creating a unique Renaissance style that arose largely from papal policy.[16] Popes of this period also became the patrons of humanist scholarship,[17] and Rome became once again the centre for canon law, which was also tied to the growth of the papal curia. Although inviting the charge that the worldliness of Rome was apostate, the sponsorship of Roman revival was seen by the

14 Julius was famously lampooned by Erasmus in his satire "Julius Exclusis," in which the pope is refused entry into heaven by St Peter. See Shaw, *Julius II.*

15 Stinger, *The Renaissance in Rome,* 2, 3, 14–82. However, the most significant papal expenditures on secular sites did not come until the middle of the sixteenth century. Partner, *Renaissance Rome,* 162, and "Papal Financial Policy in the Renaissance and Counter-Reformation," 55.

16 Frommel, "Papal Policy." The art and architectural policy of the papacy arguably begins with Pope Nicholas V (1447–55); see Westfall, *In This Most Perfect Paradise.*

17 For example, Machiavelli's *History of Florence* was commissioned by Pope Leo X in November of 1520 (coincidentally during the most contentious clash with Luther).

papacy as part of the church's mission in the world. Thus, a renewed Petrine city would also renew the authority of the papacy and thereby aid the salvation of the church's flock. The more the divine mission of the church (with the pope at its head) was furthered by Rome's revival as an important capital city, the more the papacy regained its ecclesial and political standing.[18]

The papacy also tried to reassert its political standing in the late fifteenth and early sixteenth centuries by securing and centralizing its control of the Papal States. Throughout the medieval period, the Papal States gave popes a measure of independence from secular powers; by the sixteenth century, they had become the cornerstone of papal power and a crucial source of its financial support. Like the rebuilding of Rome, the consolidation of the Papal States was deliberately undertaken to augment the political power of the papacy, particularly since effective control had been lost to the powerful Colonna family in the aftermath of the Avignon papacy and the Great Western Schism.[19]

In attempting to centralize their control over the Papal States, popes found themselves confronting belligerent, family-dominated fiefs and vicariates, as well as general instability (often rooted in conflicts with other national or regional civic powers) in the eastern and northern regions. Until the turn of the sixteenth century, popes dealt with these difficulties through military and administrative nepotism that, in the short term, ensured the loyalty of recalcitrant lords and hostile families. In the long term, however, nepotism created more difficulties: once a patron died, familial loyalty died with him, and thus each new pope had to face a lukewarm, if not antagonistic, host of appointees installed by his predecessor; to make matters worse, the papal throne itself was contested by powerful Italian families.[20]

18 See O'Malley, *Praise and Blame in Renaissance Rome*; Stinger, *Renaissance in Rome*, 83–155.

19 See Partner, *The Lands of St. Peter*, and Prodi, *The Papal Prince*.

20 This is one of Machiavelli's criticisms of the "Ecclesiastical Principalities" in chapter 11 of *The Prince*. Papal nepotism reached its height under the pontificate of Alexander VI (r. 1492–1503). Alexander was arguably the most notorious of all the Renaissance popes, fathering several illegitimate children, including the equally notorious Cesare Borgia. The notoriety of the Borgias ought not obscure the fact that they at least partly succeeded in ridding the Papal States of their political difficulties, particularly rival factions, and clearing the way for the subsequent consolidation of papal power.

Pope Julius II instituted direct rule over the Papal States by conquering the border territories and consolidating recalcitrant papal fiefdoms and principalities. He diminished the impact of nepotism and eradicated much of the factionalism that prevailed. Julius also centralized the administration of the Papal States in Rome, effectively making them forever subject to the pope.[21] Although the motives of several of the Renaissance popes were dominated by nepotism at the expense of the best interests of the papacy, Julius's motives appeared to be dominated by the interests of papal power and authority and a Christian faith welded to the centrality of the papal office. Despite his unseemly wars for papal territory and temporal power, Julius appeared convinced that strengthening the independence of the Papal States and the papacy would strengthen the church.[22]

Thus, by the early sixteenth century, papal policy was a major factor in any political consideration or dispute in Italy. Furthermore, the papacy regained its foothold as a significant actor in pan-European politics. By these measures, the efforts of popes such as Julius were successful. Yet the re-emergence of papal political power did not dissolve the quandary of the institution, which continued to struggle to maintain any sort of effective political power while the secular dynasties and authorities across Europe grew with nascent nationalisms and administrations, along with larger armies. Moreover, the rebuilding of Rome and the administration of the Papal States exerted pressure on already strained papal revenues.[23] This financial pressure, in turn, encouraged (among other expedients) the widespread and popular sale of indulgences.

The Impasse of Late Medieval Political Theory and New Foundations

These problems of pope and emperor at the beginning of the sixteenth century contributed to a general political conundrum that permeated the political thought of the age: once-dominant medieval theories of spiritual and temporal power had long faded without new

21 Delumeau, "Rome: Political and Administrative Centralization in the Papal State in the Sixteenth Century"; Black, "Perugia and Papal Absolutism in the Sixteenth Century."

22 Shaw, *Julius II*, 311–15.

23 For the financial pressures and revenues of Julius's pontificate, see Gilbert, *The Pope, His Banker, and Venice.*

ones to replace them. The institutions of pope and emperor remained, but effective power over Western Christendom eluded both. For much of the medieval period, the "two swords" doctrine, with some variations, explained the relationship of the church to secular powers. Generally, this doctrine placed papal authority above secular powers, although sometimes this supremacy was nuanced and apolitical. But in the thirteenth century hierocratic interpretations of ultimate papal supremacy over temporal powers abounded, reaching their zenith with theorists such as Giles of Rome (c. 1250–1316) and his work *On Ecclesiastical Power* (1302). Supported by the writings of canon lawyers of the previous centuries, the authority of papal acts and legislation came to be seen as absolute. Popes proclaimed famously hierocratic papal bulls, such as Boniface VIII's *Unam Sanctam* (also of 1302, in the midst of a clash with the emperor), boldly declaring that every *human being* was a subject of the pope.[24]

However, in the thirteenth and fourteenth centuries opposition to papal supremacy also rose to prominence. For example, in his *On Royal and Papal Power* John of Paris (c. 1255–1306) called for limits over papal power with arguments that can be seen as an early ancestor of constitutionalism and conciliarism.[25] Several antipapal theories displaced papal monarchical claims with imperial ones. Dante Alighieri (1265–1321) defended universal imperial power in his only major political work, *Monarchy*.[26] In the three divisions of the work, Dante defended, respectively, the necessity of a universal temporal power, the importance of Rome as its seat of power, and its divine sanction to rule independently from papal authority. For Dante, the corollary of his imperial political theory was a revitalization of the church and its mission. But perhaps the most extreme imperial theory opposing papal power was Marsilius of Padua's *The Defender of Peace* (1324).[27] Countering papal absolutist claims that temporal power was given by God through the pope, Marsilius maintained that sovereignty was essentially derived from the people; he even went so far as

24 For a concise account of papal monarchy and hierocratic theory, with a helpful bibliography, see Banner, "Hierocratic Arguments."

25 Ibid., 626. For an English translation of his text, see John of Paris, *On Royal and Papal Power*.

26 Dante, *Monarchy*.

27 Marsilius of Padua, *Defensor Pacis*.

to argue that contemporary papal and imperial conflicts ultimately resulted from the illegitimate political claims of papal authority.

This very brief sketch of late medieval political theory is not meant to suggest that Luther was directly influenced by these earlier thinkers – in fact, he gave no indication that he had any substantial knowledge of their theories – but only that his own political ideas emerged in a world where imperial and papal claims to power and authority had long been openly contested, without any particular doctrine or school of thought emerging supreme. Moreover, since the exercise of those powers was so far from matching many of these theories anyhow, it is little wonder that we find several of Luther's famous contemporaries asking what temporal government was and how it ought to be used, and, in answering these questions, returning to ancient sources of political thought to begin anew.

Consider two famous works written around the time that Luther struggled with the doctrine of justification. Only two years separate the composition of Erasmus's *The Education of a Christian Prince* (1515) and Machiavelli's *The Prince* (1513).[28] Although these were both famous examples of "mirror for princes" literature, they presented starkly contrasting counsel for what constituted political virtue. For Erasmus, the prince was well served by cultivating his Christian faith and studying the ancient ethical philosophers; the common interest and the prince's hold on power were both upheld by the practice of traditional moral virtues, which Erasmus sought to renew through his humanist revival of rhetoric.

By contrast, for Machiavelli, the virtue of a prince included knowing how and when *not* to be morally good, lest he fail "to maintain the state" (*mantenere lo stato*) and thus negate any gains he had made by strictly following traditional morals. Machiavelli's princely advice warned that strict adherence to moral virtues, especially liberality, could lead to political calamity, and that a return to order could then require him to resort to even greater vices.[29]

Despite these antithetical visions of political virtue, both "mirrors" were in agreement on the general problem: the age was plagued by ignorance of the source of political authority and confusion over what princely conduct begot the best rule. Hence both works, at

28 However, *The Prince* was published only posthumously in 1532.

29 See *The Prince*, chapter 16.

least in part, claimed to be going back to ancient sources of sound political teachings to resolve this broad impasse in political thought. Erasmus looked to Cicero, the great statesman, philosopher, and orator of the Republic. Machiavelli looked to the hidden political teachings of pagan history, particularly Rome's productive conflict between plebs and nobles. They also presented their political thought as new, even though it was based on ancient lessons. In this respect, in his *Discourses on Livy* Machiavelli went much further than Erasmus when he wrote, in the preface to the first book, that his account was a discovery of "new modes and orders" or "a path as yet untrodden by anyone," since no modicum of political wisdom seemed to remain in the age.[30]

Luther's own political thought shared their prognosis: plagued by ignorance and the abuse of temporal government, the age needed new lessons from ancient wisdom. For Luther, however, these new lessons must also be based on biblical revelation, which taught humanity about divine justification through faith. The ethical and political implications of that theology of justification would lead Luther to construct his theory of temporal government. But, fundamentally, it shared the perspective of many thinkers of the sixteenth century that the age was ripe for a new account of the source and purpose of political authority. Thus, it was fitting for Luther to consider his *Temporal Authority* as one of the most important works of his enormously productive career: it sought to resolve the destructive political ignorance of the age and to lay a foundation for reform upon what he believed to be a sound biblical theology.

EARLY INFLUENCES ON LUTHER'S POLITICAL THOUGHT

The topic of justification at first appears far removed from any foundational political theory, or from political affairs altogether; but in fact, since it is at the core of Christian belief and doctrine, it can have major implications for political life. Since justification explained how God made humankind righteous, it supported all of institutional Christianity's doctrines of the sacraments, the church's ministry in

30 Machiavelli, *Discourses on Livy*, 5.

the world, and (most importantly for this study), the nature and limits of secular power. Thus, Luther's preoccupation with justification was no "ivory tower" issue; it would soon challenge the highest ecclesial and political powers of the early sixteenth century. Luther's early life and his career as a cleric and academic unfolded against the backdrop of several significant intellectual movements that influenced and shaped his theology of justification and, ultimately, his theory of temporal government. Among the late medieval influences upon Luther's thought, two broad intellectual movements stand out for particular consideration: humanism and observantism.[31]

Humanism

One major intellectual influence on Luther's thought was the early modern cultural and educational movement known today as "humanism."[32] Although this term was not applied until the nineteenth century – and its meaning has been debated ever since – "humanism" generally denotes the movement begun in fourteenth-century Italy (but quickly becoming pan-European) to implement an educational curriculum based on the *studia humanitatis*, or the study of rhetoric, moral philosophy, grammar, poetry, and history after the models from pagan and Christian antiquity.[33] Defined as such, humanism exerted an immense and wide-ranging influence on the Renaissance and Reformation periods.

Luther's inquiries greatly benefited from humanism's influence over his age.[34] One of its most obvious effects was in the renewal of philology, particularly the study of Hebrew and New Testament Greek; humanist philology liberated scripture from problematic Latin translations and scholastic commentary, and encouraged the study of the Bible in its original languages and the re-examination of

31 The scholarly literature on the intellectual influences upon Luther's early life is very large. For a concise account of the "theological situation" in Erfurt and Wittenberg, see Lohse, *Martin Luther's Theology*, 18–27.

32 For a criticism of this influence, see McGrath, *The Intellectual Origins of the European Reformation*, 32–59.

33 The definitive scholarly statement on humanism as defined above is Kristeller, "Humanism," 113–37.

34 For a deep account of its influence upon him, see Spitz, *Luther and German Humanism*. See also Spitz's "Luther and Humanism."

long-neglected patristic commentaries. Moreover, it encouraged a different approach to the study of texts. Through this humanist influence, Luther sought less to find the meaning of scripture in passages and maxims extracted from the text – a practice typical of scholastic biblical studies – and placed more emphasis on the *overall meaning* and *context* of the book, thereby reviving interpretations that he believed had been lost or corrupted. Thus, humanism provided Luther with the tools of his theological revolution: ancient languages, rhetoric, and textual criticism, along with an ability to ground this revolution in the Bible.[35] Humanism also buttressed his political thought. From the biblical interpretations of *Temporal Authority* (1523) to the (often overlooked) civic-minded educational reforms he advocated in his *To the Councilmen of All Cities in Germany That They Establish and Maintain Christian Schools* (1524)[36] and the *Sermon on Keeping Children in School* (1530),[37] Luther's political thought was deeply influenced by humanism.

Observantism

Luther's thought was also influenced by the "observant" movement that arose out of monastic reform in the fourteenth and fifteenth centuries. Essentially, observantism called on members of monastic and mendicant orders to strictly observe their order's rule of life. This call to strict observance was in part inspired by real and perceived corruptions within the orders, but it also arose from popular appeal, since monasteries were a great spiritual resource for the community, and the promise of reform strengthened their standing and reputation. In reviving the monastic ideal, observant orders inspired the laity to embody observant ideals in everyday life.[38] Prominent examples of this movement included The Brethren of the Common Life in Holland, Thomas à Kempis's *Imitation of Christ*, and the *devotio moderna*.[39]

35 For an overview of humanism in the Reformation, particularly seeing it as providing the "tools" for reform rather than the ideas themselves, see Rex, "Humanism," 51–70.

36 LW 45: 339–78; WA 15: 27–53.

37 LW 46: 207–58; WA 30 II: 517–88.

38 Cameron, *The European Reformation*, 41–3.

39 Post, *The Modern Devotion: Confrontation with Reformation and Humanism.*

By Luther's time, even though observantism had affected many of the orders of Europe, it had failed to bring about the intended world-wide church renewal or even to quell the simmering conflicts within the orders. When Luther entered the monastery in Erfurt, he joined a reformed German Augustinian congregation, an observant monastery of the rule of St Augustine. This same monastery came to the fore of an observant dispute in 1510 when Johann von Staupitz (who would be Luther's mentor in his early church career and had also been first dean of the University of Wittenberg in 1502) became both the provincial of the order in Saxony and the vicar general. Since Staupitz was both an observant and sympathetic to church reform, his office was protested by opponents of monastic reform, forcing the Augustinians to appeal to Pope Julius II. They sent Luther as one of the two representatives to Rome, where the pope ordered them to obey Staupitz.[40] Thus, observantism brought Luther before Rome and the papal court for his first and only time.

Observantism brought Luther's attention to a theological tension within strict Augustinian observance: a monk's life seemed to promise divine justification with a life lived by the rule. Luther would vehemently reject that notion of justification. Much later, Luther would claim that he was an *irreprehensibilis monachus* ("irreproachable monk")[41] but also argue that the "most pious monk is the worst scoundrel."[42] For the observant movement, the scoundrel monk was to be rooted out: rules of the order made godly men and nurtured holy lives. Luther would conclude otherwise: perfect monks – however good – were still scoundrels, for strict observation of the rule had no power to justify them before God. The influence of observantism forced Luther to resolve for himself the problem of justification.

Contemporary Debates over Justification

Luther developed his theology of justification within an intellectual context that had been debating profound ontological questions arising from medieval philosophy and theology. The late medieval

40 Brecht, *Martin Luther: His Road to Reformation*, 98–105. See also Steinmetz, "Luther and the Late Medieval Augustinians" and *Luther and Staupitz*.

41 LW 34: 336; WA 54: 186.

42 LW 54: 340; WATR 3: 306.

scholastic debate over "nominalism" centred on notion that the metaphysical status of universal categories of things was distinct from that of the particulars of these things. Do only specific human beings exist, or does humanity, as a universal category, also exist? The "realists," in following the *via antiqua*, the "old" philosophy of Thomas Aquinas and Duns Scotus, affirmed the existence of universals. The "nominalists," who followed the *via moderna*, the "modern" philosophy of William of Ockham and others, argued that only particulars existed.[43] Toward the beginning of the sixteenth century, contemporary heirs to the *via moderna* debated with another intellectual movement now labelled the *schola Augustiniana moderna*, although recent scholarship has cast doubt on whether this was in fact a cohesive school of theology.[44] Nevertheless, textual evidence remains of debates between the *via moderna* and representatives of this supposed *schola Augustiniana moderna*.[45] One crucial issue in this debate was divine justification, adherents of the *via moderna* asserting that the covenant between God and human beings established the necessary conditions of salvation that involved doing good works; in contrast, proponents of the *schola Augustiniana moderna* denied outright that human beings could in any way initiate their own justification and thus accused the *via moderna* of being neo-Pelagian.[46] One such prominent critic, Gregory of Rimini (c. 1300–1358), a member of the Augustinian Order, appropriated the radical soteriology of Augustine by arguing that the power to resist sin and turn to righteousness was entirely an action of God.

Although it is tempting to assume otherwise, there is no evidence that Luther had any knowledge of Rimini or the criticisms of the *via moderna* views of justification until *after* he had begun his own revolution on justification. In fact, before this revolution Luther appears to have accepted a general *via moderna* outlook on the matter. For example, Gabriel Biel (c. 1420–1495), a prominent Occamist of the *via moderna* and author of *Commentary on the Canon of the Mass*, had thoroughly impressed the young Luther, along with the thought of

43 For a useful but critical synopsis of late medieval scholasticism and the Reformation, see McGrath, *Reformation Thought*, 66–85.

44 McGrath, *Intellectual Origins of the European Reformation*, 82.

45 Ibid., 87.

46 After the ancient opponent of St Augustine, Pelagius (354–420). In church councils of the fifth and sixth centuries, Pelagius's views were deemed heretical.

another prominent Occamist, Peter D'Ailly (1350–1420).[47] Only later, after his reformation "discovery" of *sola fides,* would he argue in his *Disputation against Scholastic Theology* that Biel's notions of the will and justification were contrary to the gospel.[48] Before arriving at his *sola fides* teaching, Luther had held Biel's work in such esteem that he claimed it made his heart bleed to read it.[49]

LUTHER'S REFORMATION RIGHTEOUSNESS

Luther's lecture notes document his radical change of position on justification. On the recommendation of Staupitz, Luther was appointed to the chair of biblical studies at the recently founded University of Wittenberg after receiving his doctorate in 1512. Part of Luther's charge was to lecture on several biblical texts, beginning with the Psalms (1513–15), followed by Romans (1515–16).

In Luther's extant notes on the Psalms lectures, known as the *Dictata super Psalterium,*[50] the theology of justification resembles that of the *via moderna*: through the convenant, God is obliged, by his liberality, to justify anyone who meets certain minimum preconditions.[51] The sinner who met the preconditions was justified not by the merits of his own efforts per se, but he nevertheless took the initiative in his own salvation.

A complete turn away from this understanding took place sometime in 1515 or 1516, for by the time he was lecturing on Paul's epistle to the Romans, Luther had spawned a theological revolution on justification and began to reject any idea that the sinner was the initiator of his own salvation.[52] This shift was propelled by his reinterpretation of the meaning of *iustia Dei,* or the "righteousness of God." Before Luther's discovery, his interpretation of the phrase squarely

47 Lohse, *Martin Luther's Theology,* 23, n. 13.

48 LW 31: 9; WA 1: 224.

49 LW 54: 264. However, the remark comes to us second-hand (in the *Table Talk*), several decades later in 1538, and thus well into the Reformation.

50 LW 10: 11; WA 3, 4, 1–414. These lectures were based on Luther's notes on a wide-margined Psalter and separate extensive notes on each Psalm. It is difficult to tell when the notes were made or how Luther may have revised them in later publications. See McGrath, *Luther's Theology of the Cross,* 74–5.

51 McGrath, *Reformation Thought,* 106; for an elaborated account of Luther's early theology of justification, see McGrath, *Luther's Theology of the Cross,* 72–92.

52 McGrath, *Luther's Theology of the Cross,* 141–7.

sided with the *via moderna* understanding of the righteousness of God: if the sinner met the preconditions for justification, then he was justified; if he did not, and thereby remained unrighteous, he met the wrath of a judging God. Late in his life, Luther recalled how terrifying this righteousness seemed; it had even caused him to secretly hate God.[53] But by the end of 1515, Luther understood the *iustia Dei* as the work of God within human beings, freely directed toward them, such that only their faith would render them worthy of justification.[54] The sinner did not have to meet the preconditions for justification or to initiate his justification, because by faith alone (*sola fides*) in Christ's death and resurrection, as an unmerited gift from God, the sinner was already justified. "And this is the meaning," Luther wrote with respect to his radical change of view, "the righteousness of God is revealed by the gospel, namely, the passive righteousness with which merciful God justifies us by faith, as it is written, 'He who through faith is righteous shall live.'"[55]

INDULGENCES AND DEBATES

Within a few years of the radical change in his view of justification, Luther was at the centre of a controversy that would permanently divide the Western church and contribute to an enormous social and political upheaval that would echo through the centuries. Although at first the controversy centred upon indulgences, it soon shifted to the far broader and very explosive topic of papal authority. It did not start this way: Luther's initial criticism of indulgences in 1517 *appealed to* papal authority instead of challenging it. But by the time of the debates at Augsburg, Heidelberg, and Leipzig, the central issue had become papal authority, which Luther had come to see as the chief agent of theological corruption and one of the most formidable threats to salvation in the world. Thus, by the time he wrote his *Babylonian Captivity of the Church* in 1520, Luther was

53 LW 34: 328–9; WA 54: 178. The *Preface to the Complete Edition of Luther's Latin Writings* was written in 1545, less than a year before Luther's death. Given both Luther's age and the amount of time that passed after his pre-Reformation struggles, the *Preface* does not provide an accurate account of the chronology of events. However, there is no reason to doubt the veracity of this claim.

54 McGrath, *Luther's Theology of the Cross*, 131–2.

55 Again, the Latin preface. LW 34: 337; WA 54: 186.

calling for a reformation of the universal church that included a nearly complete rejection of papal authority as it had been hitherto understood and defended.

It all began with Luther's criticism of the sale of indulgences in the autumn of 1517.[56] Indulgences were sanctioned reductions or commutations of penitential acts or temporal punishment that would otherwise have been imposed on the penitent. Although the theology behind them was never quite settled, generally it was believed that Jesus's sacrifice upon the cross had made a surplus of merit, not only eternally justifying all humanity before God, but essentially justifying *all* trespasses and injustices, rendering, at least in principle, no further need for the contrite to make right with God beyond confessing their sins. Eternal righteousness was considered granted through absolution after confessing. Yet the contrite always had to do something in the world to repair the wrongs they had committed, for the sake of themselves and their neighbours, and so confessors imposed punishments and/or penitential acts that had to be performed after absolution. Here, the surplus merits of Christ could be used to reduce or commute these punishments as an indulgence. Since the pope was generally considered the successor to Peter and thus the bearer of the "power of the keys" given to the apostle by Jesus (Matthew 16:19), authority over indulgences rested ultimately with him. Indulgences could be gained through a variety of penitential acts, but almsgiving and monetary donation had become a regular means of commuting punishments for penitents *and* raising badly needed papal revenues.

In fact, by the beginning of the sixteenth century indulgences had become a *major* source of much-needed papal revenue; indeed, Pope Leo X's "plenary" indulgence proclamation on 31 March 1515 (a commutation for all penitential acts) was expected to finance the rebuilding of St Peter's Basilica in Rome. These indulgences were sold in Germany after the election in 1514 of Albrecht of Brandenburg to the archbishopric of Mainz, see of the primate of Germany, and an elector of the Holy Roman Empire. But holding this office came at an enormous cost: Albrecht owed the pope the huge sum of twenty-four thousand ducats. For, in addition to steep pallium fees paid simply to occupy the office, according to canon law Albrecht had to pay for

56 For an overview of Luther and the controversy, see Lohse, *Martin Luther's Theology*, 96–109; Brecht, *Martin Luther: His Road to Reformation*, 175–237.

special papal dispensation because he was too young and already held two church offices (including another archbishopric). Financed by the Fugger banking house of Augsburg, Albrecht settled on an arrangement through which the proceeds from the indulgences would be split between the Fuggers and the papacy.[57]

From the outset, Luther's objections to indulgence trafficking were strictly theological; in fact, only much later did he show any knowledge of the financial and political details.[58] That same autumn he wrote his *Treatise on Indulgences*,[59] wherein he challenged no ecclesial authority, affirmed some of the theology of indulgences, and wrote in a cautious and pious tone.[60]

Even when Luther published his *Disputation on the Power and Efficacy of Indulgences* (commonly known as the Ninety-Five Theses) on 31 October 1517, he appeared unaware of the controversy that would soon be provoked. In the accompanying letter to Archbishop Albrecht of Mainz on the same day, Luther implored the archbishop only to correct the false understandings of indulgences, saying nothing about papal authority.[61] At the end of his life, Luther argued that the theses did not even challenge indulgences themselves, but only their misuse, and that with them he had intended to defend the papacy.[62]

Despite what Luther had intended, within months of publication several prominent theologians considered the theses to be a heretical attack on papal authority.[63] Sylvester Mazzolini Prierias, a Dominican

57 Brecht, *Martin Luther: His Road to Reformation*, 179; Nischan, "Albert of Brandenburg," 15–16.

58 LW 41: 232; WA 51: 539.

59 WA Br 12: 5–9.

60 Brecht, *Martin Luther: His Road to Reformation*, 188–9.

61 See Letter 16, Cardinal Albrecht, Archbishop of Mainz, Wittenberg, 31 October 1517. LW 48: 43–9; WA BR 1: 108–12.

62 WA DB 11 (II): 104; WA TR 5, 5346, 5349. Cf. Brecht, *Martin Luther: His Road to Reformation*, 198. Obviously, the veracity of Luther's claim is subject to debate. But Luther could not claim that he was not challenging the common understanding of confession. Undoubtedly, the theses questioned the sacrament of penance in its current practice and supporting theology. For this point we need look no further than the very first thesis: "When our Lord and Master Jesus Christ said 'Repent,' he willed the entire life of believers to be one of repentance." LW 31, 25, WA 1, 223. (The Latin for "Repent," *poenitentiam agite*, could be rendered in two ways: "repent" or "do penance." Luther wished to challenge the latter interpretation.)

63 Brecht, *Martin Luther: His Road to Reformation*, 202–21.

whom Pope Leo X had named "Master of the Sacred Palace," declared them heretical a mere three days after he had first read them. Prierias's response, *Dialogue Concerning the Power of the Pope,*[64] accused Luther of heresy and countered with a doctrine of papal infallibility: since the church could determine matters of faith and morals, and the pope was its highest authority, to question sanctioned church practices such as indulgences was to undermine the pope and faith alike. In March 1518, after Luther had published his *Sermon on Indulgences and Grace,*[65] Johannes Tetzel, commissary of the indulgences in Germany, similarly charged Luther with heresy in his own published theses.[66] Even Johannes Eck, a theologian at Ingolstadt and one-time friend of Luther, had published his *Obelisks* against him, accusing him of heresy chiefly for his supposed anti-papalism.

Within the next two years, several debates, disputations, and hearings would shift the controversy from a relatively minor scuffle over the misuse of indulgences to a major conflict over papal authority and sweeping church reforms. At the Heidelberg Disputation in April 1518, Luther made no mention of papal authority.[67] Yet by the October 1518 Imperial Diet of Augsburg, where Luther was examined by Cardinal Cajetan – the papal legate attending the diet[68] – papal authority (and particularly Luther's opinion on the papal bull *Extravagante*[69] that justified it) was foremost on the agenda. By the Leipzig debate of July 1519, papal authority had become the central issue for Luther's opponents. At Leipzig, though Luther had prepared thirteen theses for the disputation with Johannes Eck, it was the last thesis on papal primacy that drew the most fire from Eck.[70]

64 *D. Martini Lutheri Opera latina varii argumenti,* 1: 341–77.

65 WA 1: 243–6. This sermon was preached and published nearly five months after the publication of the theses.

66 *D. Martini Lutheri Opera latina varii argumenti,* 1: 306–12.

67 Luther was warned by Staupitz to avoid controversial subjects and concentrate on free will, sin, and grace. The events at Heidelberg occurred during a triennial meeting of the Eremite Augustinians; the *Heidelberg Disputation* was Luther's account of the events; LW 31: 35–70; WA 1: 353–74.

68 Cajetan attended the diet to gain approval for a crusade indulgence against the Turks, but he was flatly refused.

69 This was the common name of the papal bull *Unigenitus* of Pope Clement VI in 1343. Luther cited it in thesis fifty-eight of the Ninety-Five Theses; contrary to the bull, Luther argued "that the merits of Christ did not constitute the treasury of merits of indulgences." LW 31: 261; WA 1: 236.

70 LW 31: 307–25. WA 2: 158–61.

The debate at Leipzig was a turning point for Luther: he started to consider the need for comprehensive church reform. At Leipzig, Luther began to clearly state his conception of the church and affirmed the Word of God as the final authority in matters of doctrine and faith. Against Eck, he argued that both popes and councils had erred, and that in upholding false teachings over indulgences the pope was *in error*. Luther's stance on papal fallibility would soon provoke his excommunication, and with it the loss of any hope for a quiet reconciliation with Rome. Starting with the Leipzig debates, Luther began to understand the scope of the conflict and its massive theological and political implications.

REFORMATION ON LAW AND GOSPEL

By 1520, Luther had committed himself to programmatic church reform by publishing several of the most important treatises of the entire Reformation.[71] *To the Christian Nobility of the German Nation Concerning the Reform of the Christian Estate*, published in August, was one such major treatise; it audaciously called for such enormous reforms that no one could now doubt that a major conflict had begun. Luther's opponents, such as the Franciscan Augustin von Anveldt and Prierias,[72] continued to publish works denouncing him, particularly emphasizing Luther's antipapal heresies and attacking his supposed conciliarist and Hussite[73] sympathies. On 15 June, with the help of Johannes Eck, Pope Leo X promulgated the bull *Exsurge Domine*, which condemned Luther's teachings (although this was unknown to Luther until December).

71 Brecht calls this Luther's "Reformatory Program" in *Martin Luther: His Road to Reformation*, 349–88. Compare this to Lohse's account of this period, which divides it into two overlapping theological battles over the sacraments and the monastic idea, in *Martin Luther's Theology*, 127–43.

72 Von Anveldt published *The Apostolic See* in May, and Prierias the *Epitome of a Reply to Martin Luther* in June. Luther responded, respectively, with *The Papacy of Rome, an Answer to the Celebrated Romanist at Leipzig* and an annotated reprint of Prierias's work.

73 The Hussites were followers of Jan Hus (c. 1372–1415), a Czech reformer in Bohemia and Moravia. Hus and the Hussites denied papal supremacy and argued for a renewed emphasis on the Bible and ancient church teachings which included, among other teachings, giving laypersons communion in both kinds (consecrated wine and bread). Hus was condemned as a heretic in the Council of Constance and burned at the stake.

Meanwhile, *To the Christian Nobility* made it abundantly clear that Luther had begun to see the papacy (and, in fact, much of the clerical hierarchy under it) as *the* major obstacle to reform. Hence, the treatise began by attacking the "Romanists" (by which he meant papalists) and the "three walls" they had constructed to buttress their claims for papal supremacy: that temporal authority had no jurisdiction over it; that only the pope possessed the authority to interpret the Bible; and that only the pope had the ability to call a worldwide church council.[74] With the idea of the "priesthood of all believers," Luther battered and breached each "wall" until no foundation was left on which the church might claim *any* temporal authority whatsoever. In mere pages, Luther had demolished the two swords of the medieval age in favour of a church that had no roles other than preaching and teaching the gospel and administering the sacraments. Even these – including Christianity's central rite of communion – would be sweepingly altered, as he would make clear only two months later, in October, in his treatise *The Babylonian Captivity of the Church.*

Whereas the church would be stripped of its political power – Luther had even boldly advocated an abolition of the papal court[75] – temporal authorities would be restored to what Luther considered their proper jurisdictions, including taking control of church revenue systems (such as the sale of indulgences and fees for offices) so as to arrest the massive export of wealth from Germany to Rome. With more wealth kept at home, secular tax revenues would fund what Luther outlined to be major social and public works projects, ranging from supporting the poor, to investing in universities and schools, to promoting a generally upright moral life by curbing luxuries, oppressive financial practices (such as usury), and various social ills caused by gluttony, drunkenness, and lust.[76] Clearly, even by the title and addressees of the treatise, Luther had by this early point already envisioned a crucial role for noble families and secular powers in the efforts to reform. Since the church hierarchy was the obstacle to reform, the necessary work fell to notables among the priesthood of all believers.

74 LW 44: 124–38; WA 6: 405–14.
75 LW 44: 142–44; WA 6: 417–9.
76 LW 44: 189–90, 200–4, 212–5; WA 6: 450–1, 457–60, 465–7.

But lest Luther's commitment to comprehensive and programmatic reform appear to be an ecclesial revolution unmoored from a strong theological foundation, his next major treatise of 1520, *Christian Liberty*, provided a theological basis by which Luther's entire Reformation career – including his political thought – could be understood. In his epistle dedicatory, Luther called the treatise "the whole of Christian life in brief form."[77] Historically, the treatise came about as an attempt to reconcile the conflict with Rome, as a certain papal diplomat, Karl von Miltitz, had approached the now-retired Johann von Staupitz and the current Augustinian vicar, Wenceslaus Link, to persuade Luther to write to Pope Leo X, and even to date his letter prior to the bull, so as to ease tensions and move toward conciliation. Luther agreed and attached *Christian Liberty* to the letter. But even though Luther claimed that the "little treatise [was] dedicated to [the pope] as a token of peace and good hope,"[78] the letter accused the papal curia of subverting the gospel and showed that he considered his position to be clearly and emphatically grounded on a sound biblical theology.

Christian Liberty defended two apparently contradictory ontological propositions: a Christian is perfectly free and subject to none; and a Christian is also a perfectly dutiful servant of all, subject to all. For Luther, these were paradoxically true, since all human beings have a twofold nature or being: a spiritual one and a temporal or bodily one. For Luther, it was through the spiritual nature that a Christian became free and justified; justification had *nothing* to do with anything bodily or external. No external thing could produce that freedom; only through the inner acceptance of the gospel – the promise that through faith in Christ the law is fulfilled and sins absolved – could one be justified and become perfectly free.

For Luther, this perfect Christian freedom had three major implications. First, all good works were rendered unnecessary for righteousness or justification, and so a Christian was "free" from the law in the sense that the works that the law demanded did not in any way merit him salvation. Second, having faith in God's promise freed the Christian from the condemnation of the law, thus making him an unblemished child of God. Third, by faith, the Christian was freed

77 LW 31: 343; WA 7: 11.
78 Ibid.

from the bondage or slavery of sin: a Christian's sins, by faith, became shared (as in a marriage, Luther argued) by the union of faith with Christ, and thus as such the sins were justified by the spiritual bond.[79]

Yet Luther also held that servitude was a necessity of the outer or bodily nature or being of humanity. In this mortal life, prior to the resurrection and thus in a state not "wholly inner and perfectly spiritual," subjection to worldly authority would continue as long as human beings needed to control their own bodies and to deal with one another. Only by discipline and authority, Luther argued, was the outer being made complementary to the inner being in a unified life dedicated to God. Only by good works and lawfulness did the outer join the inner in its service and dedication to God. For Luther, subjection to temporal authority was one type of godly bondage, to which the outer nature was bound; in this, he echoed the message of Paul in Romans 13:1–7.[80]

Thus, *Christian Liberty* grounded Luther's reform in a theology that would come to define much of his career as an evangelical reformer. Elsewhere, and with a slightly different emphasis, Luther would refer to this theological core as the law and gospel distinction. Many times throughout his career he argued that this was at the centre of *all* proper understanding of the Bible and theology.[81] Although somewhat analogous to Augustine's "letter" and "spirit" and Paul's "body" and "spirit" distinctions, Luther's law and gospel differed from these other theological treatments of the human condition by considering the law and gospel as a dialectical ontological dyad, rather than as two stark alternatives of perdition and salvation. In fact, Luther thought that although the "law" dealt with and punished the body or the outer human being, it was wholly complementary to the gospel by underscoring what it had no power to do: namely, to save souls by faith. Hence, for Luther, the law and gospel distinction intimately cohered with his doctrine on justification. In fact, Luther would develop a twofold "use" of the law in the years that followed his publication of seminal treatises such as *Christian Liberty*.[82] One use was theological, or the ultimate spiritual sense: the law showed people

79 LW 31: 353–6; WA 7: 56–8.
80 LW 44: 358–60, 363–5, 368–72; WA 7: 59–60, 63–4, 66–70.
81 Lohse, Martin Luther's Theology, 267; WA 7: 502.
82 Luther arguably had a threefold distinction of the law's use. See chapter 3, 81–4.

their sins and thus was accusatory. Through this use of the law, human beings were condemned and could not by their own powers be justified (hence pointing to justification by divine grace). The other use of the law was political: by promoting human welfare and maintaining order, the law – via government, parents, educators, and justices – was used to bring the temporal government a worldly peace intended by God to enable the flourishing of both bodies and souls.

Luther's law and gospel doctrine, first articulated in *Christian Liberty* and other early works, defined human existence through two distinct relationships to God and to one another. The spiritual part of humanity, governed by the gospel – salvation through faith in the righteousness of Jesus Christ – formed one part of being. In this relationship with God, humanity was subject wholly to God's grace and election, made clear by revelation and taught by the church, rendering all who received this gospel wholly justified and made perfectly right in the judgment of God. In the temporal, outer, or worldly part of humanity, the "law" provided both self-awareness of the ultimate inability of human beings to *justify themselves* in the eyes of God, and guidance for a peaceful, orderly life with neighbours and with all of creation. As an ontological dyad of humanity's relationship to God, Luther's law and gospel doctrine was meant to account for the whole of human life and being in relation to God. It explained how human beings could be made perfectly justified by God spiritually, and yet still subject to laws temporally. Therefore, *Christian Liberty*'s opening paradox of Christians being perfectly free and perfectly subject was for Luther a true paradox: both propositions had to be accepted to understand human existence and God's beneficent sovereignty over it.

Luther's two kingdoms teaching was most basically and essentially derived from the law and gospel ontology. It began as an articulation of the realms of authority God had given over both modes of human existence. Luther called these distinct ontological realms "kingdoms" to emphasize their distinct yet concurrent jurisdictions and to underscore that, for each one, there was no other authority to answer to or serve: the spiritual and temporal kingdoms were sovereign (under God) over each of their own spheres or modes of human existence. The spiritual and temporal *governments*, as distinct from kingdoms, were simply the practical institutions designed to exercise these sovereignties.

Luther's political thought was inextricably rooted in the law and gospel theology, for it came out of his struggle with the doctrine of justification and his subsequent perception that the church had horribly corrupted its proper understanding of justification. To be clearly interpreted and understood, Luther's political thought must therefore be seen as an integral part of his overarching law and gospel understanding of human beings in relation to God. The two kingdoms and temporal government make little sense as coherent political doctrines without heeding the law and gospel teaching.

Accordingly, as an early articulation of that teaching, *Christian Liberty* showed not only that theological doctrines were of paramount importance to Luther's reform program, but also that his political thought was also intimately related to it. It is no surprise, then, that *Christian Liberty* contained one of Luther's first and clearest statements on his two kingdoms teaching, and that this teaching would become the cornerstone of his theology and political thought. A full articulation of that political thought would soon come in his 1523 treatise *Temporal Authority: To What Extent It Should Be Obeyed.* But even before the publication of that work, Luther was writing forcefully about the divine purpose of temporal government in the quickly developing and deepening Reformation.

2

Luther's Political Thought

THE BASICS OF LUTHER'S POLITICAL THOUGHT

The Two Kingdoms

In his seminal political work, *Temporal Authority: To What Extent It Should Be Obeyed* (1523), and throughout the rest of his life and career, Luther argued that Christians were governed by God through *zwei Reiche*, or two kingdoms: the *geistliche Reich*, or spiritual kingdom, and the *weltliche Reich*, or worldly kingdom. Each kingdom or regiment (Luther used the German terms *Reich* and *Regiment* either interchangeably or else to describe different aspects of the same reality[1]) had its own proper sphere and structure for effective, godly rule over life.[2] For Luther, the spiritual kingdom was ruled by Jesus Christ through his revealed Word. Although not equivalent to the visible church, the spiritual realm had the means to justify humanity and thus worked *within* the visible church by sanctifying it by grace. Luther sometimes called this kingdom's sphere of influence the "inner" part

1 Further discussion of Luther's terms is found later in this chapter, 45–6.

2 This study's account of Luther's political thought builds on several important works of historical theology analyzing Luther's "two kingdoms." See Lohse, *Martin Luther's Theology*, 314–24. For a focus on the political and ethical ramifications, a classic analysis of the two kingdoms is Althaus, *The Ethics of Martin Luther*, 43–82. Wright's recent study *Martin Luther's Understanding of God's Two Kingdoms* not only explains the theology of Luther's two kingdoms but also helpfully traces the historical appropriations and misunderstandings of his teaching. For a recent critical theological analysis, see Barth, *The Theology of Martin Luther*, chapter 12, "Division of Labor: God's Left and Right Hands," 313–48. For the two kingdoms in the history of political thought, see Cargill Thompson, *The Political Thought of Martin Luther*, 36–61.

of humanity: it ruled over the hearts of human beings, justifying them in spite of their sinfulness and freeing their souls from all other authorities and powers.

In contrast, the temporal or secular kingdom was the realm of the "outer" human being, comprising all worldly goods and affairs. For Luther, the temporal realm did not only assume responsibility for what we might today designate as properly political, for it included under its purview *all* "outer" matters of human life, such as marriage and the household. The chief means of rule and order within the temporal kingdom's realm, however, were those of the princes and magistrates, who were the pinnacle of temporal government's effective governance through the rule of law and the use of coercion. For Luther, the temporal government's primary responsibilities were peace, order, and the protection of life and property. Thus, these responsibilities fell foremost to the political powers and offices, even though parents, teachers, and petty magistrates were also office holders in the temporal regiment.

In Luther's thinking, the temporal kingdom was exclusively the realm of coercive force, and this exclusivity was directly connected to its divine mandate to uphold the rule of law and protect life and property. In fact, for Luther the rule of law *necessitated* the threat and use of force: although the law was divinely instituted for the sake of peace and order, and insofar as it ruled toward these ends it was rational and natural, it also had to rule over human beings, who were plagued by sin and an all-too-fallible reason. Coercion, therefore, was not only useful for temporal government but also had a divine sanction to fulfill its purpose. Law required punishment for transgression; executing the law required, at times, going to war or executing people. There were limits, however, to this coercive power; moreover, coercion was for Luther in no way legitimate within the spiritual kingdom. For instance, the Word could not be coerced upon souls for salvation. Contrary to outlandish claims about Luther's endorsement of force in the temporal kingdom, such as the accusation that he was a proto–National Socialist, he considered the authority and power of princes and magistrates as being far from absolute. Luther's magistrates had no legitimate jurisdiction over their subjects' "spiritual" beings, and were mandated by God to rule for the sake of peace, order, and the love of neighbour.

Following directly from his thought on the spiritual kingdom, Luther – unlike most church reformers in the sixteenth century, including some of his closest German colleagues, such as Johannes Brenz and Philip Melanchthon – did not consider political authority intrinsically Christian, even though the spiritual kingdom was a realm governed by Christ. Luther considered *all* political powers, Christian or pagan, ancient or contemporary, as manifestations of the same divine gift of temporal government. In the same vein, Luther also argued that political wisdom was not exclusive to Christians, even though they alone could distinguish the two kingdoms. In his *Commentary on Psalm 101*, for instance, Luther advised that political wisdom was perhaps best exemplified in the ancient Greeks, and that classical authors such as Aristotle and Homer were its best sources.[3] Luther's thinking here, the evidence in this commentary and in several places elsewhere suggests, was that all human beings had access to and some knowledge of natural law, which was generally given to humankind as the Golden Rule, and that classical thinkers such as Aristotle were the most adept in discerning its meaning and discussing its principles and guidance for living justly and in a good political order.[4]

Luther did forcefully argue, however, that the two kingdoms were biblical. From his early studies on Paul's Romans and 1 Peter to his *Lectures on Genesis* late in his life and career, Luther's two kingdoms remained a mainstay of his biblical teachings and interpretation. That they were ubiquitous in his thinking and in scripture (as he interpreted it) was indicative of their importance for grasping how

3 LW 13: 216–17; WA 51: 258. For a discussion of this commentary, see chapter 3, 78–80.

4 See for example LW 40: 98; WA 18: 69–70. Luther's praise of Aristotle here might first appear to be a very remarkable about-face to his excoriation of the classical philosopher in the theses of the Heidelberg Disputation of 1518, or in the polemics of the *Babylonian Captivity of the Church*. However, several major factors complicate any assertion that Luther greatly changed his views on the value of Aristotle's philosophy. First, theses like those at Heidelberg were meant as controversial starting points for debate; they did not necessarily reflect Luther's settled views, and they are not greatly explained and defended by Luther in writing. Second, and most importantly, these negative assessments of the philosopher were less about the value of his philosophy, than about what he perceived to be the negative influence of Aristotle upon contemporary *theology* in general, and salvation in particular. See Lohse, *Martin Luther's Theology*, 48–9.

much God cared for humanity. In essence, the two kingdoms were two complementary means through which God graciously directed all humanity. For Luther, the Bible abundantly confirmed this: God directed peace and order through temporal government, and the peace of the soul through the spiritual realm.

Although the *zwei Reiche* were biblical and universal, they could also be corrupted. For Luther, the primary mode of corruption was the failure to keep the kingdoms separate and distinct. Popes and priests, as office holders in the spiritual kingdom, had no business with human law, whereas political authorities had no claim on the affairs of the soul and the ministering of God's Word. The sinful ambitions of men pushed them beyond their duties in the two realms: clerics wished to rule the world, and secular authorities sought to rule over the soul. Thus, Luther's conception of the two kingdoms and their corruption became a foundation for programmatic reform; the Roman Church, he believed, was abandoning its role in the spiritual kingdom for the temporal kingdom and must be returned to its spiritual mission. Meanwhile, temporal authorities, particularly those who coercively resisted church reform, but also those who neglected the protection of life and property, were shirking their divinely ordained duties to the temporal kingdom.

However, for Luther, exceptions could be made in times of emergency, particularly when caused by the resistance of the Roman Church. Thus, he believed that a secular magistrate could conduct affairs in the spiritual realm as a *Notbischof* or "emergency bishop," but that this was only a temporary means to the full restoration of temporal government as a means of divine governance alongside a complementary (but otherwise separate) ecclesial realm of spiritual authority centred on grace alone in Jesus Christ.[5] How was this separation of kingdoms to be maintained? What were the boundaries between these realms? These would prove to be some of the most contentious and difficult questions for Luther and his followers to answer.

5 The difficulties of Luther's position is treated more fully in chapter 5.

Temporal Authority and the Two Kingdoms

Temporal Authority was Luther's most famous political text and one of his few treatises that focused on a political topic. He considered it one of his most important and best works. As a key source for his two kingdoms theory and the political applications he derived from it, it is foundational to an understanding of Luther's political thought, for it informed the subsequent development of all of Luther's political ideas.

Luther wrote *Temporal Authority* in three parts, each part addressing a particular question. He began the first by asking what temporal authority was and on what was it based. For the answer, Luther looked to scripture, particularly Romans 13:1–2 and 1 Peter 2:13–14, both of which affirmed the divine institution of government and demanded obedience to it. In these New Testament passages Luther saw more than just Paul and Peter's counsel to Christians to be obedient; he also saw an emphasis on the divine institution of government as a universal, transhistorical foundation for all political legitimacy. Temporal government, Luther argued, had existed since the beginning of the world. Coercion had been legitimated since the condemnation of Cain, and so the foundations for temporal authority were laid in the antediluvian age.[6]

Yet Jesus himself, in the Sermon on the Mount, taught his followers to love their enemies and turn the other cheek.[7] At first glance this might appear to undermine temporal authority and its use of coercion: Christians and the polities they lived under (it seemed) were to turn the other cheek in the face of all violence and disorder. Moreover, it seemed also that the words of Paul and Peter were at least in tension (if not contradiction) with Jesus's commands in the sermon; on the one hand, Paul counselled obedience to the Roman emperor (who at the time was Nero) and claimed that he, even as an author of state coercion, was a servant of God's will, and yet Jesus's ethic of loving enemies appeared to undermine the legitimacy of Roman law, order, and coercion. What was an earnest Christian prince to do?

6 LW 45: 85–6; WA 11: 247–8.
7 Matthew 5: 38–48.

In *Temporal Authority*, Luther argued that neither of the teachings of the Epistles and gospels could be rejected, nor did they contradict one another. The two kingdoms provided the way out of the apparent conundrum. Luther explained that although all of humanity was divided into two kingdoms, true Christians were part of the spiritual kingdom and as such had no need of either temporal government or the sword, since the justified exceeded the righteousness that worldly law demands. In contrast, the temporal kingdom needed temporal government and its sword, since those, being neither justified nor righteous, needed "the law to instruct, constrain, and compel them to do good."[8] But Luther added a critical point: *no one* is by nature Christian and righteous; thus, *all* human beings are subjects of the temporal kingdom. In this life, *both* governments must remain, since human beings are both spiritual and temporal. A Christian, Luther argued, as a Christian, needs no temporal government; but he is also inescapably in this life a subject of the temporal kingdom, and thus cannot do without the divinely ordained government to provide order and at times even coerce his body. For Luther, both governments were necessary: "neither one is sufficient in the world without the other."[9]

With the "two kingdoms," Luther argued, the "word of Christ is now reconciled, I believe, with the passages that establish the sword."[10] Any crisis of conscience for the Christian could be reconciled by the fact that service to temporal government was also divine service, and thus "there must be those who arrest, prosecute, execute, and destroy the wicked, and who protect, acquit, defend, and save the good." The hangman could do his duty to temporal government and thereby help curb sin and love his neighbour.

In the treatise's second part, Luther treated the extension and limits of temporal authority. Luther called this section the "main part" of the work, since by knowing its ends and limits, temporal government could keep steadfastly focused on its divinely assigned roles and functions as one of the "two kingdoms."[11] Temporal government had jurisdiction over life and property, or what Luther, echoing his

8 LW 45: 89; WA 11: 250.
9 LW 45: 92; WA 11: 252.
10 LW 45: 103; WA 11: 260.
11 LW 45: 104; WA 11: 261.

famous 1520 treatise *Christian Liberty*, called "external" things. The soul – the "internal" world – was strictly beyond its domain and authority. Thus, temporal authority could not, for instance, require or forbid beliefs without weakening its role as arbiter of external things as well as hurting souls and the spiritual kingdom itself, the proper realm for the soul. The inner person could not be persecuted or prosecuted by temporal government, and so neither could faith be commanded by it nor could heresy be prosecuted by it (a point over which Luther was in the minority in the Reformation). Luther argued that the banning of his German New Testament by secular princes transgressed the boundaries of the *weltliches Reich*, as did any magisterial attempts to curb church reform.[12] In time, although *Temporal Authority* appeared to have settled the boundaries of political control over spiritual things, the issue would become, even among evangelical reformers themselves, one of the most contested in the late sixteenth and seventeenth centuries.

The third section of *Temporal Authority* served as a kind of mirror for princes treatise, or *Fürstenspiegel*, with a distinctly pastoral bent. The question for this section was not just how to be a good prince, but how one could be a good *Christian* prince. Nevertheless, it too, like the rest of the famous treatise, reinforced the place of the two kingdoms in Luther's political thought. Although Luther was not about to expose the methods of effective rule – he readily admitted that this necessary knowledge was beyond his expertise – he did wish to expose how a prince could rule within the bounds of temporal government's "external" things while at the same time being a Christian believer in God's unmerited grace. This *Fürstenspiegel* was a prince's guide to living in the two kingdoms as both a good prince and a Christian. Hence, what remained of *Temporal Authority* was Luther's attempt to "instruct [the ruler's] heart" on how to see his duties and princely affairs as godly duties to the temporal kingdom.[13] Luther listed four pieces of advice. First, the prince ought to dedicate himself to benefiting his subjects, and thereby also resist the temptations and distractions of aristocratic and courtly life.[14] Second, Luther advised that the prince be wary of the "high and mighty and his

12 LW 45: 112; WA 11: 267.
13 LW 45: 119; WA 11: 273.
14 LW 45: 120–1; WA 11: 273–4.

counsellors" and not simply trust that his own selflessness is found in others.[15] Third, Luther argued that the prince "must deal justly with evildoers" and, likewise, as part of the overarching duty to be just, obey his own superiors and conduct only justified war waged for the ends of peace and order.[16] Fourth and last, a matter that "should really have been placed first," the prince must place in God "true confidence and earnest prayer."[17] Following these counsels, a prince would come to respect the holy office of temporal government that had been given to him.

Beyond Temporal Authority *and the Two Kingdoms*

Since it was his most direct statement on political affairs, *Temporal Authority* is justly considered to be Luther's best work of political thought (thinking so puts one in good company, as Luther took the same view himself). Unfortunately, it is too often considered his *only* politically relevant work, and this had led to a neglect of Luther's place in the history of political thought.[18] Considering it the only political treatise worthy of note ignores the enormous breadth of writings Luther devoted to the subject throughout his life and career.[19] An even more important point, however, is that reading *Temporal Authority* in isolation inevitably leads to several significant errors in the interpretation of Luther's political thought. One such error is the idea that this treatise can be understood without much reference to its historical context and, in particular, to the reasons Luther felt compelled to write on political subjects in the midst of a growing church schism. Another error, closely related, is to interpret *Temporal Authority* without much recourse to or understanding of Luther's theology – in particular, how his theology of law and gospel undergirded the two kingdoms and his understanding of temporal government in general. Indeed, Luther boasted that

15 LW 45: 121–3; WA 11: 274–6.

16 LW 45: 123–6; WA 11: 276–8.

17 LW 45: 126; WA 11: 278.

18 This can be the unintended consequence of books like Höpfl's *Luther and Calvin on Secular Authority*: the only one of Luther's works that it considers is *Temporal Authority*.

19 For example, my edited anthology, *Divine Kingdom, Holy Order: The Political Writings of Martin Luther*, contains excerpts from twenty-nine different texts, including biblical commentaries and sermons.

Temporal Authority was one of the most important works since antiquity, but he had made such a claim with the assumption that it was to be considered in tandem with the reforming evangelical theology that he had made his life's work and mission. Finally, an error that can persist even if the others are avoided is the idea that *Temporal Authority* was Luther's final word on government, that his thinking on the matter did not change and develop, and that new political challenges and great questions did not thereafter arise. *Temporal Authority* did not answer several of the crucial questions that dogged the Reformation as it grew in Germany and demanded more of the magistrates of the territories in which it settled. Most notably, of course, *Temporal Authority* did not adequately answer the problem of revolt or the limits of obedience: these acute questions would arise within the decade after 1523. There were plenty more questions, such as magisterial oversight of education or clergy, and, in time, Luther would address these matters and more. *Temporal Authority* doubtless provided the sure foundation for Luther's political thinking, but it did not provide a comprehensive sum of his political thought.

An overemphasis on *Temporal Authority*, even with due attention to context and theology, has led many scholars of the past century to sum up Luther's political thought firmly within what came to be called the *zwei Reiche Lehre*, or "two kingdoms doctrine." First coined by theologian Karl Barth in a book review in 1922,[20] the *zwei Reiche Lehre* came to posit that Luther's political ideas could be understood *only* within a systematic and rigid distinction between the two kingdoms; therefore, Luther's early writings, such as *Christian Liberty* and *Temporal Authority*, were foundational and thus useful for understanding Luther's ideas, whereas later texts that did not fit into that paradigm (such as Luther's "three estates" teaching in his *Lectures on Genesis*) were dismissed or ignored altogether.[21] Beginning with the assumption of a *zwei Reiche Lehre*, scholars combed the early writings, particularly *Temporal Authority*, for consistent use of terms to determine the precise boundaries of the *Lehre*. The problem was that Luther, having not started with a rigid *zwei Reiche Lehre* to begin with,

20 Barth, review of *Religiöser Sozialismus: Grundfragen der christlichen Sozialethik*, by Paul Althaus, 461–72; see Lohse, *Martin Luther's Theology*, 154.

21 Skinner's *The Foundations of Modern Political Thought*, vol. 2, omits any mention of Luther's "three estates" or any of his biblical commentaries.

began to appear inconsistent regarding his own supposed doctrine![22] In *Temporal Authority* and elsewhere, Luther used the German words *Reich* and *Regiment* to describe two slightly different aspects of the same divine reality: generally, *Reich* referred to the sphere of rule, and *Regiment* referred to the means of rule. But Luther also used the words *Oberkeit* ("authority") and *Gewalt* ("power") as synonyms of *Reich* and *Regiment*. This confusion and imprecision become far less problematic if the two kingdoms are considered in relation to his ontology of the inner and outer parts of humanity and his theology of justification. Luther's two kingdoms concept was not meant to be a philosophical doctrine in which *Oberkeit* and *Gewalt* could be precisely defined and distinguished.[23]

To look at the whole of Luther's writings is to see considerable breadth and depth in his political thought that went far beyond the confines of the important but relatively narrow questions of *Temporal Authority*. The following chapters attest to this breadth: the political teachings Luther gleaned from the Bible (chapter 3) and the responses Luther gave to various political challenges of the German Reformation (chapter 5), such as support for the poor, magisterial oversight of clergy, and the reform of education. Luther's biblical commentaries, his *Lectures on Genesis* in particular, deserve special attention in considering the place of the two kingdoms in his political thought. Instead of two kingdoms, Luther there distinguished three estates comprising clergy, marriages and households, and political authorities. Rather than undercutting or contradicting the *zwei Reiche*, this construction provides what Bernhard Lohse has called an instructional "supplement" to them in showing that the idea of the temporal kingdom was not a narrow doctrine of political authority.[24]

Luther's political thought was grounded in his law and gospel theology and his ontological distinction between the inner and outer natures of humanity. Temporal government was the sovereign sphere of outer humanity; temporal authority was the divine gift in charge of the order and well-being of that realm. God mandated that temporal authority exercise its power as a love of neighbour and refrain from

22 See Cargill Thompson's excellent treatment of this problem in "The Two Kingdoms and the Two Regiments: Some Problems of Luther's *Zwei-Reiche-Lehre*."

23 Lohse, *Martin Luther's Theology*, 157.

24 Ibid., 322–3.

trespassing the spiritual realm. Given its crucial role in upholding human existence, Luther deemed temporal authority a divine gift as precious as life itself. He also considered his teaching on it a restoration after a long, dark period of abuse and neglect, mostly at the hands of power-assuming clergy and their subservient princes. But this core of Luther's political thought was not simply and clearly exposed in *Temporal Authority*. Luther's political reflections were very episodic, and much of his thinking would be written in reaction to Reformation disputes to come.

At the time Luther was writing *Temporal Authority*, major controversies were on the horizon: the Radical Reformation and the right of resistance to the empire would challenge his thinking on temporal government and demand he publish his answers. So significant were these controversies that they deserve to be considered as addenda to the core of Luther's political thought, for they shaped how he subsequently saw the temporal kingdom and the divine purpose of political authority. Luther's works on these episodes were also shaped by the political context of the early sixteenth century. This chapter turns therefore to these crucial episodes in Luther's career, but first with due attention to the political landscape from which he took his bearings and then began to consider his own efforts as the most significant political thought since late antiquity.

LUTHER'S POLITICAL THOUGHT IN HISTORICAL CONTEXT

Worms to Wartburg

Luther's trial in April of 1521 at the Diet of Worms remains one of the most famous events of European history, and so it is difficult to believe that the imperial diet had any other business aside from Luther. However, like any other diet, most of the agenda of Worms (months of work, in fact) was taken up with the multifarious matters of imperial governance, including the imperial supreme court, police procedures, the emperor's relations with the Pope, economic matters, and foreign policy; in fact, the "Luther affair" was not even originally on the agenda.[25] Yet the imperial authorities could not

25 Brecht, *Martin Luther: His Road to Reformation*, 433.

ignore the controversy as they met in the winter and spring of 1521. It was at the Diet of Worms that the political implications of Luther's protest began to be clear to the political authorities themselves.

In the fall and winter of 1520–21, shortly before the diet began, Luther's teachings were condemned by Pope Leo X in his bull *Exsurge Domine.* On 3 January 1521, he was finally excommunicated. Condemned heretics could normally expect swift justice – typically public execution by burning – to come from the secular authorities, but the current secular authorities, under the influence of Frederick the Wise, decided to give Luther a hearing at the diet and even guarantee him safe passage there and back by imperial escort.[26] As it unfolded, it became clear that the trial's purpose was not to give Luther a forum for simply explaining himself (as the imperial invitation led him to believe) but to allow him to recant or else suffer an additional imperial ban.[27] Although he asked for a day to ponder the situation, Luther famously did not recant.[28]

Although many political authorities at Worms tried to avoid an imperial ban through intense negotiations in the days following Luther's defiance, their efforts failed: on 21 May 1521, Emperor Charles V issued the Edict of Worms, putting Luther under imperial ban and essentially making him an outlaw in the empire. Several temporal powers feared that the ban and subsequent execution would halt what many considered to be desperately needed church reform. Thus, the Edict of Worms put many princes and magistrates in a vexingly difficult position between supporting reform and promoting heresy.

The Luther controversy at Worms presented even more fundamental questions for secular authorities. What were their duties and prerogatives over their subjects? To what degree were they bound to the authority of the emperor or of the pope? Although these had been perennial questions of empire in the medieval era, in the aftermath

26 There was solid legal basis for a hearing: as of diet proceedings of 1519, the emperor guaranteed a hearing to any citizen before being put under imperial ban. Aulinger, *Deutsche Reichstagsakten unter Kaiser Karl V,* 873, 9–14.

27 Oberman, *Luther: Man between God and the Devil,* 39.

28 Luther's petition for a day's reprieve has sometimes been interpreted as a lack of nerve. Martin Brecht argues to the contrary, noting that Luther did not anticipate being asked to wholly confess or recant his writings. Brecht, *Luther: His Road to Reformation,* 455; LW 48: 202; WA Br 2: 305.

of Worms they became acutely pressing with an immediate (or at least imminent), practical importance. To be sure, deferring these questions to "buy time" was possible: Frederick the Wise, after the emperor's edict, negotiated his way around it, thereby rendering impotent a condemnatory imperial edict in the very territory that housed the condemned heretic. But this evasion did not settle the pressing political questions.

In fact, Luther's theology of *sola fides* appeared to many to undermine the value of being a good subject: since ethical life had no bearing on divine justification, it seemed as though Luther's theology countenanced a shocking antinomian position that encouraged a revolt against all worldly powers. Luther had argued that Christians were free with respect to the law; therefore, many reformers began to ask, what ultimate value was it to respect and obey temporal authority? Could Christians simply take or leave their political authorities at their own discretion?

Instead of facing prosecution and almost certain execution or assassination, on his way back from Worms Luther was secretly taken, by the authority of his prince, to the Wartburg. There he would stay sequestered for the next ten months (from 4 May 1521 until 1 March 1522), concentrating on his writing and translating the New Testament into German.[29] But it was during this period in hiding that the controversial political questions came to the forefront of Luther's thinking. His letter from the Wartburg to his colleague and fellow reformer Philip Melanchthon on 13 July 1521[30] provides ample evidence of the consideration he was giving to questions of temporal authority. In fact, as this letter indicates, Luther and Melanchthon had been discussing the topic for some time. Luther replied to several matters elicited by another letter (no longer extant) from Melanchthon. When Luther turned to temporal authority, he maintained that he had kept to the thoughts he had *previously* held and discussed with Melanchthon; thus, the two men had debated the matter before the Diet of Worms, showing that the topic was important enough to have already been developed by them over time.

29 Brecht, *Martin Luther: Shaping and Defining the Reformation*, 1–56.

30 Although it was written earlier; Luther complains that it was supposed to have been sent "some days ago." LW 48: 256–63; WA Br 2: 356–9.

However, this letter also shows that Luther's thoughts on temporal authority were not driven by particular political affairs or crises but, first and foremost, by the difficulty of interpreting the two seemingly contradictory commands of the New Testament that at once seemed to uphold *and* to undermine political authority. Of course, for Luther and Melanchthon the biblical teaching on government had immediate contextual importance in the aftermath of Worms, but the emphasis in Luther's letter was clearly on determining this teaching, rather than addressing any immediate political crisis.

Hence, Luther argued that the words of Paul from Romans 13:1 could not be jettisoned: even though temporal authority "is neither commanded nor counselled in the Gospel," yet it is "commended to us and affirmed, as is the law of matrimony, which is also not directly connected by the Gospel."[31] Whereas Melanchthon was looking for some commandment from Christ regarding political authorities, Luther remained "caught in these Scripture passages [and had] nothing to challenge [his] position" that the political authority of the world was affirmed as a divine gift, "something to be honoured and remembered in our prayers."[32] Though without a direct command from Christ, Luther was emphatic: the Bible nevertheless affirmed the divine origins and purpose of temporal government.

Yet, by the fall of 1521, controversies over the proper course of reform and the nature of temporal authority were brought home to Wittenberg. During Luther's long absence from the town, several soon-to-be-considered radical reformers, such as Andreas Karlstadt (1486–1541), assumed leadership of the reform cause and sought to quickly institute major liturgical changes in the local churches, including radically altering the central rite of Christianity, the Eucharist, and conducting a general program of iconoclasm that sought destruction of all sacred images.[33] Thus, the winter of 1521–22 saw a clamorous mix of clergy, students, professors, and laity foment threatening demonstrations, angry debates, and even violence and destruction of property. So disruptive were these events that Luther, still at the Wartburg, learned of them through his Saxon court contacts and wished to personally investigate them. For three days in

31 LW 48: 259; WA BR 2: 357.
32 LW 48: 261; WA BR 2: 359.
33 Brecht, *Martin Luther: Shaping and Defining the Reformation*, 25–45.

early December, disguised with a beard and in a knight's garb, Luther secretly paid the first visit to Wittenberg since Worms under the identity of "Junker Jörg."[34] Although the worst disturbances were to come at the end of month, Luther had seen enough to prompt him, after returning to the Wartburg, to pen his *Sincere Admonition to All Christians to Guard Against Insurrection and Rebellion.*[35]

The *Sincere Admonition* is a pivotal text for the shift in focus between Luther's July 13 letter to Melanchthon and *Temporal Authority*. With the unrest on the ground in Wittenberg, and the threat of anarchy and complete disorder afoot, Luther insisted that serious reflection and coherent action needed to accompany church reform. In particular, a clear understanding of the temporal kingdom would have to accompany ecclesial reform, especially since – given the protection granted to him by his prince – reform was beginning to rely on the cooperation of princes and magistrates.

Two critically joined ideas, central to Luther's political thought, emerge in the *Sincere Admonition*, albeit in nascent and undeveloped form. First, coercion was legitimate – in the eyes of God – only in the hands of what Luther called the *ordenlicher*, or "duly constituted"[36] temporal authorities (which he did not define); second, the subjects of such authority had thus no legitimate grounds for rebellion against them. To be sure, this was not a highly developed political theory, but nevertheless it showed, in retrospect, the foundation for one that was soon to come. For now, echoing the inner/outer distinctions of *Christian Liberty*, Luther wrote that he was content to leave to temporal government the work of the "hands" and direct his teaching toward the "hearts" of fellow reformers.

The Historical Context of Temporal Authority

In the summer of 1522, Luther's preaching on 1 Peter was a formative influence upon *Temporal Authority*. The printed commentary, published in the following year,[37] contains an extensive treatment of

34 Ibid., 29.

35 LW 45: 51–74; WA 7: 676–87.

36 LW 45: 61; WA 7: 679.

37 The Weimar edition originally dated the preaching to 1523; however, nineteenth-century evidence pointed to the summer of 1522; see the introduction in *LW* 30: ix.1 Luther had in fact preached on 1 Peter in the summer of 1522, after he had returned from

the "two kinds of government." In his study of this epistle, Luther began to see not only that the temporal kingdom was a great divine gift worthy of service and honour but that this teaching was entirely complementary to the gospel and to his emphasis on *sola fides.* The commentary came in the aftermath of Luther's return to public preaching and his renewed emphasis on the law and gospel. Months earlier, at the beginning of March, Luther secretly returned the Wartburg; within days, he returned to preaching and teaching, producing some of the finest sermons and writings of his career.[38] The famous eight "Invocavit Sermons," beginning on March 9 and continuing throughout the week,[39] were exemplary of his law and gospel teaching and a concomitant reining-in of radicalism.

Seen in this context, his preaching on 1 Peter in the summer of 1522 was apt and timely, reinforcing the apostolic grounds for his views on temporal authority. In the foreword to the commentary, Luther argued that this "noblest" epistle contained "genuine and pure gospel."[40] Before saying so, Luther explained that by "gospel" he meant not a *particular* gospel account (such as Luke), but "nothing else than a sermon or report concerning the grace and mercy of God merited and acquired through the Lord Jesus Christ with His death."[41] Thus, for Luther, the gospel "is not what one finds in books and what is written in letters of the alphabet; it is rather an oral sermon and a living Word" that "announces to us the grace of God bestowed *gratis* and without our merit, and tells us how Christ took our place, rendered satisfaction for our sins, and destroyed them, and that He makes us pious and saves us through His work."[42] 1 Peter was one such conduit of the gospel; in fact, for Luther the epistle was as great as Paul's epistles to the Romans and *greater* than the four "gos-

Wartburg but before he penned *Temporal Authority* in the fall. His commentary on the epistle, based on his preaching, was published (like *Temporal Authority*) early in 1523. Although greater precision in the dating of both the commentary and the great political treatise eludes us, the importance of the epistle in the formation of Luther's two kingdoms teaching and in the writing of *Temporal Authority* is undeniable regardless of which text preceded the other.

38 Brecht, *Martin Luther: Shaping and Defining the Reformation*, 59.

39 Invocavit Sunday was the first Sunday of Lent; thus, Luther preached every day from Sunday to the following Sunday. LW 51: 70–100; WA 10 III: 1–64.

40 LW 30: 4; WA 12: 260.

41 LW 30: 3; WA 12: 259.

42 LW 30: 3; WA 12: 259.

pels," since the latter, Luther wrote, "do little more than relate the history of the deeds and miracles of Christ," whereas Paul and Peter were the "best evangelists" in teaching the living Word.[43]

How striking it was for Luther, therefore, that Peter and Paul's epistles were united in both gospel *and* a political-ethical teaching: 1 Peter 2:13–17, like Romans 13:1–2, counselled obedience, honour, and service to the political authorities as part of Christian life in light of the gospel. Thus, just as these epistles taught the "genuine and pure gospel," they also imparted a complementary political teaching. For Luther, the fact that Romans and 1 Peter agreed on the divine nature of political authority and the respect and obedience that it demanded showed not only that there was an apostolic teaching on the temporal kingdom but also that this would be a key teaching to accompany the programmatic reform that he and others were beginning to effect. It was this rediscovery of the complementary political teaching to the gospel that would later lead Luther to claim that he was one of the most important political thinkers since the age of the apostles. The ground for this outlandish claim becomes clear in his study of 1 Peter and its subsequent influence on *Temporal Authority*. Luther saw in the epistle very clearly that temporal government was a gift from God, and that it was supposed to be independent from the church and spiritual affairs. Programmatic reform would have to restore it to its proper divine purpose, and that most certainly did *not* entail some kind of radical political revolution, such as that attempted in the city of Münster in the 1530s. Again, the epistle helped shape Luther's thinking: living in light of the gospel meant that service and general obedience were due to the secular order, even if that order was unchristian or unjust. 1 Peter counselled honour and obedience to Roman emperors, just as Paul in Romans counselled honour to Nero. Revolutions for the sake of establishing a Christian polity would be breaking with the Petrine teaching. Of course, Luther would have to elaborate on the matter in *Temporal Authority* and in his writings on the Peasants' War of 1525, but the commentary on 1 Peter in 1522 shows that the foundation for his answers in these works was already there and being built on his interpretation of a key "gospel" epistle.

43 LW 30: 4; WA 12: 260.

After studying and teaching 1 Peter in the summer of 1522, but before writing *Temporal Authority* in late December, Luther showed in several of his writings his preoccupation with the "temporal kingdom." In fact, Luther wrote that he was intending to write a definitive treatise on the matter in the near future: on September 21, in a letter to jurist Johann von Schwarzenberg in Bamberg, Luther, apparently in disagreement with von Schwarzenberg's published ideas (in a book that has been lost), promised that a "booklet" (*Büchlein*) on reconciling temporal power with the gospel was forthcoming.[44] One month later, Luther preached a series of six sermons for the court of Duke John the Steadfast in Weimar, one of which – preached on 25 October 1522 – became something of a rough outline for *Temporal Authority*.[45] Although these sermons survive only as notes from someone in attendance, Luther's exposition of the tasks of temporal government and its separation from spiritual government was, at least in this piecemeal form, essentially the same as it would be in the definitive treatise to come.[46] Evidently, Luther's ideas had made a favourable impression on the court and his Duke, for John asked Luther if he would expand on his views in a treatise – which of course, as the letter to Schwarzenberg showed, Luther had already intended to do. Thus, in late December 1522, when Luther wrote *Temporal Authority*, he dedicated it to John the Steadfast, claiming that it was the product of the prince's wishes, but that it also came about out of "necessity" and the "entreaties of many."[47]

Temporal Authority was not written in response to an immediate political crisis in Luther's home principality. Rather, his most famous political work was chiefly the product of his developing theology while he preached the gospel and effected church reform. To be sure, as seen in the preceding chapter, Luther's age and German context were rife with political tensions and problems, and the Reformation would heighten many of them (such as the problem of resistance). But, relative to the rest of the early sixteenth century, the

44 WA BR 2: 600–1. This letter is not included in *Luther's Works*. Brecht, *Martin Luther: Shaping and Defining the Reformation*, 116.

45 WA 11: 371–93. These sermon notes are not translated in *Luther's Works*.

46 See Brecht's summary in *Martin Luther: Shaping and Defining the Reformation*, 116.

47 LW 45: 81; WA 11: 245.

autumn of 1522 was not a particularly tense time in the empire, nor is there much evidence for a shared belief between Luther and his close contemporaries of an impending political crisis in the empire. Such fears and crises would come later.

The most pressing political matter that influenced the composition of the treatise was addressed only as an "illustration" well into the second part: Luther's German translation of the New Testament, published in September of 1522, was put under publication bans, confiscated, and destroyed in Albertine Saxony, Bavaria, and Brandenburg. This ban, under the authority of Duke George of Saxony, Elector Joachim of Brandenburg, and Duke Wilhelm IV of Bavaria served for Luther as a negative example of the limits of temporal authority. These princes, Luther believed, had overextended their authority – as in Herod's murder of Christ![48] – into the jurisdiction of the spiritual kingdom and were imperilling souls through the ban. Nevertheless, while the controversy was high on Luther's mind, it was clearly not a *sine qua non* for the treatise's publication; it was for him yet another example, among many past and many to come, of the misunderstanding of the nature of temporal authority.

Luther's dedication to John the Steadfast and the outline of the treatise (in particular, the third part, on how to be a *Christian* prince) clearly show how he intended *Temporal Authority* as, foremost, a *pastoral* treatment of government for princes and magistrates who found themselves troubled by their competing obligations to fulfill the worldly duties of their office – especially prosecuting and punishing wrongdoers – and to live as Christians. The dedication and content clearly show that Luther first intended this treatise as pastoral advice to help Christians who occupied political offices negotiate between "turning the other cheek" and the necessities of law and order. Nevertheless, that overarching pastoral concern launched the definitive and foundational work of Luther's political thought.

48 LW 45: 112; WA 11: 267. This accusation, among many, is why Johannes Cochlaeus concluded that by *Temporal Authority* Luther had attacked princes with hatred and contempt. Johannes Cochlaeus, *The Deeds of Martin Luther From the Year of the Lord 1517 to the Year 1546 Related Chronologically to all Posterity*, 113–4.

The Restorative Emphasis in Luther's Political Thought

In the several instances in which Luther would later reflect upon the importance of *Temporal Authority* and its message, the degree of self-praise was so hyperbolic as to appear almost comical today. In his 1526 work *Whether Soldiers, Too, Can be Saved,* he claimed, "I might boast here that not since the time of the apostles have the temporal sword and temporal government been so clearly described or so highly praised as by me."[49] In his 1529 treatise, *On War Against the Turk,* he wrote, "I have written in such glorification of temporal government as no teacher has done since the days of the apostles, except, perhaps, St Augustine."[50] Such statements might easily be dismissed as vain self-aggrandizement if they did not provide a coherent basis for the whole of Luther's political thought as a restorative project to return temporal authority to its place as a precious gift of God that brings law and order to the world. For Luther, this was the lesson of Paul and Peter in their epistles, but it had been lost or corrupted in his age. *Temporal Authority* and Luther's two kingdoms and law and gospel theology were restoring it. Luther's boasts, therefore, were entirely serious: he was leading the way in nothing less than a reformation of the temporal order by restoring what he considered to be the apostolic teachings on government.

Throughout his life and career, Luther's political ideas would change and develop, but nevertheless they remained clear on the basic nature of temporal government: that it was divinely made to bring order and to curb sin, and thus deserved honour and service. Through this consistent teaching, Luther believed he was restoring government to its proper biblical and natural understanding. In his *On War Against the Turk,* one reads Luther framing his thought on temporal authority within an account that places him as recovering it from the ignorance and corruption of his contemporary world, and restoring service of temporal authority as service to God:

> This was the state of things at the time: no one had taught, no one had heard, and no one knew anything about temporal government, whence it came, what its office and work were, or how it ought to serve God. The most

49 LW 46: 95; WA 19 II: 625.
50 LW 46: 164; WA 30 II: 110.

learned men (I shall not name them) regarded temporal government as a heathen, human, ungodly thing, as though it jeopardized salvation to be in the ranks of the rulers. This is how the priests and monks drove kings and princes into the corner and persuaded them that to serve God they must undertake other works, such as hearing mass, saying prayers, endowing masses, etc. In a word, princes and lords who wanted to be pious men regarded their rank and office as of no value and did not consider it service of God.[51]

Though significant, Luther's boasts over his contributions were few. However, the emphasis on restoration in his thinking permeates much of what he had to write about temporal authority. Time and again, in a variety of works and contexts throughout his career, Luther excoriates his age for misunderstanding temporal authority while positing his own ideas as restoring honour and godly service to government through a true understanding of its nature. From his biblical commentaries to his treatises and even his hot polemics, Luther's theory of temporal government, with the reformation theology on which it was built, was presented as the complementary reformation of the political order that would restore it to its divine purposes.

Consider two of Luther's generally neglected biblical commentaries: his works on Psalm 2 and Ecclesiastes. In both of these commentaries, Luther's own position on temporal authority was presented as the foil to Satan and the sinful influences that perennially sought to corrupt and denigrate government. In his *Commentary on Psalm 2*,[52] published in 1532, Luther's interpretation of the first two verses of the psalm turns them into an attack on the two kingdoms:

Why do the nations conspire,
And the peoples plot in vain?
The kings of the earth set themselves,
And the rulers take counsel together,
Against the LORD and his anointed, saying
"Let us burst their bonds asunder,
and cast their cords from us."[53]

51 LW 46: 163; WA 30 II: 109.
52 LW 12: 1–136; WA 40 II: 193–212.
53 Psalm 2: 1–2. *New Revised Standard Version.*

For Luther, this conspiracy of nations, these kings counselling one another against God and his anointed, did not amount to a general indictment on political authority (though at first glance it might appear so), but an indictment of those who misunderstood its godly purpose and misused its authority. Using language similar to the two cities of Augustine of Hippo's *City of God*, Luther sketched a contrast between what he called the kingdom of Christ (*regnum Christi*) and the kingdom of the world (*regnum mundi*). Like the city of man in Augustine's classic work, Luther's kingdom of the world rejected the love and wisdom of God for the sake of futile self-love. But lest anyone confuse these two *regni* with his two kingdoms, Luther was explicit: temporal authority was an extraordinary gift from God that, though made for good, was abused by the *regnum mundi*. "It does not follow," Luther wrote, "that because the kingdoms of the world fight against the kingdom of Christ, they are evil in themselves."[54] In fact, temporal authority's purpose and limits, Luther argued, had been restored when the gospel had once again come to light. Luther argued that the gospel "does nothing else but liberate consciences from the fear of death so that we believe in the forgiveness of sins and hold fast to the hope of eternal life."[55] The gospel, Luther wrote, does not condemn temporal authority, nor remove or change it: "these things remain in their proper place." The evangelical reform, Luther's *Commentary on Psalm 2* showed, was restoring not only the gospel but the "proper place" of the precious gift of temporal authority, after a long reign of darkness of the *regnum mundi*.

Luther's interpretation of Ecclesiastes (published in 1532, though based on lectures from 1526) also displays the restorative emphasis consistent with his boasts. Luther viewed the book as the "Politics" or "Economics" of Solomon, meaning that it was a work of *pastoral counsel* to those who ruled governments and households (but not meaning that it taught *how* to rule them).[56] In seeing it so, Luther also argued that many of the received medieval interpretations of the book were "noxious," since these taught that the book imparted a general "contempt for the world" such that political office and household rule were best forsaken in favour of monastic withdrawal. Luther

54 LW 12: 11; WA 40 II: 203.
55 LW 12: 19; WA 40 II: 214.
56 LW 15: 5; WA 20: 7

countered such "monstrosities" and "loathsome idols" with his interpretation that the "point and purpose of this book [was] to instruct us, so that with thanksgiving we may use the things that are present and the creatures of God that are generously given to us and conferred upon us by the blessing of God."[57] Chief among those gifts, for Luther, was government. Luther's commentary on Ecclesiastes was intended as a corrective – and an ambitious one at that, considering the number of medieval commentaries on the book that preceded him – to the long neglect of government as a precious gift of God worthy of honour and service.

These two biblical commentaries also show how Luther sought to restore temporal authority to its divinely instituted purposes as the Bible had expressed it. Luther's two kingdoms and law and gospel theology, as well as the teaching on temporal authority that accompanied it, was first and foremost, as Luther understood it, biblically rooted. Thus, a fuller understanding of Luther's political thought must grapple with how Luther read and interpreted the Bible and in what ways scripture led him to articulate a coherent political teaching that complemented the evangelical message of salvation by faith.

57 LW 15: 10; WA 20: 13.

3

Luther's Political Thought and the Bible

THE BIBLE'S IMPORTANCE IN LUTHER'S POLITICAL THOUGHT

It would be hard to overstate the place of the Bible in Luther's thinking: throughout his career, in nearly all contexts when serious thought was required, he used scripture to guide him. Luther's hearing at the Diet of Worms famously showed the regard he had for the Bible as the foremost and final source of Christian authority. There, while facing imperial condemnation for his heresies and the pressing demands to retract his works and recant, he repeatedly claimed that unless his ideas were shown to him to contradict scripture he would remain steadfast to them. He had even claimed that his very conscience was captive to the Word of God and so could not be moved to adopt anything that would violate it.[1] His "captivity" to the Bible continued even after he was whisked away by Prince Frederick to the Wartburg, for he would spend much of his time in the next year of hiding furiously translating the New Testament into German.

But Luther's *use* of scripture – for any issue or dispute – demanded that it comply with what he considered to be the central truths God had revealed *through* the Bible. Luther did not merely quote passages from the Bible as proof of divine sanction or prohibition. For Luther, regardless of the topic or how strongly it pleaded its case, if a particular biblical passage failed to cohere with the gospel proclamation of

1 LW 32: 112; WA 7: 838.

salvation by faith alone, it simply could not be considered an authoritative biblical teaching.

All of Luther's politically relevant treatises were written with what he believed to be a solid foundation in biblical revelation. This relationship of Luther's political thought to the Bible went far beyond mere biblical references he made in his works; thus, as he repeatedly invoked Paul's command to be subject to the political authorities (Romans 13:1), he was not merely citing a topically convenient scriptural passage on a marginal issue, but drawing attention to the deep and immeasurable connection of the purpose of government to God's salvation.

In the history of political thought, however, this deep connection to the Bible has sometimes been ignored or misunderstood, leading in turn to misrepresentations of Luther's political ideas. One such misrepresentation is to see Luther's political thought as an attempt to parse off the political realm of action from Christian ethics, leaving the political order, as Sheldon Wolin put it, "without counterweight."[2] In this view, Luther's temporal government becomes something independent and autonomous, and thus a direct precursor to the modern state that engulfs the ethical worlds of individuals and communities, all the while distancing itself from theological considerations on the purpose of government. Such an interpretation of Luther, however, cannot be squared with the intimate relationship of his temporal kingdom with his biblical hermeneutic. For Luther at least, the Bible was a very heavy counterweight to any supposed political autonomy.

Ignoring Luther's works on the Bible – such as commentaries and lectures – has greatly skewed his place in some of the most well-known and influential interpretations of the history of political thought. Quentin Skinner, in his 1979 political history of the Reformation, correctly argued that the Bible was the final authority for Luther's political ideas, yet he not only failed to account for what that authority meant for Luther but also failed to consider even one

2 Sheldon Wolin, *Politics and Vision*, 143. For further treatment of this argument, see chapter 7.

commentary, lecture, or sermon on a biblical book.[3] Consequently, without consideration of the biblical basis of Luther's political thought, Skinner concluded his study with the erroneous claim that the reformer "made no appeal to the scholastic concept of a universe ruled by law" and "scarcely any appeal even to the concept of intuited law by nature."[4] On the contrary, as the *Commentary on Psalm 101* and his *Lectures on Genesis* clearly show, Luther's considerations of the rule of law and scripture were much broader than any narrow reading, based only on explicitly political treatises from the 1520s, has argued. For Luther, the Bible *affirmed* that law ruled the universe and that Christians and pagans alike could discover this fact – by reason.[5]

Because of his rich biblical theology, as well as the importance of law and the temporal kingdom in it, Luther's commentaries and lectures on biblical books contained some of his most intriguing and insightful political works and provide a corrective for common misunderstandings. In particular, many of Luther's lectures and commentaries on the Bible help reinforce how he considered not only that the two kingdoms are biblically grounded, but also that temporal government was a universal divine gift ubiquitous in God's creation and grasped and understood by reason. From his commentaries on Psalms to his famous lectures on Genesis, Luther showed that political teachings abounded in scripture and validated his effort to praise government as one of God's most precious gifts.

But how did Luther become convinced that the Bible taught a clear and coherent political teaching? How was he convinced that his interpretation and appropriation of it was sound? The answers to these questions are found in the way Luther held to the principle of *sola scriptura* and the hermeneutic of law and gospel that he used to adhere to it.

3 *Foundations of Modern Political Thought*, vol. 2, *The Reformation*. Skinner did make some introductory remarks on glosses and *scholia* on Romans and the Psalms from the reformer's early professorial career.

4 Skinner, *Foundations of Modern Political Thought, Volume* 2, 19. Skinner's erroneous claim is baffling, since the evidence to the contrary is overwhelming. Whitford noted that Luther uses "natural law," "laws of nature," and "command of God" – the latter being something written in human hearts as distinct from commandment – 583 times in the *Luther's Works* translations; "*Cura religionis* or Two Kingdoms," 57.

5 This fact is clear even in his early polemical works from the 1520s. Consider, for example, his argument for natural law in *Against the Heavenly Prophets*, LW 40: 97.

LUTHER AND *SOLA SCRIPTURA*

One of the most powerful general principles of the Reformation was *sola scriptura*, the belief in the Bible alone as an authoritative source. Essentially, the principle of *sola scriptura* in the sixteenth century taught that other authoritative sources, such as tradition or philosophical argument, no matter how time honoured or how reasonable, could not by themselves reliably sanction church doctrine and practice if these in their particulars could not be first demonstrated biblically. To be sure, the Bible had always been the first and most important source of Christian theology and doctrine; medieval scholasticism, despite being a usual target of reforming polemics, prioritized the Bible above all else for authoritative theology and doctrine.[6] What generally distinguished reformers in the sixteenth century from their predecessors was both their emphasis on this principle and their development of distinct biblical hermeneutics that guided it. But even an agreed emphasis on *sola scriptura*, especially when biblical hermeneutics differed, did not translate into widespread agreement on biblical meaning and the liturgy and doctrine that derived from it.

The public disagreement between Luther and Huldrych Zwingli at the Marburg Colloquy in 1529 was a prescient indication that reform based on *sola scriptura* was by no means as simple as the principle might at first have seemed.[7] Although the colloquy was intended to foster unity among reformers before the second imperial diet of Speyer, Luther and Zwingli failed to agree on the meaning of none other than Christianity's most sacred rite – the Eucharist – because of conflicting positions of biblical interpretation over the meaning of Jesus's words "This is my body."

Rather than providing a simple and clear unifying principle, *sola scriptura* would be the source of great disagreement and conflict. It proved to be philosophically complex and politically explosive. Philosophically, disagreement over the meaning of *sola scriptura* would embroil reformers (such as Luther and Zwingli) in the ontological status of particulars and universals, the limits of language for

6 See the extensive account of what McGrath calls the "medieval priority of scripture" in *Intellectual Origins of the European Reformation*, 119–47.

7 Brecht, *Martin Luther: Shaping and Defining the Reformation*, 325–44.

expressing theological reality, and the meaning of God's eternal presence in a world of becoming. Politically, some versions of the *sola scriptura* were very dangerous to Luther's own view of temporal authority as a divine gift worthy of honour and respect. Many radical reformers, on the basis of a version of *sola scriptura*, had begun fomenting revolt against princes and magistrates because the Bible, they believed, had taught them that political authority was hopelessly demonic.

Sola Scriptura *for Luther: the Gospel*

Luther's adherence to the *sola scriptura* principle was qualified by a theology that distinguished the words of the Bible from the Word of God. The Word of God, or the gospel, was not equated with the Bible, but was transmitted or proclaimed by it. The Word or gospel, in its simplest form, was the message of Christ's gift of righteousness. The whole biblical canon of both the Old and New Testaments was understood as proclaiming this Word. Although the Old Testament predated the life of Jesus, it pointed to Christ as a divine promise to be fulfilled. The purest proclamations of the Word were to be found in the New Testament, but the epistles therein could nevertheless be divided and distinguished by how strongly and clearly they each proclaimed the Word. For Luther, because both of the testaments were conduits of the Word and ultimately Christocentric, all authoritative Biblical interpretation must also be Christological. "Take Christ out of the Scriptures," Luther wrote to Erasmus in *The Bondage of the Will*, "and what will you find left in them?"[8] In Luther's view, this did not mean that any given passage must be reduced to an immediate Christological meaning, but that any given biblical interpretation had to cohere with the overarching proclamation of the Word.

Luther's Christ-centred hermeneutic sought to revise the prevailing medieval approach to the Bible, namely the *Quadriga*, or "fourfold sense of Scripture." This old hermeneutic looked for four possible meanings in biblical passages: the *literal* meaning, or face value of the text; the *allegorical* meaning, or the meaning derived from words that were otherwise obscure or unacceptable in their

8 LW 33: 26; WA 16: 606. Lohse, *Martin Luther's Theology*, 189.

usual meanings; the *tropological* meaning, or the lessons on moral conduct; and the *anagogical* meaning, or the hope in a fulfillment of divine promises. In the wake of humanist criticism of the *Quadriga*'s literal meaning of scripture, most notably that of Jacques Lefèvre d'Étaples (c. 1455–1536), Luther was convinced that the supposedly singular literal meaning could in fact be understood in two distinct ways: a literal-historic meaning, or the face-value account of events, and a literal-prophetic meaning that placed those events in a larger prophetic context of scripture.[9]

Luther's early lectures on the Psalms (1513–15) show how he had begun to break off from the *Quadriga* method of interpretation and develop his Christological hermeneutic. In the preface to his *Dictata super Psalterium,* he wrote that there was a great contrast between the words understood by the flesh, known as the "letter," and the words made clear by God as the "spirit" of scripture.[10] With this distinction, plus the scholastic fourfold meaning of scripture, Luther listed eight possible interpretations of the phrase "Mount Zion."[11] This multiplicity of meanings would create a mass of confusion, leaving biblical authority a "mockery" unless an interpretation could be affirmed elsewhere in scripture by another, "literal-spirit" meaning. Thus, for Luther, the literal-spirit meaning of scripture was the governing meaning of scripture: there were no doubt allegorical, tropological, and anagogical meanings, but they were "valid" only if they were "expressly stated [literally] elsewhere."[12] In Luther's thinking, there was a hierarchy of biblical meaning that the *Quadriga,* even for its advantages, had failed to privilege; central truths were proclaimed in the Bible, and these truths validated (or invalidated) *all* biblical interpretation.

9 Roland Bainton, "The Bible in the Reformation," 25; McGrath, *Intellectual Origins of the European Reformation,* 152.

10 LW 10: 3; WA 3: 11. The contrast of "spirit" and "letter," though greatly expanded upon by theologians such as Augustine of Hippo, originated with Paul in 2 Corinthians 3:4–11; it is also closely related to his law and spirit distinction in other epistles (Romans 7:7–13, Galatians 3:19–29). There is also an approximate Hebrew Bible analog in living the law and "circumcising the heart" in Deuteronomy 30: 1–19.

11 LW 10: 4; WA 3: 11. See also Ebeling, "Der vierfache Schriftsinn und die Unterscheidung von litera und spiritus," 51–61.

12 LW 10: 4; WA 3: 11.

In 1515–16, a mere year or so after lecturing on the Psalms, and around the same time as Luther had reached his theological breakthrough over justification while lecturing on Paul's Epistle to the Romans, he also discovered he had not only settled an immensely important pastoral question but had also uncovered a hermeneutic key to all biblical authority and revelation. Justification by faith alone was so important and so central a truth, Luther believed, that it was an architectonic truth to all biblical understanding. Once Luther saw that the core of the gospel message was salvation by faith alone in Christ, he wrote in the Latin preface to his collected works, "A totally other face of the entire Scripture showed itself to me."[13] No longer was Luther either grappling with justification or struggling for meaning in opaque passages or texts of the Old and New Testaments, for the whole Bible became for him one coherent revelation of the mercy and righteousness of God given to humanity through the death and resurrection of Jesus.

Through his "discovery" of *sola fides*, Luther came to believe that the Bible was its own interpreter, for it revealed through the gospel proclamation its own standard for authoritative teaching that was dependent not on traditions or reasoned argument as such, but on the reception of God's revelation of the Word through scripture. It was not that Luther dismissed traditional doctrines and practices or powers of human reasoning in his biblical interpretations – far from it – but that all reasoning, tradition, and interpretation had to first be validated by the proclamation of the Word. Moreover, it was not that Luther ignored the many styles of literature, including prayers, laws, and prophecies; rather, for Luther, all these seemingly disparate works gained their unity either in the proclamation of Jesus Christ as the Word of God or in the prophetic coming of that Word. This unity of proclamation and interpretation was the essence of *sola scriptura* for Luther: the Bible was at once the message and its interpretation.

With his hermeneutic centred on *sola fides*, Luther prioritized certain texts of the Bible for their clear proclamations or prophecies of the gospel over others that he considered weak. One of Luther's clearest statements on the matter was in his 1522 preface to his translation of the New Testament, in which he gives Christian readers

13 LW 34: 337; WA 54: 186.

advice for prioritizing certain books in their devotions and in their attempt to receive and understand biblical revelation:

From all this you can now judge all the books and decide among them which are the best. John's Gospel and St Paul's epistles, especially that to the Romans, and St Peter's first epistle are the true kernel and marrow of all the books. They ought properly to be the foremost books, and it would be advisable for every Christian to read them first and most, and by daily reading to make them as much his own as his daily bread. For in them you do not find many works and miracles of Christ described, but you do find depicted in masterly fashion how faith in Christ overcomes sin, death, and hell, and gives life, righteousness, and salvation. This is the real nature of the gospel, as you have heard.[14]

But, just as Luther gave priority to the Gospel of John and the writings of Paul, he minced few words in relaying what books confused or inhibited the proclamation and reception of the Word. Foremost among them was the Epistle of James, which he called an "epistle of straw" in that it appeared to praise the righteousness of "good works" and thus had "nothing of the nature of the Gospel about it."[15] Luther considered Revelation, Hebrews, and Jude inadequate for similar reasons; although these books contained "fine teaching with all honour ... we cannot put it on the same level with the apostolic epistles."[16]

The "Law" in the Bible

For Luther, although the Bible cohered in Christ, the whole of scripture was not only a revelation of the gospel but also a revelation of what he distinguished as "law." Perhaps the most obvious example of this law was the enormous body of ethical, communal, and ritual code contained in the first five books of Moses. With what he believed to be based on the apostolic teaching of Paul in his epistles (and indeed, for most of the Christian tradition), Luther considered many parts of this Mosaic law to be non-binding upon Christians, but this did not mean that Leviticus (for example) contained long-expired historical artifacts from ancient Israel that bore no significance to

14 LW 35: 361–2; WA DB 6: 8.
15 Ibid.
16 LW 35: 395; WA DB 7: 345.

gospel. Rather, Mosaic law was properly understood and interpreted only through Christ, since that law condemned sin, promised mercy and salvation, and ultimately (in Jesus) fulfilled that promise.[17]

For Luther, the law was neither in conflict with the gospel nor identical to the Old Testament or an old covenant with the people of Israel. Luther considered the law in the Bible as dynamically and dialectically connected to the gospel: the gospel was understood with the law, and vice versa. They were inseparable parts of the same revelation to humanity. This dyad of law and gospel pervaded *all* of scripture; law was not simply given in the explicit code of Leviticus but was intricately maintained throughout the Old and New Testaments. In fact, some of Luther's most important and expository writings on the law came in commentaries and lectures on the New Testament, such as in his 1531 lectures on Paul's epistle to the Galatians, in which the apostle emphatically taught that faith in Christ, not observing the Mosaic law, made people justified before God.[18]

There and elsewhere, though hardly in any systematic fashion, Luther wrote of multiple uses or purposes of the law as they were revealed in the Bible.[19] Foremost for him was the theological purpose of the law, which accuses and convicts us for our sins. The law under this use, and in stark contrast to the gospel, could not in any way aid us in achieving righteousness, but rather made us aware of our unrighteousness. But for Luther, by making men aware of their unrighteousness and their powerlessness to justify themselves, the theological use of the law directed an accused and convicted humanity straight to the gospel. In his lectures on Galatians, Luther claimed that the "law is a minister and a preparation for grace."[20] Hence, law and gospel were an inseparable dyad at the core of biblical revelation.[21]

But preparing for the gospel was not the only use of the law. God also willed the law to govern the "outer nature" of humankind for the worldly purpose of peace and order. Through government

17 Lohse, *Martin Luther's Theology*, 273–5.

18 See his discussion on the function and use of the law beginning in LW 26: 306; WA 40 I: 473. These lectures were delivered in 1531 but were not published until 1535.

19 See Engelbrecht, *Friends of the Law*. See Engelbrecht's appendix on Luther's phrases for use of the law, 259–60, for a list of primary source references on the matter.

20 LW 26: 314; WA 40 I: 477.

21 Lohse, *Martin Luther's Theology*, 270–1.

authorities, teachers, and parents, humanity was instructed by the law through reasoned argument and just practices; meanwhile, to deal with transgressions, the law also legitimated the coercive punishment of sin and the standards by which it was to do so. With some variations throughout his works, Luther called this use of the law "civil" or "political." Though secondary to the spiritual use of the law, the political use was nevertheless also biblically revealed: for Luther, its use was clearly present in the laws of Moses and even in Paul's teaching of obedience to imperial jurisdiction. Thus, Luther believed that the Bible gave a clear corrective to what he considered to be the sinful corruptions of antinomianism or moral and legal relativism. God instituted the law for peace and order, and so wherever this second use was encountered in the world, such as in temporal government, it was to be honoured and respected for its divine purpose.

In a few instances in his works, Luther wrote explicitly of a third use of the law as an instruction or guide to living for the faithful.[22] This third use of the law was adopted by Melanchthon in his *Loci Communes Theologici* in 1535,[23] and it soon became a matter of theological controversy in the German Reformation, even leading to explicit affirmations of a "third use" in the *Formula of Concord* of 1577 against accusations that the doctrine implicitly revived a belief in justification by works. In recent times, Luther's second explicit passage (from his second Antinomian Disputation of 1538) has been considered to be an interpolation by one of Melanchthon's students into the transcript.[24] Even more recently, however, this conclusion has been questioned, and Luther's commitment to the third use of the law, even if not often explicitly stated, has been affirmed.[25]

The consistency of the third use of the law with Luther's thought is reasonable, especially given that in no way did he see the law diminish in the lives of Christians as distinct from unbelievers. For Luther, Christians remained both righteous *and* sinful; therefore, the first accusatory function of the law remained active (in fact, it was still essential to the dyad of law and gospel, and thus to faith in

22 WA 10 I: 456; WA 39 I: 485. These are not translated in *Luther's Works*.

23 CR 21: 405–6.

24 See Ebeling, "On the Doctrine of the *Triplex Usus Legis* in the Theology of the Reformation."

25 This is the convincing argument of Engelbrecht in *Friends of the Law*.

Christ's salvation), and as human beings in this world, the second use remained as well. Luther *always* argued that humanity was subject to temporal government, and so the third use concept was complementary to his unfeigned praise of the divine gift of government. Thus, the third use, the idea that the law tutored believers in living good lives while in no way contributing to their justification, seems quite reconcilable to Luther's writings even if it remained only in rudimentary form. It fits with his overall biblical interpretation.

Through the Bible Luther came to see that temporal government was inextricably part of God's will for all humanity. For Luther, the Bible had clearly revealed the law not only to point to salvation in the gospel but also to bring peace and order to humanity on earth. The Bible's representation of law, such as the Mosaic law of Deuteronomy or Paul's treatment of imperial jurisdiction, clearly showed how God had instituted the law for multiple functions, and thus how the political uses of the law, and hence temporal government in general, had to be respected and honoured as a divine gift. It was the Bible, therefore, that revealed to Luther the nature and purpose of the temporal kingdom and the extent to which it brought order to human life.

THE TWO KINGDOMS IN SCRIPTURE

Many studies in the history of political thought have rightly focused on Luther's two kingdoms thinking as the cornerstone of his political ideas, but seldom have any studies given an account of the Bible as the paramount source of this teaching. Instead, attention has often been paid to supposed antecedents in late antiquity and the Middle Ages of Luther's two kingdoms, including Augustine's two cities and the long-standing medieval doctrine of the two swords epitomized by Pope Boniface VIII's *Unam Sanctam.*[26] These likely exerted some influence on Luther's two kingdoms thinking, but since he never acknowledged or discussed them, and given that his own ideas differed significantly from them anyhow, the measure of these influences can only remain amorphous and vague. The Bible, by

26 See Figgis, *Studies of Political Thought from Gerson to Grotius*; Schwiebert, "The Medieval Pattern in Luther's View of the State," 98–117. Figgis's Luther bridges medieval political thought to modern absolutism; Schwiebert's Luther is in continuity with the medieval conceptions of political authority.

contrast, especially the Epistles of Paul and Peter and the Gospels of the New Testament, was overwhelmingly acknowledged by Luther as the source of his two kingdoms teaching and, in turn, his ideas on temporal government.

As the definitive statement on the two kingdoms and its meaning for political and ethical life, *Temporal Authority* deserves its place as the most significant political work of Luther's career, as well as one of the most important political writings of the Reformation. But it cannot be denied that the formation of Luther's ideas in *Temporal Authority* came directly from his wrestling with the gospel's relationship to political authority and ethics in the New Testament. Once again, Luther's letter to Melanchthon on 13 July 1521 (a year and a half before *Temporal Authority* was published) attests to this fact, clearly showing Luther's struggle with the statements of the apostles Paul and Peter regarding the "sword" and governmental authority and its meaning in the light of the gospel: "I cannot allow you to reject the statements of the Apostles Paul in Romans 13[:1–2] and Peter in I Peter 2[:13–14] as if they were not applicable here, or as if they were only instructing the citizens. You will not accomplish this, my Philip! These are words of God – of great importance – when Paul says: [temporal] authority is from God, and whosoever resists [temporal] authority resists God's ordinance, and [temporal authority] is the servant of God."[27] The gospel affirmed and commended the sword, Peter and Paul had emphatically commanded it, and thus the apostolic epistles became the guiding texts on Luther's early political thought.

Returning once again to the commentary on 1 Peter, based on his summer lectures in 1522, we see that Luther had discovered that this "genuine and pure gospel" epistle had a coherent and compelling teaching on government. In his understanding, 1 Peter reconciled the gospel and the sword by teaching how God had ordained "two kinds of government" throughout the world, one for Christians (i.e., the spiritual government of the gospel) and one for "unbelievers" (i.e., the government of law and order). Temporal government, including its use of the sword, was ordained by God to bring peace to "external matters" among sinners. As such, these governments were

27 LW 48: 260; WA BR 2: 358.

entirely complementary to one another, and it was therefore a work of Christian love for neighbours to serve and respect the political authority, even though Christians – insofar as they were Christians – were governed purely by the Holy Spirit. Governments of pagan Romans, as in the case of 1 Peter, or of heretical Turks (for, as he preached on the epistle, the Turkish invasion of Eastern Europe encroached on German-speaking lands),[28] provided they refrained from infringing the gospel and spiritual government, were all alike to be obeyed and served in their times as the instruments of God for peace and order among men.

For Luther, 1 Peter revealed that gospel freedom was reconcilable with the enforcement of laws because God had ordained two governments for very different but concurrent jurisdictions over humanity. Apparent conflicts between the demands of the gospel and the demands of secular authorities were *only apparent* conflicts: this was a prevailing teaching in 1 Peter's second chapter, and it was also the pastoral crisis upon which *Temporal Authority* began. Luther emphatically believed that reconciliation between the commands of Christ and the demands of princes was an authentic teaching of the Word of God.

But another text of the New Testament appeared to oppose the divine legitimacy of the sword in no uncertain terms: none other than the sayings of Jesus found within the discourse known as the Sermon on the Mount. "Do not resist an evildoer," Jesus said, "but if anyone strikes you on the right cheek, turn the other also."[29] Such a teaching appeared to counsel a radical ethic for Christian life, one that seemed to demand jettisoning the duties of subjects or citizens to uphold justice and to serve the temporal order. Wielding the sword, such as serving in war, or executing punishment, or even in self-defence, appeared to be irreconcilable – or at least in great tension – with Jesus's teaching on how to live as a disciple. Thus, the interpretation of Jesus's teaching was of immense importance, since it spoke directly to the essence of Christian living under government. In the Reformation, many radical reformers had been taking Jesus's words as an endorsement for withdrawal from the exercise of all political authority, so it behoved Luther to preach on how Jesus's

28 LW 30: 75; WA 12: 329.
29 Matthew 5:38–9 (NRSV).

teaching was reconcilable to the Pauline and Petrine injunctions to serve and honour government.

Christian Liberty and *Temporal Authority* answered this directly with an account of the two kingdoms: both Peter's command to obey and serve authority and Jesus's command to "turn the other cheek" must be taken seriously, and these commands were reconciled by seeing Christians as at once both "inner" and "outer," or spiritual and temporal, beings. But Luther's two kingdoms was no mere external or *sui generis* solution to an otherwise intractable biblical problem, even though reading only *Temporal Authority* and ignoring his biblical commentaries may indeed give that impression. Rather, Luther believed that the two kingdoms doctrine was a wholly biblical teaching, a fact confirmed by his insistence on the idea when he preached on the Sermon on the Mount to the *Stadtkirche* in Wittenberg from 1530 to 1532.[30]

Even though Luther's sermons were redacted into the published commentary of 1532, they were unmistakably his, for they contained one of the most clear and succinct explanations of his two kingdoms as a reconciliation of the ethical demands of Jesus and Paul. In short, Luther argued, "Christ is addressing His sermon only to His Christians."[31] A Christian was subject only to Christ, but a subject was under the law and must uphold it for himself and his neighbour. But one man was both Christian and subject: in this life, he would always be a "Christian-in-relation" and thus would always have an obligation to himself and others to protect property and persons.[32] "Thus when a Christian goes to war or when he sits on a judge's bench, punishing his neighbour, or when he registers an official complaint, he is not doing this as a Christian, but as a soldier or a judge or a lawyer," Luther argued, but "at the same time he keeps a Christian heart" and "lives simultaneously as a Christian toward everyone."[33] With the whole person living in two kingdoms, Luther believed he had saved both Jesus's and Paul's teaching as *applicable*

30 Luther took over preaching duties while the regular pastor (and Luther's friend, confessor, and fellow evangelical reformer), Johannes Bugenhagen (1485–1558), was away reforming the church in Lübeck. Brecht, *Martin Luther: Shaping and Defining the Reformation*, 434.

31 LW 21: 107; WA 32: 388.

32 LW 21: 109; WA 32: 390.

33 LW 21: 113; WA 32: 393.

and *binding* for all Christians. The heretical alternative, Luther believed, was to consider Christ's commands as counsel only to "those who would be perfect" and not to all Christians. Luther considered this view a blasphemous abomination that overturned the Word. By contrast, his interpretation saved the integrity of the Bible: "I do not doubt that here I have presented their true, pure, and Christian meaning to my friends and to anyone else that is interested," Luther wrote in the commentary's preface; "it is beyond understanding how through his apostles the wicked devil has managed so cleverly to twist and pervert especially the fifth chapter, making it teach the exact opposite of what it means."[34] For Luther, only a biblically centred hermeneutic could retain in full force the teachings of Christ and the apostles as one consistent divine Word.

Government as Divine Gift in the Bible

Luther believed that the Reformation, with its re-emergence of the gospel, was restoring temporal government to its rightful place as a divine gift worthy of honour and service. Luther saw this restoration as essentially biblically based: the Bible clearly taught that political government was one of God's most precious gifts, as valuable as life itself. It is no surprise, therefore, that many of Luther's meditations on the meaning of this divine gift are found in his lectures and commentaries on various parts of the biblical canon. From his lectures on Genesis to his commentaries on several psalms and wisdom books, Luther found an abundance of biblical teachings on temporal government.

Luther's *Commentary on Psalm 82* (1530)[35] is one of the most striking, for it clearly distances him from supporting autocratic authority and counselling unquestioning obedience to tyranny. Written during his stay at the fortress of Coburg during the tense Diet of Augsburg and the imperial crisis, the commentary commanded sober pause from any political authority who believed a renewed respect for the temporal kingdom now gave them unlimited authority over the affairs of their territories. Luther argued that Psalm 82 strongly affirmed government as a divine gift, but that with the use of that gift

34 LW 21: 3; WA 32: 299.
35 LW 13: 39–72; WA 31 I: 189–218.

came profound duties and responsibilities that must be fulfilled lest the government incur God's wrath.

Luther wrote that because Psalm 82 so clearly praised temporal government for its nobility and virtues (even repeatedly calling rulers "gods") and implored rulers to use the office with such great care, "every prince should have [it] painted on the wall of his chamber, on his bed, over his table, and on his garments" as a constant reminder of the divine purposes of political authority and the specific duties God commanded that it exercise.[36] In the first few verses of the psalm, Luther saw several princely virtues that the temporal government was to practice, such that it would be "the highest service of God and the most useful office on earth."[37] First among these virtues was to "secure justice for those who fear God and repress those who are godless."[38] For Luther, this virtue demanded that the temporal power was to secure a place for the teaching and preaching of the gospel in its land. More than supporting the construction of grandiose churches and Renaissance artwork, Luther's example showed that even though the two kingdoms were separated, the godly purposes of political authorities included some degree of magisterial support for pastors. Although he always insisted that they be strictly separated, it was unclear where exactly in this pastoral oversight Luther would draw the line separating the two kingdoms.[39]

The second virtue in Psalm 82 was to bring the "poor, the orphans, and the widows to justice, and to further their cause."[40] In Luther's view, this virtue demanded that the temporal authority maintain good laws and customs so as to protect the most vulnerable, found hospitals for the whole nation and thereby protect the poor from beggary, and protect beggars from becoming destitute.[41] Luther offered St Elizabeth of Thuringia, princess of Hungary and Landgravine of Thuringia, and perhaps one of the most venerated saints of the

36 LW 13: 51; WA 31 I: 198.

37 LW 13: 51; WA 31 I: 198.

38 LW 13: 52; WA 31 I: 199.

39 It is in Luther's *Commentary on Psalm 82* that James M. Estes detects a change in Luther's thinking over the *cura religionis*, or magisterial oversight of church reform, and thus Luther moves toward Melanchthon's position; Whitford's "*Cura religionis* or Two Kingdoms" counters Estes's argument.

40 LW 13: 53; WA 31 I: 200.

41 LW 13: 54; WA 31 I: 201.

Middle Ages, as the princely model: she had founded a famous hospital near the Wartburg and tirelessly served the poor and ill until her early death at twenty-three.

Psalm 82's third virtue demanded that temporal government guard against violence and force and thus become a general peacemaker that upholds the rule of law and enforces the punishment of wrongdoing. This virtue decidedly prioritized the rule of reasonable law: "[L]aw is wisdom and should be the first of the two," Luther wrote, "for government by force without wisdom does not last."[42] Peace was a heavenly stronghold, more useful than the strongholds of walled cities and impenetrable fortresses, and more heavenly than anything brought to the world by monks and priests. It is from peace, Luther wrote, "that we have our bodies and lives, wives, and children, houses and homes, all our members – hands, feet, and eyes – and all our health and liberty."[43] The status of temporal authority as a most esteemed gift of God meant that it was duty bound to promote its most sacred end, peace; "lack of peace," Luther wrote, "may be counted half of hell, or hell's prelude and beginning."

Luther's *Commentary on Psalm 82* chided princes for not being *Heilande*, "saviours of the country," or *Landesväter*, "fathers to the people"; they did not bring peace, aid the poor, provide for the preaching of the Word, or rule justly.[44] Contrary vices, rather than virtues, were in fact ruling the day and thus corrupting God's precious gift and jeopardizing the souls and bodies of rulers and ruled alike. Luther's commentary focused on a particularly timely vice for German powers: the failure to deal properly with heresy.[45] For Luther, it was the duty of temporal government to suppress heresy because it often counselled rebellion or sedition, such as the abandonment of property or family, and thus failed to respect the proper jurisdiction of temporal government. Even the suppression of heretical doctrines was within the sphere of temporal government, Luther believed, since the teaching and proclaiming of such doctrines was blasphemous and, as such, a threat to public order and lawfulness. This would prove to be one of the most troubling and

42 LW 13: 55; WA 31 I: 201.
43 LW 13: 55; WA 31 I: 202.
44 LW 13: 53; WA 31 I: 200.
45 LW 13: 61–62; WA 31 I: 208.

difficult responsibilities of government for Luther to explain.[46] Yet in this commentary Luther even viewed temporal government as a proper arbiter for peacefully settling disputes between "papists" and "Lutherans" when clear and determinative demonstrations in the Bible were wanting.[47] If biblical demonstrations *were* clear, or if certain persons taught against the Word and refused to stop teaching their doctrines, they were to be coercively treated by temporal powers as rebels against the public order and corrupters of the divine gift of government.

In his *Commentary on Psalm 82*, Luther's good prince, as a saviour, father, and deliverer, and thus with powers to guarantee the rule of law, to maintain order, and to oversee the preaching and teaching of the gospel, seemed to be approaching the absolutism that he has often been accused of encouraging. But Luther's own reading of Psalm 82, and the Bible in general, dispels such a conclusion. Psalm 82 strongly asserts the role of God's judgment and wrath (in the forms of rebellion, invasion, and collapse) for failing, for instance, to give justice for the weak and the orphan (v. 3). Years earlier, in his *Exposition of Psalm 127 for the Christians in Livonia* (1524), Luther had warned princes not to believe that even their own good diligence preserved regimes, lest they become either worrisome or arrogant, for in the end governments were upheld only by the will of God.[48] But while the *good* prince lived precariously, the abusive and neglectful prince, the psalm warned, would be destroyed by God's wrath and lose his power. Psalm 82 warned authorities who shirked their duties that damnation was near. "They do not believe this terrible threat and condemnation," Luther wrote, "but must be made to experience it. All history is full of illustrations of this."[49]

Further reflections on the neglect of God's gift and the limits of political power came in Luther's *Commentary on Psalm 2* (1532). Based on lectures that he had completed after having famously taught on Paul's epistle to the Galatians,[50] this commentary was preoccupied with Paul's contrast of life in the Spirit with life in the flesh,

46 See chapter 5, 119–22.
47 LW 13: 62–3; WA 31 I: 209.
48 LW 45: 329; WA 15: 370.
49 LW 13: 72; WA 31 I: 218.
50 Brecht, *Martin Luther: Shaping and Defining the Reformation*, 455–6.

except here the Pauline contrast is translated into an apocalyptic and eschatological clash of warring *regna* or kingdoms, quite similar to Augustine's two cities in his *City of God*. The kingdom of Christ, along with its saving gospel, and the kingdom of the world that ceaselessly sought to destroy it were obviously distinguished from Luther's *zwei Reiche*: the former two kingdoms were radically opposed to one another, one kingdom furthering the rule of God and the other devilishly opposed to it. Luther's temporal kingdom, by contrast, had always been the means by which God brought order to the external world, and was thus entirely complementary to the spiritual kingdom. In this commentary, Luther saw temporal powers on *both* sides of the apocalyptic war of kingdoms. Temporal powers were godly and thus served the "kingdom of Christ," if they ruled in accord with their own proper jurisdiction. "[God] does not condemn the wisdom and righteousness of kings, then, if they stay in their place, that is, if with their wisdom they control and govern things subject to reason and with their honourable conduct they invite others also to obey the laws and serve the common peace."[51] The moment the government began to war against the Word, it trespassed into the spiritual kingdom. Doubtless Luther had current Reformation disputes in mind in this commentary: active political persecution of evangelical reform was thus for him a violation of the liberating good news of God's salvation *and* a violation of the gift of temporal government. Trespassing into the spiritual kingdom was as much a corruption of God's purposes for temporal authority as it was an attack on the salvation of souls.

For Luther, although temporal government provided for the preaching of the gospel, understanding its nature and purpose did not require its officers to be Christian, or even exposed to biblical revelation. Luther said as much, interestingly enough, in *Commentary on Psalm 101*.[52] Although Luther has been unjustly accused of antinomianism and neglecting natural law, in this commentary he discussed natural law at length. His abundant knowledge of classical sources has often passed unnoticed by scholars, but in this commentary he displayed his impressive familiarity with Greek and Latin authors. Luther's use of natural law and classical authors was in service of one of the commentary's clearest arguments: the divine gift of

51 LW 12: 67; WA 40 II: 277.
52 LW 13: 143–224; WA 51: 200–64.

temporal government was not bound to Christian civilization, but was known by pagan antiquity and discoverable by natural reason.

In Luther's view, this psalm was a song of David in praise of the gift of secular authority.[53] But God's purpose for temporal government could be seen in the political and philosophical leaders of pagan antiquity: great political actors such as Cyrus and Alexander ought to be emulated and the works of Homer, Plato, Aristotle, Cicero, and Livy read and digested for their sage political-philosophical lessons. Positive law was to be seen (and evaluated) as a reasoned application of natural law, although Luther cautioned that "everyone likes to think that natural law is encased in his head."[54] This commentary indicated a maturing shift in Luther's thinking: whereas once he had rejected the adoption of Roman law (which had superseded German customary law)[55] and rejected Aristotle's influence in the study of theology,[56] the 1530s he was urging the study of classics and natural law to inform understanding of the nature of temporal authority.[57] His *Commentary on Psalm 101* was not, therefore, some great departure from earlier political thought, but an extension of what Luther thought the Bible had revealed to him about the temporal order. To be sure, the Reformation was maturing, and he was heavily engaged with thinkers such as Melanchthon over the value of law and pagan antiquity. Moreover, the succession of another new Saxon prince was bringing the education of princely virtues back into focus, and Luther's commentary hinted at serious doubts over the

53 LW 13: 146; WA 51: 200.

54 LW 13: 160; WA 51: 211.

55 His original position against Roman law was articulated in *To the Christian Nobility of the German Nation*; LW 44: 203–4; WA 6: 459–60.

56 This appears as early as his *Disputation Against Scholastic Theology* in 1517. Theses 43 and 44: "It is an error to say that no man can become a theologian without Aristotle. This in opposition to common opinion. Indeed, no one can become a theologian unless he becomes one without Aristotle" LW 31: 12; WA 1: 226. Was this commentary signalling a significant departure from his earlier stance? Luther's early polemics excoriate the influence of Aristotle in *theology*, particularly as it related to divine justification, salvation, and the sacraments; in these writings he had little to say about the value of pagan philosophy overall. Here Luther's praise for classical antiquity is for its political wisdom over the laws that God had given them through their natures and written on their hearts.

57 Luther had taught on Aristotle in his early career at the University of Wittenberg; thus, it is no surprise that when he needed to cite such classical sources, he was adept. See Luther's *Lectures on Titus*, in which he treats the Greek virtue of *epieikeia*, or gentleness, as a crucial political virtue of both rulers and ruled (LW 29:71–5; WA 25:56–60).

licentiousness – particularly the alcoholism – of John Frederick's court.[58] But this psalm, and indeed the whole Bible, showed Luther that temporal authority was a divine gift to all humanity, and that often in the pagan world it was well received and rightly understood.

The Bible praised this gift, sometimes in the most extraordinary ways. Perhaps the most notable, for Luther, was the Bible's encomium of temporal government, the Song of Songs.[59] That Luther saw this canonical poem between a "lover" and a "beloved" in this political way made his interpretation unique in the entire history of biblical interpretation, Jewish or Christian. That distinction was no mean feat: the Song of Songs was one of the most discussed books of the Christian canon in the Middle Ages, with over thirty known commentaries that survive from the twelfth century alone. Dismissing all commentaries known to him as "immature and strange," Luther began his "brief but altogether lucid" interpretation as a "new path" to understanding the book as praise for the divine gift of government.[60]

Rather than allegorizing away and transcending its eroticism, Luther considered the earthiness and sexual passion of the Song of Songs to be entirely fitting for an encomium of government. Conjugal love and marriage and government were gifts of God, encoded in the order of creation; therefore, both the literal meaning *and* the allegory similarly praised these natural gifts. Unlike previous commentaries, Luther's interpretation did not shun, for instance, the lover's praise of his beloved's breasts (4:5), "for the Holy Spirit is pure and so mentions women's bodily members that he wants them to be regarded as good creatures of God."[61] Luther wrote that only our own sinfulness led to misuse of our genitals; thus, he continued, "there is nothing that pleases me more than the fact that I see Solomon speaking in such sweet figures about his highest gifts which God has conferred upon his people." The world-weary ruler, Luther argued, should take great consolation in the Song of Songs, for like the consoled lovers of the poem, it reassured him that the vicissitudes of political life were in service of "matters of the loftiest and greatest kind, with divinely ordained [government], or with the people of God."[62]

58 LW 13: 216; WA 51: 257.

59 For a study of the commentary, see Carty, "Martin Luther's Political Interpretation of the Song of Songs."

60 LW 15: 191, 195; WA 31 II: 586, 588.

61 LW 15: 231; WA 31 II: 686.

62 LW 15: 192; WA 31 II: 587.

Luther's political interpretation of the Song of Songs has been dismissed by historians and is either unknown or ignored in the history of political thought.[63] Although at first glance it appears bizarre, it is in fact quite fitting for both his biblical interpretation and his political thought. How to receive and understand temporal authority was a major ethical lesson of Christian freedom. The church of the past, according to Luther, had been plagued with views that denigrated political service and marriage as somehow less holy and worthy than clerical life. Luther's interpretation of the Song of Songs, therefore, fit perfectly with what he believed to be the purpose of scripture: "to teach, reprove, correct, and train in righteousness" and to dispel false teachings that undermined God's merciful gifts. Political authority, like the creative union of male and female, was divinely instituted and sanctioned as a most precious service to God and neighbours for the ends of bringing order and peace to the world. The Bible had abundantly affirmed this teaching throughout the Old and New Testaments, and through the words of Solomon it was getting a proper biblical song of praise.

Temporal Government as Holy Order in the Lectures on Genesis

From June 1535 through November 1545, twice weekly (unless some crisis or illness prevented it), Luther lectured on Genesis at the University of Wittenberg. These lectures were compiled and redacted through the notes of his students and today fill multiple volumes of *Luther's Works* and the *Weimarer Ausgabe.*[64] Dismissing earlier suspicions that the authentic Luther was lost in the redaction, recent scholarship has come to see the lectures as genuine and reliable works for divulging Luther's thought.[65]

Despite this recent acceptance of their authenticity, the significance of the lectures for Luther's political thought has gone largely unnoticed, even though they articulate a new and distinct idea of temporal government not found in the rest of his writings. In these lectures, Luther designates government as one of three *ordines*

63 Brecht simply dismissed the interpretation as incorrect in his *Martin Luther: Shaping and Defining the Reformation,* 249; neither Skinner nor Cargill Thompson mentions it at all in their studies on Luther's political thought.

64 LW 1–8; WA 42–4.

65 See Pelikan's assessment in his introduction to LW 1 (xii).

divinitus, or "holy orders," including the church and the household, which God had instituted for His rule over the world. These "orders" or "estates" were part of a God-given order both embedded in creation and revealed by scripture.[66] For Luther, service to each holy order was a divine calling; thus, for him, being called to marriage or to political service was on par with a ministerial calling to the church. To consider only church service as divine service, or even to prioritize it over the others, as Luther argued the papacy and Roman Church had done, corrupted the church, household, and temporal government alike. "Let the clergyman teach in church, let the civil officer govern the state, and let parents rule the home or household," wrote Luther, for "these human ministries were established by God."[67]

Luther's commentary on the twentieth chapter of Genesis, featuring the story of Abraham and Sarah settling in Gerar under the Canaanite king Abimelech, provides the richest source for the holy orders in the lectures.[68] Though the king had wished to lie with Sarah, having been deceived into thinking she was only Abraham's sister rather than also his wife, he is warned by God in a dream to leave her alone. He then restores her to Abraham, who in turn blesses the king. Abimelech then gives livestock and slaves to the couple and allows them freedom to settle where they wish. Luther argued that this story represented the three holy orders in Abraham (the church), Sarah (the household), and Abimelech (the temporal order) and how they ought to interact with one another. Abimelech was a model of the temporal order because he supported and provided for the other two: "this king belongs in the catalogue of the saintly rulers whose duty it is to support the prophets and defend the Church of God."[69] Abimelech maintained the dignity of his own authority while protecting the household (the sanctity of the marriage and their promised progeny) and fostering the church (specifically here

66 There is some faint affinity between government as a "holy order" in the *Lectures on Genesis* and government as the last level of God's fourfold rule over the earth in his *Commentary on Zechariah* (LW 20: 169–74; WA 23: 511–4). Other than this brief appearance in this commentary on the minor prophet, Luther gives no further elaboration of this fourfold rule of God.

67 LW 2: 83; WA 42: 320.

68 LW 3: 328–41; WA 43: 110–20.

69 LW 3: 357; WA 43: 131.

the furthering of the covenant through the birth of Isaac immediately after the story).

Abimelech modelled the just treatment of the spiritual order by the government because he supported Abraham in his ministry even though the king was a Gentile. The king's material support of Abraham through goods and property, after it became clear that a prophet was in his kingdom, showed how he had recognized the godliness and goodness of the patriarch's ministry but did not in any way interfere with it. The response of the spiritual order – in this case, Abraham's intercession, which led to the healing of Abimelech's family – in turn modelled its rightful relationship to the government. Abraham honoured and obeyed Abimelech's authority and law while maintaining the integrity of the spiritual order.

This reading of government as holy order, with Abimelech as a praiseworthy example, meant that Luther considered the divine purposes and jurisdiction of government to be both biblically revealed *and* discoverable by human wisdom and experience. Abimelech was a king of the Philistines, yet he knew the nature of secular government. Abimelech knew how his holy order ought to rule over Yahweh's prophet. Knowing his own responsibility in the affair with Sarah, he pleaded on behalf of his people, insisting that his error not be attributed to them, and thereby proving his just and equitable rule. Moreover, once reconciled with Abraham and Sarah, he supported them, thus upholding the orders of household and spirit that God had written into creation. Therefore, according to Luther's reading of Genesis 20, temporal authority could be known and wisely used, according to its divine design, outside of revelation of the covenant but not in any way contrary to it.

Luther's designation of temporal government as one of three holy orders in his *Lectures on Genesis* raises the question of whether he had abandoned the two kingdoms teaching, or at least significantly departed from it. That Luther also made the household a holy order did signal some kind of change from the earlier two kingdoms, for he had earlier argued that the temporal kingdom included its jurisdictional oversight of households and marriage. In these lectures, the emphasis is on different but concurrent modes of service to God in this world. Hence, Luther emphasized the divine calling of married life and political life as similar to clerical life. All were holy services to God; there was no biblical basis for privileging clerics and monastics,

Luther argued. There was certainly no basis for a hierarchy of church authority over the temporal order or over the household. For Luther, Genesis was an appropriate text for extolling the godly service of marriage and the household, going a great distance to explain the household's inclusion: in this first biblical book, God's covenant with Abraham was seen to vitally depend on families and the creative and holy command (given both to the first human beings and then again to the children of Noah) to "go forth and multiply."

However, beyond the addition of the household as another means by which God had brought order to the world, the similarities and differences leave us with some degree of ambiguity with respect to how the two kingdoms and three orders or estates were to be understood together.[70] What can be concluded, however, is that even in the holy order teaching temporal government remained one of God's greatest gifts by bringing peace and order to all aspects of worldly life. Luther's two kingdoms doctrine was much more precise with respect to how that gift was used and applied. Thus, in general, the *Lectures on Genesis* put temporal government in the larger context of a world divinely ordered since the beginning of creation.

CONCLUSION

Luther's political thought was deeply informed by his interpretation of the Bible. His two kingdoms doctrine was born out of his struggle and reconciliation with seemingly contradictory but binding biblical imperatives. The purposes and limits of temporal government were set by Luther's biblical hermeneutical key of law and gospel. The honour, praise, and service due to temporal authority were all, for Luther, biblical revelations. In short, Luther found authority and inspiration for his political thought in the Bible; no other source comes remotely close in importance to an understanding of the grounds for his political ideas, or at least as he understood and articulated them himself. Thus, a clear understanding of how Luther's political ideas were founded on scripture must be considered, lest misinterpretations and anachronisms follow and the remarkable extent to which he devoted time, thought, and writing to political matters be neglected or forgotten in the history of political thought.

70 Lohse, *Martin Luther's Theology*, 322–4. For further discussion of the three orders, see chapter five, n. 76.

4

Radicalism and Resistance

LUTHER'S CONSISTENT DEFENCE OF TEMPORAL AUTHORITY

Of all the controversies Luther was embroiled in over his life, two stand out as the most politically explosive: the Peasants' War of 1525 and the Protestant resistance to the Holy Roman Empire beginning in the 1530s. From the sixteenth century onward, Luther's contributions to these controversies have been scrutinized and debated, making him sometimes a fomenter of revolt, or a hero of conscience, or even a champion of autocratic and oppressive government. In the eyes of his contemporary enemies, Luther's errors and foibles led directly to massive peasant and societal upheaval and to deep political and cultural divisions that would cripple the empire. Even in the late modern period Luther would not escape blame for the tragedy of the Peasants' War: Marxist and Catholic historians alike would blame Luther as the instigator of peasant rebellion who thereafter utterly abandoned the peasant cause to the violent reprisals of the German princes and nobility.[1] In Marxist history, for example, the peasant leader and one-time friend turned enemy of Luther, Thomas Müntzer, would come to be a proto-revolutionary leader, looking for proletarian revolt early in the bourgeois age.[2]

1 In 1850, shortly after the failed revolutions of 1848 (which provide a comparative reference for understanding the historical progress of bourgeois capitalism), Friedrich Engels published *The Peasant War in Germany*. Engels denounced Luther as a "middle-class" betrayer of the peasants. An emblematic nineteenth-century version of the polemical Catholic history of Luther is Johann Joseph Ignaz von Döllinger's *The Reformation*.

2 From 1975 until the collapse of the regime, Müntzer appeared on the five-mark note of the communist *Deutschen Demokratischen Republik*.

Across ages, ideologies, and confessions, Luther has also been accused of being baldly inconsistent or contradictory in his dealings with both the Peasants' War and Protestant resistance. Luther had, after all, proclaimed complete freedom in the gospel – though, of course, coupled with complete bodily submission to worldly authority – and so it appeared to many that a new revolutionary political order had begun, one that called on ordinary Germans, including peasants, to re-examine their societal and political standing in light of evangelical freedom. Yet Luther came to vigorously and angrily reject any attempt to justify the Peasants' War on the basis of the spiritual freedom he had proclaimed. His opponents, whether radical reformers such as Müntzer or Catholic detractors, considered his very public rejection of the peasants' gospel freedom as an astounding and inexcusable about-face: not only had Luther incited the revolt, they argued, but he was now denying them the theological grounds he had given them. They believed he had shirked his responsibility for what would become one of the most violent and deadly upheavals of the century.[3]

Luther's endorsement of "protestant" resistance at the meeting of Torgau in October of 1530 and afterward has likewise been charged (both then and lately) with hypocrisy and contradiction. Up to Torgau, Luther emphatically counselled obedience to political authorities: *Temporal Authority*, for instance, gave no grounds for armed resistance of political authorities, and it appeared to argue that there could *never* be a legitimate resistance against any duly constituted superior authority. Thus, when Luther joined several colleagues in defence of armed resistance against the Holy Roman emperor – the most superior and duly constituted political authority in all of Europe – it appeared as though Luther had completely abandoned his earlier stance.

However, Luther's treatment of radical political reform and armed resistance was largely consistent with the core of his political thought. In fact, in seeking to restore temporal authority to its God-given role of keeper of law and order in all "outer" human affairs, Luther came to see that he had to oppose the Radical Reformation's political revolutions *and* advocate a limited armed resistance to the Holy Roman

3 For example, see Cochlaeus's vehement condemnation of Luther's role in the revolt in *Luther's Lives*, 165–6.

Empire. The adoption of these stances was not made without some changes or developments to positions he had previously publicly defended, but they were essentially in accord with his defence of temporal authority as a most precious gift of God, as it had been presented in *Temporal Authority*. Luther came to believe that the Peasants' War and the armed alignment of Catholic authorities against the evangelical territories were both lethal threats to the two kingdoms. This chapter examines how that came to be.

LUTHER AGAINST THE RADICAL REFORMATION

The Peasants' War of 1525

LETTER TO THE PRINCES OF SAXONY CONCERNING THE REBELLIOUS SPIRIT

Well before the outbreak of the Peasants' War, Luther had begun to denounce radical reformers who sought to transform the political order into new evangelical kingdoms. His position was made especially clear in the case of Thomas Müntzer and a small band of prophetic followers, whom Luther had derisively called the "Zwikau prophets" ever since Müntzer began his zealous reforms at the Church of St Katherine in the Saxon city of Zwickau. There, Müntzer became known for his radical liturgical reforms and fervent apocalyptic preaching, but also for his claims to a particular divine revelation that was calling him to a worldwide mission to lead radical church reforms. When he was dismissed from Zwickau in the spring of 1521, he took two missionary trips, to Bohemia and to Prague, and continued to wander about until March 1523, when he was appointed pastor of St John's Church in Allstedt, Thuringia, in Electoral Saxony.[4]

At Allstedt, Müntzer's career boldly took a more political turn, and his preaching began to raise the concern of several secular rulers. First, his advocacy of radical reforms resulted in some public unrest and destruction, such as the iconoclastic destruction of a Marian chapel in neighbouring Mallerbach. Second, he began to consider himself a prophet in the mode of the Hebrew Bible's Daniel, offering

4 Ulrich Bubenheimer, "Thomas Müntzer," 99–100. See also Gritsch, *Reformer without a Church*.

himself as a preacher to political authorities – including the Elector John and his son John Frederick – and denouncing several princes and magistrates who opposed him. He even called for the violent destruction of all enemies of the gospel. Finally, after hearing the news that Müntzer had been forming a league of like-minded reformers and minor magistrates, a concerned Duke John called Müntzer and his followers to a council in Weimar at the beginning of August 1524. Thereafter Müntzer was forbidden to publish or preach.

Prior to the council, in July, Luther responded to the situation with his *Letter to the Princes of Saxony Concerning the Rebellious Spirit.* As even the title would make clear, Luther's simple position was that Müntzer was guilty of insurrection and ought to be expelled. He reminded the princes of the divine purpose of their office: "[Y]our power and earthly authority," Luther wrote, "are given you by God in that you have been bidden to preserve the peace and punish the wrongdoer, as Paul teaches."[5] Inaction against insurrection, Luther warned, would be called to account before God, the people, and the world, for it was one of the most basic responsibilities of temporal authority. Throughout the coming upheaval in the Peasants' War, Luther would continue to focus on maintaining order as the most pressing need of the hour, and he urged temporal authorities not to be taken in by theological debates and radical spiritual doctrines at the expense of keeping worldly peace.

In fact, Luther's *Letter to the Princes of Saxony* abstains almost entirely from any substantial treatment of Müntzer's theology. For one thing, as Luther acknowledged in the letter, he had already publicly criticized Müntzer's spiritual doctrines several years ago in a number of sermons and treatises.[6] The more important issue, however, was not Müntzer's theology so much as his invocation of the sword to defend and propagate it. In Luther's thinking, once Müntzer invoked coercion and armed revolt to transform the temporal authorities into like-minded theocracies, he was violating the clear division between the two kingdoms. Luther admitted that Müntzer was free to preach whatever spiritual doctrines he wished, and that "time would tell" the

5 LW 40: 51; WA 15: 213.

6 LW 40: 51, n. 1: a reference to the *Eight Wittenberg Lenten Sermons* (1522), WA 10 III: 1–64, and *On Both Kinds in the Sacrament* (1522), WA 10 II: 11–41.

divine truth of his doctrines. Luther also assumed – especially since the Bible was rife with examples of it – that in this life there would always be a plurality of spiritual doctrines and sects and that there would also always be spiritual conflict. Insofar as that conflict remained in the spiritual kingdom, Luther argued, temporal authority was not to interfere with it.

But as soon as Müntzer endorsed the sword for the propagation of spiritual ends that ought to be directed only to "hearts and souls," Luther argued, he became subject to the laws and punishments of temporal authority. For Luther, Müntzer's own behaviour betrayed his spiritual cause and showed that he had knowingly trespassed into the affairs proper of the temporal kingdom: he avoided his enemies and eluded hostile powers and assemblies. "Tell me," Luther asked, "who is this bold and defiant holy spirit who confines himself so closely that he will not appear except before a harmless assembly?"[7] For Luther, the true preacher of the Word would not fear his enemies and could humbly account for himself before anyone, great or small. Luther cited his own case: he had appeared before enemies at Leipzig, Augsburg, and Worms, before the emperor and papal legates, and had clung to the Word while respecting the jurisdiction and duties of temporal authorities. Luther sought to reform the spiritual kingdom and restore the temporal, but Müntzer appeared to threaten temporal order with theological revolutions wherever he went. The *Letter to the Princes of Saxony* made it clear that fomenting revolt was never to be tolerated by temporal government, nor was this to be considered any kind of legitimate implication of the evangelical reform Luther and his colleagues had begun in Electoral Saxony and elsewhere.

Luther's treatment of the Müntzer affair in 1524 was an early harbinger of his treatment of the Peasants' War in the following year, as well as part of a clearly demonstrable body of evidence that he adhered consistently to his ideas on temporal authority and to the theology of *sola fides* and the dualistic anthropology of works such as *Christian Liberty*.

7 LW 40: 52; WA 15: 213–4.

THE OUTBREAK OF THE PEASANTS' WAR AND LUTHER'S ADMONITION TO PEACE

In May 1524, the Peasants' War began as a peaceful protest against feudal obligations at the abbey of Saint Blasien, in the Black Forest, southwest of Freiburg. Soon, however, after quickly spreading across southern Germany and Switzerland and becoming more radical and violent, it became one of the largest popular revolts in all of European history, resulting in the deaths of approximately 100,000 peasants.[8] Within months of the summer uprisings, peasant alliances had been formed to spearhead negotiations with feudal lords and temporal authorities. Although some disputes were particular to certain territories, a common list of grievances emerged against the long-standing privileges of clergy and nobility, particularly with the publication of a pamphlet from a revolutionary peasant alliance named the Christian Union of Upper Swabia. Their "Twelve Articles of Memmingen"[9] was reprinted and published widely, becoming a manifesto for like-minded peasantry and, to the movement's detractors such as Luther, a prime example of the movement's excess and licentiousness.

In seeking to redress grievances and ameliorate the barely subsistent lot of the peasantry, the Twelve Articles called for an eradication of the traditional prohibitions on peasant hunting, fishing, and foraging. The pamphlet also called for the abolition of serfdom, tithes on grain, taxes on inheritances, and a reform of services owed to feudal lords. Showing its Reformation pedigree, the Twelve Articles also demanded "that in the future the entire community have the power and authority to choose and appoint a pastor," as well as "the power to depose him" if he did not "preach the holy gospel to us clearly and purely," thereby adding "no teaching or commandment of men to the Gospel."[10]

The Twelve Articles sought to eliminate all human convention from the gospel teachings so that peasant life could be purely lived *according to* it. For the Christian Union of Upper Swabia, their grievances were based on nothing else but the gospel, and so accompanying

8 For an overview of the Peasants' War, see Blickle, *The Revolution of 1525*. For a collection of historical documents from the conflict, see Scott and Scribner, *The German Peasants' War*. For a study of Luther's role in the conflict, see Kirchener, *Luther and the Peasants' War*.

9 These articles are translated in LW 46: 8–16.

10 LW 46: 10.

each article were passages from scripture that demonstrated each demand's biblical basis. Of course, there were long-standing and legitimate injustices that German peasants had demonstrably suffered, and even several legal bases upon which the peasants could claim redress against feudal abuses. But rather than invoking these, the Twelve Articles claimed that the *only* ground for legitimacy was the Bible. In fact, the Christian Union was so confident in its biblical footing that it claimed (in the last article of the pamphlet) that it would withdraw any one of its demands if – and only if – scripture could be shown to conflict with it.

Luther took the Christian Union at its word.[11] His *Admonition to Peace* bluntly argued that "not one of the articles teaches anything of the Gospel," and that the biblical footings of each article were falsely assumed.[12] For Luther, the gospel required complete submission to temporal authority, and scripture showed this with sundry examples. The substance of the articles, however, was "concerned [only] with worldly and temporal matters."[13] The reform of taxes and tithes and even the power to appoint and dismiss pastors (which Luther believed had to meet the approval of temporal powers) all fell under the jurisdiction of the temporal kingdom. The effect of the Twelve Articles, Luther argued, was to turn Christian freedom into a "completely physical matter."[14] But just as Luther had argued in *Christian Liberty* and *Temporal Authority*, Christian freedom was a spiritual freedom in the spiritual kingdom: to be sure, it influenced the temporal kingdom, but for Luther it could not simply and effectively change the affairs of the temporal world without compromising both kingdoms. Luther went further: as an evangelist, he had little to say about the substance of the articles, leaving it to lawyers to discuss. Christians qua Christians should have nothing to do with the affairs of the temporal kingdom.

In dismissing the gospel foundations of the revolt, Luther's *Admonition to Peace* emphasized that it was a threat to the two kingdoms and thus an assault against both the preaching of the gospel *and* the upholding of law and order. In this treatise, Luther was at

11 Brecht, *Martin Luther: Shaping and Defining the Reformation*, 174–8.
12 LW 46: 35; WA 18: 320.
13 Ibid.
14 LW 46: 39; WA 18: 326.

once practical and apocalyptic. Rupturing the integrity of the kingdoms would have disastrous consequences for body and soul. Diametrically opposing the pamphlet's claims, Luther wrote that the status of gospel preaching in Germany – particularly at this critical juncture in the early Reformation – was threatened by the revolt and thus imperilled the souls of all in the affected lands. The rule of law and civil peace was also threatened, Luther warned, and this could very well result in the apocalyptic destruction of Germany. Luther's warnings over the potential for violence, it must be noted, were written before he knew that violence was already taking place. He had this vision of apocalyptic upheaval because it was for him the necessary outcome of the destruction of the two kingdoms, and especially the neglect of the temporal one; Luther claimed he was giving this warning to all "out of brotherly love."[15]

Luther's practical advice in the *Admonition to Peace* was divided between the authorities and the peasants. As for the princes, lords, and clergy, he denounced their courtly extravagances and their hostility to the gospel. Luther insisted that the gospel and evangelical reform were not responsible for the revolt: "I have taught with all quietness, have striven earnestly against rebellion, and have energetically encouraged and exhorted people to obey and respect even you wild and dictatorial tyrants."[16] He then *defended* the Twelve Articles, calling them fair and justified, and arguing that the refusal to acquiesce to these justified grievances would bring God's judgment upon the nobility and clergy.[17]

As for the peasants, Luther insisted in a pastoral tone that they desist from revolt, for no "Christian association" could justifiably defy temporal authority, even if the rulers were wicked. Moreover, even if the peasants were legitimately aggrieved, in judging their own case Luther argued that they were breaking both natural law and common equity.[18] Luther urged both sides to negotiate for peace, along the model of the Weingarten Treaty between the Swabian League and the Lake Constance Peasants, which he had republished and appended to his treatise.

15 LW 46: 17; WA 18: 292.
16 LW 46: 20; WA 18: 295.
17 LW 46: 22; WA 18: 298.
18 LW 46: 24–5; WA 18: 301–3.

Through the *Admonition to Peace,* Luther had intended to encourage peace, rescue the evangelical cause from accusations of rebellion and civil disorder, and clarify his own positions on Radical Reformation politics. Unfortunately for him, he failed all three: extreme violence was already spreading, as was confusion over the evangelical gospel, and accusations that he had fomented rebellion was coming from all corners, even from his allies within the reform movement. In part, these failures were a matter of bad timing, for when Luther had penned and published the *Admonition to Peace* in April of 1525, all-out, violent rebellion had already begun.[19] Luther wrote the treatise on a trip to Eisleben with his fellow reformers Philip Melanchthon and John Agricola in order to establish a school at the request of Count Albrecht of Mansfeld. The very fact that he was on such a trip suggests that Luther had no idea how serious the situation had already become. In fact, while Luther was still travelling throughout Thuringia, he would witness at first hand the horrors that would come to characterize the uprising all over Germany. This experience – a mere two weeks after the publication of the *Admonition to Peace* – would inspire one of his most infamous and polemical treatises, *Against the Robbing and Murdering Hordes of Peasants.*

ATTACKING RADICAL POLITICS: LUTHER'S POLEMICS IN THE PEASANTS' WAR

Luther was outraged by the revolt. He was shocked at how far it had affected Thuringia (including the seizure of Erfurt, where he had been a student). He was incensed at the radical leadership of Thomas Müntzer and his followers, who had helped it spread through their millenarian prophesies of a new world order. This outrage was first expressed in a letter Luther wrote on May 4 to Johannes Rühel, a lawyer from the court of Duke Albrecht who had been keeping Luther up to date on the uprisings. "If God wants to pour out his wrath upon us and devastate Germany," he wrote, "then these enemies of God, these blasphemers, robbers, and murderers, these unfaithful and perjuring peasants are suitable for this."[20] Rühel's sovereign, Luther argued, had no greater duty than to crush the revolt as long as he was

19 Brecht, *Martin Luther: Shaping and Defining the Reformation,* 178–9.

20 LW 49, 110; WA BR 3: 481.

able, and to be comforted and confident that such action was the fulfillment of God's purpose for temporal government.

Written around the same time as the letter (the precise date of publication is unknown), Luther's *Against the Robbing and Murdering Hordes of Peasants* gave a scathing attack on the Peasants' War.[21] Luther was no stranger to publishing polemics and vitriol against his enemies (whomever they were), but this polemic was one of the harshest he would ever write. With his hostility came an explanation: Luther gave three major reasons why the peasants in revolt deserved his wrath. First, they were violating the feudal oaths that required them to be "true and faithful, submissive and obedient," and Christ and Paul, as Luther quickly reminded them, upheld these oaths.[22] Second, they were starting a rebellion in which they demanded authority and right to *all* property, and in so doing had become the worst robbers and plunderers. For Luther, this also meant that everyone else was a judge and executioner of rebels: just as, with a rabid dog, "if you do not strike him, he will strike you," Luther wrote, "let everyone who can smite, slay, and stab, secretly or openly, remembering that nothing can be more devilish than a rebel."[23] Third, the peasants had become the "worst blasphemers of God and slanderers of his holy name" because they clothed their rebellion in the gospel, believing their actions to be divinely sanctified by scripture and Christ and their revolt obligatory for all baptized followers of Jesus.[24] For Luther, baptism did "not make men free in body and property, but in soul";[25] thus, living in common property was not meant to render the whole world in common, and thus erase all property distinctions and social classes, but only for the disciples who freely entered such a community (such as those in Acts 4:32–37). In proclaiming the goods of other men – particularly the nobility and clergy – for themselves, the peasants were essentially thieves. They had violated *both* of the two kingdoms: spiritual freedom in Christ was taken as temporal

21 An early title of the work, *Against the Robbing and Murdering Hordes of the Other Peasants,* showed that Luther intended it to be directed against actively rebelling peasants and not as a diatribe against all peasant claims. Brecht, *Martin Luther: Shaping and Defining the Reformation,* 181, 187.

22 LW 46: 49–50; WA 18: 357. Luther quoted from Luke 20:25 and Romans 13:1–2.

23 LW 46: 50; WA 18: 358.

24 LW 46: 50–51; WA 18: 358.

25 LW 46: 51; WA 18: 359.

freedom, and so both divine grace *and* worldly peace were destroyed by their rebellion.

Luther wrote that he would not oppose temporal authorities that put down the rebellion without judicial ruling, since it would be within their rights to do so. Even the Christian prince, though he should "humbly pray for help" and "offer the mad peasants an opportunity to come to terms," must otherwise fulfill his duties with a clear conscience and smite the rebellion. Dying in the process, Luther added, would even be a kind of "martyrdom" for the temporal kingdom, and succeeding in quelling the revolt an act of love to one's neighbour.[26] Thus, Luther infamously concluded "let whoever can stab, smite, slay" and then added at the very end of the document, as if anticipating the storm of controversy this polemic would arouse, "if anyone thinks this too harsh, let him remember that rebellion is intolerable and that the destruction of the world is to be expected every hour."[27]

Shortly after writing *Against the Robbing and Murdering Hordes of Peasants*, and shortly before Müntzer's execution at the end of May, Luther had four of the radical leader's letters published under the title *A Dreadful Story and a Judgment of God Against Thomas Müntzer*, with the purpose of revealing his arrogance, violence, and inability to compromise.[28] But this publication also buttressed Luther's own arguments: although he himself sounded uncompromising and violent, it was in fact the radical leadership that had led the revolt down the path to God's wrathful judgment for its radical denigration of the gospel and the destruction of the temporal order.

However, Luther's writing on the Peasants' War was badly outpaced by events. By the time his *Against the Robbing and Murdering Hordes of Peasants* was widely read, the revolt in Thuringia had been largely

26 LW 46: 52–3; WA 18: 360. In designating a death in the service of temporal order as martyrdom, Luther was likely violating his own distinctions between the two kingdoms, rendering armed service of government as a spiritual sacrifice. Janz notes that this polemical instance was not the only time Luther invoked martyrdom for the defence of the secular realm; he also used it several times in writing about conflict with the Turks: e.g., in his 1529 *Army Sermon Against the Turks* (WA 30 II: 173, 175) and in his 1541 *Appeal for Prayer Against the Turks* (LW 43: 238; WA 51: 619); Janz, *The Westminster Handbook to Martin Luther*, 138–9. Even in this polemical work, Luther's overarching pastoral purpose was clear: as in his later treatise *Whether Soldiers, Too, Can Be Saved*, Luther assured believers that temporal authority could be defended by the sword with a clean conscience.

27 LW 46: 55; WA 18: 361.

28 Brecht, *Martin Luther: Shaping and Defining the Reformation*, 184.

suppressed.[29] Though not without arms and some sophisticated military leadership, coupled with the advantages that the initially slow response of the Swabian League gave them, the peasant rebels were in almost all contexts severely lacking in arms and experience. Once put to the test on the battlefield, the revolt was swiftly crushed. In some contexts, brutal retributions followed noble victories. With his polemic read so late in the uprising, it now appeared that Luther was endorsing severe authoritarian cruelties rather than defending the integrity of both the gospel and temporal authority as he had intended. Moreover, his elector Frederick the Wise had just died, and this loss subjected Luther to the charge that his support for the princes against the peasants was an effort to ingratiate him to hitherto hostile authorities.

Friend and foe alike assailed *Against the Robbing and Murdering Hordes of Peasants.*[30] The great Catholic controversialist Johannes Cochlaeus quickly responded to the text with his own printed polemic against Luther, transferring the blame that the reformer laid against the peasants to the words and teachings of Luther himself. He would repeat this accusation again in his account of Luther's life a decade later.[31] Another Catholic antagonist, Jerome Emser, published *How Luther Has Promoted Rebellion in His Books.* Swiss reformer Huldrych Zwingli took up another common accusation by arguing that Luther's words had encouraged the harsh retributions against the peasants. Even Luther's own colleagues and allies, such as Johannes Brenz, Johannes Agricola, and Wolfgang Capito, had major reservations about Luther's polemic, holding that it was lacking in Christian charity and mercy, and even that is was inconsistent with evangelical theology.[32]

Given the poor timing of publication, Luther's harsh and uncompromising tone, and the swirling controversies of the early Reformation, the accusations against Luther were not surprising. But at base – aside from his tone and invocation of ideas such as a secular martyrdom – Luther's *Against the Robbing and Murdering Hordes of Peasants* was consistent with his earlier political thought in seeking to defend

29 Ibid., 187–9.

30 Ibid.

31 Vandiver, Keen, and Frazel, *Luther's Lives*, 159.

32 Brecht, *Martin Luther: Shaping and Defining the Reformation*, 188.

the honour and divine purpose given to temporal government. This consistency best explains Luther's motives in publishing the subsequent "open letter" that he wrote in July of 1525 and dedicated to Caspar Müller, chancellor of Mansfeld, who had implored him in a letter to answer the criticism and confusion.[33]

Rather than backtracking on or withdrawing his previous arguments, Luther's *An Open Letter on the Harsh Book Against the Peasants* showed how confident he was in them. He essentially repeated his arguments, despite all the confusion, all the accusations, and all the immense political pressures that were being applied to him in the aftermath of the revolt. The peasants were wrong to rebel, and the authorities were right to crush them. They were guilty of confusing the two kingdoms, and this was akin to "putting the devil in heaven and God in hell."[34] The harshness of his previous work was thus justified: "the peasants would not listen; they would not let anyone tell them anything, so their ears must be unbuttoned with musket balls till their heads jump off their shoulders."[35] Not only was coercion justified, but Luther argued that it was a kind of divine mercy, protecting the innocent, ensuring a general peace and order; the maintenance of temporal authority through the use of the "sword" was a kind of natural necessity, "just as necessary to a people as eating and drinking, even as life itself."[36] For Luther, the Peasants' War sought to overthrow the entire order of things, all the while indiscriminately injuring rulers and subjects, and rupturing all worldly order, from courts to families. In attacking *all* government during the uprising, the peasants could not then justify a new rule after; still less would they have grounds to appeal for clemency after they failed.

In the *Open Letter*, Luther defended himself against the charge that he had encouraged violent and cruel retributions. For all who read it fairly, he wrote, his polemic was primarily advice to "Christian and pious rulers, as befits a Christian preacher."[37] His first aim was to reassure the troubled consciences of Christian princes that they were

33 Ibid., 186.
34 LW 46: 70; WA 18: 390.
35 LW 46: 65; WA 18: 386.
36 LW 46: 73; WA 18: 392.
37 LW 46: 83; WA 18: 400.

permitted to use force to suppress rebellion.[38] Besides, any advice he might give to tyrants – those who abused their power and slaughtered peasants beyond the requirements of duty – would not be heeded anyhow. Bloodthirsty tyrants would be judged, Luther promised, for they too were guilty of abusing the divine gift of temporal authority and would soon face the wrath of God.[39] In the meantime, Luther would defend temporal authority from the apocalyptic threat of the Peasants' War. All his works concerning that tragic cataclysm were consistent with that aim, and all were ardent applications of the seminal ideas on government he had written years earlier.

RESISTANCE, OBEDIENCE, AND THE LIMITS OF GOVERNMENT

Historical Overview

Luther's endorsement of Protestant resistance to the Holy Roman Empire in 1530 is best introduced with some attention to the complex and high-pressured political context of the imperial crisis brought about by the Reformation. The crisis had been a long time in the making. Early imperial attempts at curbing the influence of Luther and other church reformers, such as the Edict of Worms, had failed to stop programmatic evangelical reform from spreading among its territories, winning the sympathies of powerful princes and city councils, and gaining acceptance among their subjects. Throughout the 1520s, the evangelical cause spread across the middle of the empire, threatening political-religious disunity at a time when the empire seemed to need unity the most: a Turkish invasion was believed to be imminent, hostile powers such as France were barely being contained in the European theatre, the race to control the New World was reaching top speed, and the pope (by the mid-1520s no friend of the emperor's) and the Roman Church were increasing pressures to move the empire to crush the German heresy.

These pressures on the empire moved the imperial diets (*Reichstage*) – by the 1520s, among the only institutions that kept the empire

38 In this respect, the work bears a notable resemblance to *Whether Soldiers, Too, Can Be Saved.*

39 LW 46: 84; WA 18: 400–1.

unified as an assemblage of estates – to become increasingly preoccupied with the *causa Lutheri*, since all other aspects of imperial affairs were affected by it. The turning point was the First Diet of Speyer in 1526, which included in its decree an article allowing the principalities and free imperial cities to rule over the religious question as they saw fit (essentially suspending the Edict of Worms) *until* a church council was called to settle the question. Thus, underscoring the sovereignty of princes and free cities *and* allowing for the evangelical cause to transform into territorial churches, the decree of the First Diet of Speyer led to the expansion of evangelical territories and ultimately to two factions of powers in the empire divided on religious grounds: the evangelical estates, and the Catholic majority. The conflict between these factions dominated the Second Diet of Speyer in 1529. The Catholic majority, emboldened by recent victories of Emperor Charles V over France in Italy, and now turning their attention to the Turkish threat, condemned evangelical "innovations," nullified the religious article of the preceding diet, and outlawed further reform until a church council was convened.[40]

With the very survival of evangelical reform at stake, six principalities (including Luther's own Electoral Saxony) and fourteen free cities officially protested the majority decision of the diet and thereby became known as "protestant" estates. Appealing to the emperor (who had been represented at both Speyer diets through his younger brother Ferdinand I, Archduke of Austria) and a church council, the Protestants argued that the majority could not overturn the unanimous decree of a former diet and did not have the authority to settle matters of religion in such a fashion. With the Protestants holding such a firm position and the Catholics entrenched in theirs, the empire appeared to be heading toward war.

The Diet of Augsburg, held during the following summer of 1530, sought to avoid conflict and reconcile the factions. The emperor himself presided and at first appeared conciliatory toward the Protestants. Because Luther was still under the imperial ban of Worms and was sequestered at the Coburg for the diet's duration, Philip Melanchthon instead represented the Protestant faction. On

40 See Brecht, *Martin Luther: Shaping and Defining the Reformation*, 352–63; Wolgast, "Protestation of Speyer," 103–5; Arand, Kolb, and Nestingen, *The Lutheran Confessions*, 64–5, 90–2.

25 June the diet was presented with the "Augsburg Confession," a summary in twenty-eight articles of evangelical doctrine and a justification for reforms that had been undertaken.[41] The Catholic "Confutation," written in part by Cardinal Lorenzo Campeggio, rebutted the Protestant confession, was read to the diet on 3 August, and was soon accepted by the emperor as the definitive imperial response to the Protestants, despite evangelical efforts to show the Confutation's weaknesses through an "Apology" of the confession. In November, the diet's recess gave the Protestants six months to accept the Confutation and return to the Roman Church, or otherwise face armed persecution from the Catholic majority. The Protestant response was swift: having learned of the recess's terms before its proclamation, a defensive league of Protestant estates was beginning to be formed, and lawyers and theologians, including Luther, were called on to defend it legally and theologically at a meeting called by Elector John for late October in Torgau, Saxony.[42]

Luther's Endorsement of Protestant Resistance

In the years after the First Diet of Speyer but before Torgau and the Augsburg Recess, Luther had already refused to endorse the formation of an armed Protestant league. One such example was his reaction to what became known as the "Pack Affair" of 1528. Otto von Pack, a counsellor for Duke George of Saxony, by using documents that were likely forged by his own hand, convinced Philip I, Landgrave of Hesse, that a Catholic alliance was forming to wage war on the evangelical territories. In response to this alleged threat, Philip began to take the lead on forming a counter alliance, including Electoral Saxony, with the purpose of carrying out a pre-emptive attack on the Catholic enemies. In his dealings with his prince over the matter, Luther was insistent: there could be no justification for aggression, and furthermore any agreement with Philip was null and void. Luther even threatened to leave Electoral Saxony before

41 See Junghans, "The Augsburg Confession," 93–7. Arand, Kolb, and Nestingen, *Lutheran Confessions*, is one of the most important and comprehensive histories of the Augsburg Confession and the formation of the *Book of Concord* to date.

42 Brecht, *Martin Luther: Shaping and Defining the Reformation*, 405–12.

Elector John withdrew from the Weimar agreement with Philip.[43] Another telling example occurred a year later, in 1529. Once again dealing with the machinations of Philip (who was now gaining a reputation for being rash), Luther refused to commit himself to the Landgrave's efforts to broker a deal that would secure evangelical support against the Turks in exchange for guarantees of imperial peace from the Catholic estates.[44]

Yet, one year later at Torgau, with the imminent threat of war over the Augsburg Recess, and in the company of Melanchthon, Jonas, Spalatin, and others, Luther signed a declaration claiming that armed resistance was a legal right of all imperial subjects – even though the signing theologians, the declaration read, were previously "unaware" of the existence of that right. Since the gospel validated civil laws, it argued, neither scripture nor civil or natural law could prohibit the Protestants from taking up arms and protecting themselves.[45] Thus, Luther became a proponent of armed resistance and soon followed up his endorsement at Torgau with a treatise on the matter. Already outlined while he was at Torgau, *Dr Martin Luther's Warning to His Dear German People* was not published until March 1531, just as the terms of the recess were supposed to take effect.[46]

At the beginning of the treatise, in light of the failure at Augsburg, Luther admitted that either war or rebellion – or perhaps both – would occur in short order. The wrath of God would soon be felt upon the empire. Still, even though Luther resigned himself to the clear message that God was not heeding evangelical prayers for their enemies, he by no means delighted in the coming conflict, nor did he condone or counsel war and rebellion. "We, who are derisively called 'Lutherans' neither counselled it nor consented to it," Luther wrote, "nor, indeed gave any cause for it" but rather "constantly and ceaselessly pleaded and called for peace."[47] But when war occurred, Luther wrote, he would be resigned to it. First of all, "it will not harm us if we die or come to grief," Luther wrote, for they were being

43 Ibid., 357–8. WA BR 4: 413–15.

44 See his letter in reply to Philip: LW 49: 250–54; WA BR 5: 203–4.

45 See the translated excerpt of the Torgau Declaration in LW 47: 8–9.

46 Brecht, *Martin Luther: Shaping and Defining the Reformation*, 415–21.

47 LW 47:13–4; WA 30 III: 278.

persecuted for the sake of righteousness.[48] Moreover, as a corollary to the first point, their opponents could not invoke the name of God, and thus they could only "wage war with a bad conscience for a blasphemous cause."[49]

As a preacher of the Word, Luther argued, it was not proper of him to conduct or counsel war, but only to push for peace. Having learned from his involvement in the Peasants' War, he added, "I will surely hold my pen in check and keep silent and not intervene as in the last uprising."[50] But Luther also included the point that although he would not counsel war, he also would *not reprove* those who defended themselves against the empire, since their actions would be "self-defence."[51] Thus, his treatise spoke from the roles of a preacher and a pastor, for he did not "want to leave the conscience of the people burdened by the concern and worry that their self-defence might be rebellious."[52]

Dr Martin Luther's Warning to His Dear German People offered several crucial arguments to assuage the troubled consciences of Protestant resisters. First, acting contrary to law was not always rebellion; otherwise, this term would absurdly apply to *all* violations of law. Imperial resistance in this case was not a refusal to submit to all government and authority other than one's own: some other term applied, and Luther would leave its designation to the "jurists."[53] Second, and more importantly, Luther argued that any movement of imperial and Catholic powers against the evangelical estates was itself *illegal*, since it violated each of divine, natural, and imperial law. The evangelical estates were being persecuted and threatened without any official imperial hearing of their positions, without any justiciable charge against their positions to date, and without any authoritative condemnations of their doctrines (the Confutations at Augsburg was not publicly released) or indications of how the Protestant estates had transgressed imperial laws.[54] Thus, in Luther's opinion, armed

48 A reference to one of Jesus's beatitudes in the Sermon on the Mount, Matthew 5:10. LW 47:16; WA 30 III: 280.

49 LW 47: 17; WA 30 III: 281.

50 LW 47: 18; WA 30 III: 282.

51 LW 47: 19; WA 30 III: 282.

52 LW 47: 19; WA 30 III: 283.

53 Ibid.

54 LW 47: 21; WA 30 III: 284.

resistance to imperial estates was much more akin to "self-defence" than to rebellion or insurrection.

Then and now, Luther's endorsement of the "self-defence" of the Protestant estates has been the subject of controversy. *Dr Martin Luther's Warning to His Dear German People* appeared to be a pivotal document showing Luther's shift from the renunciation, before Torgau, of *all* armed resistance to increasing approval of it thereafter and for the rest of his life and career.[55] Certainly, there is a noticeable contrast between Luther's early writings, before Torgau, and his later statements on the subject as the empire edged ever closer to internal collapse and war.

In *Temporal Authority* Luther had denied any legitimate grounds for resistance to any superior political authority: "To act [in war] as a Christian, I say, a prince should not go to war against his overlord – king, emperor, or other liege lord … for the governing authority must not be resisted by force."[56] In his 1526 treatise *Whether Soldiers, Too, Can Be Saved,* Luther again concluded that any warfare directed against superiors was unjust, and he emphatically denied a right of revolution against a tyrant. Even in writing to his prince, Elector John, in the months before the Diet of Augsburg in 1530, Luther had flatly denied the possibility of resistance to the empire: "It is in no way proper for anyone who wants to be a Christian to stand up against the authority of his government regardless of whether [that government] acts rightly or wrongly; rather a Christian is to suffer force and injustice, especially from his government."[57]

Nevertheless, at Torgau, and with the publication of *Dr Martin Luther's Warning to His Dear German People,* Luther clearly *had* changed his view: although he maintained that, as a preacher of the Word, he could not endorse warfare, there now appeared to be (at least in very nascent form) several grounds – imperial law, natural law, and divine law – for legitimate armed resistance against the superior authority of the Holy Roman Empire. This concession to resistance theory would grow in the coming years. At first, Luther denied that any such change

55 Two excellent studies, defending Luther from the charge of inconsistency, can be found on this topic: Shoenberger, "Luther and the Justifiability of Resistance to Legitimate Authority," and Cargill Thompson, "Luther and the Right of Resistance to the Emperor."

56 LW 45: 124; WA 11: 276–7.

57 LW 49: 275; WA BR 5: 258.

of position had taken place. In a letter to Lazarus Spengler, chancellor of the city council of Nürnberg, written on 15 February 1531 (before his *Warning* was published), he argued that while he still maintained all subjects must obey the emperor, now the issue was whether resistance to the emperor and Catholic estates was itself demanded by imperial law. Luther argued that a decision on the issue had *not* been definitively made, since the imperial legality of resistance was still subject to a convincing demonstration from legal experts, and imperial law (in Luther's opinion) would be the only solid ground for it.[58] Yet in several records of the *Table Talk* (*Tischreden*) in the subsequent years, Luther appeared to have accepted the argument for the imperial constitution's sanctioning of resistance.[59] In fact, nearing the decade's end in 1538, Luther had signed on to an agreement with his colleagues, written by Melanchthon, that resistance to the emperor was justified to protect subjects against idolatry and the confiscation of property.[60] To top off this change in his position, in his 1539 *Circular Disputation on the Right to Resist the Emperor* Luther had even come to see that the pope and emperor (as his minion) had become tyrants on a hitherto unimaginable scale, overturning the entire order of spiritual and temporal things, and, as such, were justifiable targets of tyrannicide for prince and subject alike.[61]

Luther had changed his position on resistance, and Torgau was clearly the watershed, even if his turn there was quite piecemeal and very cautious. But to conclude that Luther was *merely* pushed by the pressures of political events rather than guided by enduring principles – as many contemporaries (enemies and even some allies) and recent scholars have argued[62] – is to miss the greater and more basic consistency of his evolving views on resistance with his career-long defence of temporal government as a precious gift of God, made clear once again by the evangelical reform of the church. For Luther in 1523, reviving respect for the divine gift of the temporal kingdom seemed to make any legitimation of resistance a flat contradiction to his aim of restoring temporal authority to its proper place of honour

58 LW 50: 11–2; WA BR 6: 36–7.

59 Shoenberger, "Luther and the Justifiability of Resistance," 13.

60 Ibid., 16.

61 WA 39II: 41–42. Shoenberger, "Luther and the Justifiability of Resistance," 19.

62 See Cargill Thompson, "Luther and the Right of Resistance to the Emperor," 202.

and respect; by the 1530s, however, the threats of imperial war were making resistance theory necessary *for the sake of* respecting temporal authority. Of course, political events were shaping and guiding Luther's views. But behind those events was his enduring view that the restoration of temporal authority was one of the fruits of evangelical reform, and increasingly the emperor posed a direct threat to the restoration of the two kingdoms. Therefore, Luther's evolving thoughts on resistance, despite how it may have appeared or sounded to many (both then and now), were consistent with the core of his political thought and his stalwart theological defence of the temporal kingdom.

To consistently defend the place of temporal government in the world, Luther's stance on armed resistance changed, but the episode also appeared to encourage his thinking on the rule of law in the exercise of power and authority. To be sure, even as early as *Temporal Authority* in 1523, Luther had written about the role of codified laws and the place of legal principles in the temporal kingdom. The prince, he then argued, must learn to be prudent and wise "so that the law may prevail at all times and in all cases, and reason may be the highest law and the master of all administration of law."[63] Not long before the Torgau meeting, in the summer of 1530 Luther was scolding parents in his *Sermon on Keeping Children in School* for neglecting their children's education, decrying the decay of the rule of law (and reason) that would follow, and the implosion of temporal government. But the Torgau meeting in late October brought attention to the importance of the rule of law and legal principles against tyranny. In *Dr Martin Luther's Warning to His Dear German People*, he left specific legal judgments to the jurists, but the place of codified law in limiting the abuse of government came to the forefront of his thinking and that of his followers.[64]

Defending Temporal Authority

The priority Luther gave to defending the honour and purpose of the temporal kingdom was abundantly clear in two crucial, politically focused treatises from the 1520s: *Whether Soldiers, Too, Can Be Saved*

63 LW 45: 119.
64 On the legal thought of sixteenth-century Lutherans, see chapter 6, 146–7.

(1526) and *On War Against the Turk* (1529). Although these writings both predate the resistance controversies, and even show Luther's refusal to legitimize resistance to higher political authorities (such as the emperor), they nevertheless underscore his belief that his thought and the evangelical reform he was leading were bringing back the divinely ordained place and purpose of temporal government from the disastrous confusion of the two kingdoms advanced by a wayward church and people.

Hence, in *Whether Soldiers, Too, Can Be Saved* Luther began to tackle the ethical and pastoral question on the permissibility of Christian military service with the hyperbolic but very telling claim that "not since the time of the apostles have the temporal sword and temporal government been so clearly described or so highly praised by me."[65] Essentially, Luther's two kingdoms teaching underscored why Christians could and should serve temporal – and *coercive* – power with a clean conscience and welcome it as a divine and holy gift. For Luther, there were, of course, limits to that service and limits to the coercion that temporal government ought to exert. The treatise aimed to explain why and under what circumstances a Christian might bear arms in the service of temporal authority.

To answer why a Christian may bear arms in service, Luther argued that war or coercion in the service of temporal authority was, at its best, an act of love: although its necessity resulted from sin, it was to be used mercifully to curb evil in order to preserve peace, households, property, and effective government. Like the good physician who "sometimes finds so serious and terrible a sickness that he must amputate or destroy a hand, foot, ear, eye, to save the body," the power of the sword was ultimately directed to restoring health in the regime, even if that sometimes meant dealing violently with political abscesses.[66] Of course, abuse of the power often occurred, but as he had argued earlier in *Temporal Authority*, this fact did not confute the godliness of the institution and its vital goods of peace and order.

For Luther, the circumstances for legitimately bearing arms were much more complex, and hard and fast rules governing them were "impossible to establish." Luther gave the example of the Peasants' War: although rebels deserved death, a true and just resolution

65 LW 46: 95; WA 19: 625.
66 LW 46: 96; WA 19: 625.

would consider the variety of motives or intentions and circumstances and thus punish relatively few with death.[67] Luther attempted some rules and distinctions, such as prohibiting war against one's superiors, and refining the circumstances that were justified with equals and inferiors.[68] Of course, Luther's prohibition of revolt and revolution for Christians would ultimately be short-lived, but he noted also that revolt was usually fomented by the abuse of the temporal kingdom in the first place. For this abuse, Luther wrote, God would avenge tyranny.[69]

Luther warned princes and subjects alike to heed the divine purpose of government when contemplating war; in fact, his warning against unjust causes was not only about endangering souls but also about upholding and protecting the divine gift of temporal authority.[70] Luther thus criticized what he perceived to be the norm in his day: authorities that started wars without justification. In contrast, he hailed the example of the (by then) late Elector of Saxony, Frederick, who would defend Saxony if attacked but showed the utmost restraint against aggression and conquest.[71] Frederick, as a good Christian prince, respected the divine gift of government and thus humbly feared God in the use of government's most deadly powers. Likewise, for Luther, the subject was to fulfill his duties to the temporal kingdom with an analogous respect and honour, which meant therefore a shunning of war for unjust causes, such as riches, women, and honour.[72] Thus, a soldier, in Luther's view, fully in his rights and duties, refuses to pick up the sword for an unjust cause: in fact, such refusal was for him a binding imperative of Christian faith. A Christian soldier was bound to discern the justness of the war as best he could and, if it was just, then use the sword with confidence and offer his "outer self" to the service of the temporal kingdom. Both prince and subject, Luther the pastor reminded them, were to place their hope and trust in the grace of Jesus Christ; but bodies and swords could be given to

67 LW 46: 100; WA 19: 630.
68 LW 46: 103; WA 19: 632.
69 LW 46: 107; WA 19: 636.
70 LW 46: 118–19; WA 19: 645–46.
71 LW 46: 199–20; WA 19: 646–47.
72 LW 46: 130; WA 19: 656.

the coercive powers of temporal government if in defending the realm they were bringing peace and order for their neighbours.[73]

Defending the divine gift and purpose of government also underscored Luther's 1529 treatise *On War Against the Turk.* The treatise was written at a time when Turkish invasion of Western Europe was believed to be imminent, as the Ottoman Empire under Suleiman the Magnificent (r. 1520–66) had expanded as far west as Belgrade and most of Hungary. In fact, within the year Vienna would be under siege, although ultimately Suleiman's forces would suffer their first major defeat there and turn the tide against further Western European invasion. Like most people of his age, Luther viewed the Turkish threat in eschatological or apocalyptic terms, particularly as divine punishment for European waywardness.[74] But for Luther the sin rested primarily in its ignorance of both the gospel and temporal authority.

Once again, as in the earlier treatise *Whether Soldiers, Too, Can Be Saved,* Luther considered evangelical reform as a movement that sought to restore not only the gospel but also government to its divinely ordained purpose. At the beginning of *On War Against the Turk,* Luther wrote, in reference to the eve of reform, "This was the state of things at the time: no one had taught, no one had heard, and no one knew anything about temporal government, whence it came, what its office and work were, or how it ought to serve God."[75] For Luther, this ignorance was erased by *Temporal Authority,* a work that fought the error that government was a "heathen, human, ungodly thing, as though it jeopardized salvation to be in the ranks of rulers."[76] However, according to Luther's thinking, this restoration of tempo-

73 LW 46: 135; WA 19: 661.

74 Since an invasion of Germany was expected, Luther frequently wrote about the Turks throughout his career. In his *Explanations of the Ninety-Five Theses* (1518), Luther argued that resisting the Turkish invasion was akin to resisting God, since the invasion was divine punishment for European waywardness (LW 31: 91–2; WA 1: 535). Pope Leo X's bull, *Exsurge, Domine* (1520), designated this argument as Luther's thirty-fourth error of the forty-one. At the outset of *On War Against the Turk,* Luther defended his position (LW 46: 162; WA 30 II: 108–9). For Luther's relationship to the Turks and Islam, see Francisco, *Martin Luther and Islam,* and Miller, "Luther on the Turks and Islam." For an overall account of Protestants and Turks in the early sixteenth century, see Fisher-Galati, *Ottoman Imperialism and German Protestantism, 1521–1555.* See also Bohnstedt, "The Infidel Scourge of God."

75 LW 46: 163; WA 30 II: 109.

76 Ibid.

ral government was as yet unheeded by many who remained under the dominance of the Roman Church, and so Europe was now facing the encroachment of the Ottoman Empire as divine judgment.

On War Against the Turk answered its central pastoral question – whether Christians could go to war against the Ottomans – with the defence of the temporal kingdom. Christians could *not* wage war against the invasion as a crusade endorsed by the papacy: such a call was to further confuse the two kingdoms, and was thus a sure sign of the thorough corruption of the Roman Church. War could not be waged in the name of Christ or for spiritual benefits (such as plenary indulgences to soldiers).[77] But Christians could, in good conscience, wage war for the defence of the temporal kingdom itself, and Luther clearly saw the Ottoman invasion as an obliteration of temporal authority's divine honour and purpose that evangelical reform had been restoring back to Germany. In Luther's understanding – as the text indicates, he had just recently been reading the Koran for the first time[78] – the Ottomans also greatly confused the kingdoms: they persecuted the gospel, spread their faith by the sword, attacked monogamous marriage, advocated iconoclasm, and claimed their head of state as the successor to a holy prophet.[79] For Luther, this made the Turkish threat akin to a large-scale, Müntzer-like destruction of the two kingdoms, and thus one legitimately resisted – so long as their motives remained pure as defenders of the kingdoms – by Western European princes and soldiers.

CONCLUSION

As all of the primary sources have shown, there was a basic unity to Luther's position on major political crises of the 1520s and 1530s: although he changed his position on Protestant armed resistance, was enmeshed in the mass peasant uprising of 1525, and even considered, at times, the pope, the emperor, and the sultan as the Antichrist (or at least as the pawns of the devil in an apocalyptic struggle), throughout these controversies over radicals, armed service, and resistance he invariably considered the survival and well-being of the

77 LW 46: 165ff.; WA 30 II: 113.

78 Luther's references to his reading begin at LW 46: 176; WA 30 II: 121.

79 LW 46: 178; WA 30 II: 123.

temporal order as of paramount concern, second only to the restoration of the gospel in a reformed church. Interpretation of Luther's role in and contribution to these crises has too often neglected this larger picture in favour of specificity without a broad contextual perspective of his political thought. Hence, studies have pored over the evidence on resistance to the empire, for example, to discover when Luther had definitively changed his position, and have concluded that he had been led to his change much more by political actors and events than by principles. But underlying his writing on resistance, and indeed on the Peasants' War and the pastoral matter of military service, Luther saw himself as – in addition to a preacher and pastor of the gospel – a restorer of temporal authority to its proper and divinely ordained purpose, as revealed in the Bible and known by sound reasoning, to bring order and peace to a sinful world.

5

Luther and the Political Challenges of Reform

THE DIFFICULTIES OF REFORM

Luther's earliest calls for programmatic church reform, even in the first revolutionary treatises from the 1520s, were at the same time calls for political reform. In the broadest terms, when Luther called out the institutional church for dominating matters outside its proper spiritual jurisdiction, he concurrently advised restoring these matters to the temporal authorities. With such political consequences to his reform, Luther has often been seen as a proponent of cleansing or simplifying "the church" while at the same time acting as a champion of the expansion of "the state," despite these terms being anachronistic to the sixteenth-century. Luther's church, as a spiritual ministry, was to be strictly focused on Word and sacrament, while the temporal authority, in his vision, was to be fully restored to its powerful position as the most precious and useful divine gift to humanity. To *some* degree, a pared-down church and an empowered temporal government figured in Luther's visions for reform.

But to *what* degree, precisely? How would Luther recommend specific, practical reforms so that the two kingdoms remained intact as separate realms over the human condition? In answering these questions in relation to several major reforms, his political thought was challenged to its limits in coherence and usefulness. In many of these reforms, such as the policing of problematic subjects and of preaching, as well as education, Luther's treatment seemed to raise as many questions on the practicality of the two kingdoms as it answered.

In overseeing reform of the church and society, Luther always stuck to the principle that the gospel demanded that the church renounce any practice or doctrine that countenanced justification by works. Therefore, he attacked not only monasticism but also *any* appropriation of the idea that clerical life was somehow deemed a worthier service than other ways of life in the eyes of God. Indeed, for Luther, even the temptation to such presumption made monasticism an illegitimate calling in the wake of reform. But the fact that Luther sought to eradicate what he deemed to be the corrosive presumptions of the doctrine of justification did not mean that he also sought to eradicate the expansive services with which the medieval church had benefited Christian society.

Luther's evangelical reform did bring about an alarming social upheaval as it severed the church from its central and dominating role in aiding the poor, educating the young, marrying the baptized, and policing heresy. Over these key areas of long-standing ecclesial prerogative, Luther replaced temporal authorities as the rightful guardians of welfare. But in Luther's thinking this was by no means a carte blanche assignment in which governments and magistrates could do as they pleased to aggrandize their power at the expense of clergy or subjects. Rather, with these jurisdictional responsibilities for order and welfare necessarily came accountability, particularly from pastors, when government failed to exercise its proper duties.

Luther firmly held that the poor needed relief, the sick needed hospitals, the young needed to be educated, and the preaching in the church at times needed special oversight; the difference of his vision from the provision of these services before German reform was that temporal government was to now possess the authority and prerogative to oversee and provide them. But for Luther this did not mean that temporal authority would come to dominate its subjects in all aspects of "outer life." In fact, although Luther considered the two kingdoms as clearly distinct and separable, in the practice of governing, as is evident in his own writings concerning these areas of public benefit, temporal authority was not simply free to act *autocratically* or without any exterior standards. But the great problem was that temporal government's oversight of the church (albeit for Luther, always a temporary measure), the policing of preaching, the policing of troublesome subjects, the sponsoring of education, the oversight of marriage, and giving aid to the poor were tightly bound up with the ends and purposes of the spiritual kingdom. Rather than giving over these responsibilities to the temporal government *tout court*, Luther's own accounts show that the spiritual kingdom remained resolutely out of its jurisdiction. Luther always held that ministers of the gospel retained a prophetic and critical purpose against secular magistrates: entirely fitting of the spiritual kingdom, they had a divine duty to call temporal authorities into account for their failures to live up to the purposes God had established for their office. As will be seen in this chapter, Luther did so himself many times. However, significant problems with the two kingdoms remained in these reforms, and Luther was often unable to resolutely settle them.

MAINTAINING ORDER BEYOND LAW AND COERCION

Temporal Government and Church Oversight

As early as 1520, Luther had identified the *special* role of temporal authority in the cause of church reform. Indeed, the explosive treatise *To the Christian Nobility of the German Nation* was itself premised on the hope Luther placed on noble laymen – outside clerical orders – to effect change in the Christian church against an entrenched clergy intent on maintaining their secular privileges. Luther argued that all Christians, by the fact of their baptisms, were all equally bishops, priests, and popes, since these positions were merely offices of the church instead of some indelible mark of higher spiritual authority. In calling upon the nobility, Luther was calling upon baptized Christians, who also crucially happened to hold high office or status in the temporal world, to use their influence to lead the whole church toward reform. He had even specifically called on the emperor and the imperial estates – not the pope – to summon a church council.[1]

In so doing, Luther seemed to have already greatly complicated, if not partly undermined, the two kingdoms distinction years before he had even articulated it: temporal powers were being called to wield authority over the reforming church. Yet, despite the increasing reliance on secular magistrates and princes for a central and authoritative leadership in reform, Luther's approach to the direct role of temporal government in the spiritual leadership of the church stressed its provisional and temporary purpose in the church crisis.

1 LW 44: 136–7; WA 6: 413.

Consider, for example, Luther's call to princely oversight of church visitation in his preface to the *Instructions for the Visitors of Parish Pastors in Electoral Saxony* (1528).[2] In its preface, Luther admitted that the "true episcopal office," based on both the biblical and patristic examples of visiting churches and overseeing teaching, was in dire need of revival. He wrote that none of his fellow reformers had felt called to the task; hence, they instead called their prince, Elector John of Saxony, to ordain several persons to the office, and to do so not out of any obligations of his temporal office, but rather "out of Christian love."[3] These parish visitors, Luther went on to explain, were to be heeded out of love by the "devout and peaceable pastors who find their sincere joy in the gospel."[4] In other words, parish visits were devoid of temporal law and coercion, as they were properly an office of the spiritual kingdom. The ordination of the visitors by the prince was thus a contingent measure whereby he, like the visitors and parish pastors alike, acted out of love for the sake of the gospel. The hard distinction he had made between the two kingdoms, Luther argued, still remained.

But even at the end of this same preface Luther seemed to entangle the two kingdoms all over again. For all those who refused visitations and oversight – Luther called them "the undisciplined heads who out of utter perversity are able to do nothing in common or in agreement, but are different and self-centered in heart and life"[5] – were to be subject to the discipline of the temporal authorities. To be sure, punishment was given not for their spiritual doctrines and practices *as such*, since the Elector was "not obligated to teach and to rule in spiritual affairs," but because these same renegades from the emerging evangelical church standards were simultaneously threatening temporal peace. Preventing, quelling, and punishing "strife, rioting, and rebellion" *were* within the proper jurisdiction of the prince and thus were entirely justified in policing dissent from parish visitations.[6]

2 LW 40: 269–320; WA 26: 195–240. Philip Melanchthon authored the instructions themselves, whereas Luther wrote the preface. Brecht, *Martin Luther: Shaping and Defining the Reformation*, 267–8.

3 LW 40: 271; WA 26: 197.

4 LW 40: 272; WA 26: 200.

5 LW 40: 273; WA 26: 200.

6 Ibid.

Thus, in the matter of oversight of the evangelical church, or at least in Luther's account of it in his preface to the *Instructions*, the two kingdoms were, temporarily, entangled for a common purpose, even *if* separate. How separate the kingdoms could be in this arrangement (notwithstanding Luther's insistence that they were) is still subject to debate.[7] The situation did facilitate the aggrandizement of secular powers over church leadership. The elector prince, simply as a loving Christian with the effective ability to do so, was to appoint parish visitors who were nevertheless only spiritual teachers without temporal authority. Churches were to submit to the spiritual leadership out of Christian love. However, resistance to these visitations was at the very least a potential threat to the temporal peace, and so by not submitting to the evangelical leadership they would in turn be subject to the heightened suspicions, if not outright coercive judgments, of the prince.

In Luther's view, the role of temporal government (in this case Elector John) was a contingent and temporary measure demanded by the deplorable conditions and utter confusion that much of the church in Saxony, not to mention society at large, was experiencing in the tremendous upheaval of reform. In no way did Luther counsel a normalizing of the kind of function Elector John was to serve over the parishes. Luther *was* consistent about its emergency status. As early as 1525, Luther had implored his elector, as an emergency measure, to oversee parishes and pulpits (and also, it should be noted here, local governments) because of the depraved and worsening conditions of churches and the reluctance of the Catholic bishops, who did little to alleviate them.[8] Late in his life and career, Luther referred to secular powers in the church as *Notbischöfe*, or "emergency [hence *Not*-] bishops." Their authority was always only as temporary facilitators of proper spiritual leadership. Luther counselled church visitors to see a *Notbischoff* as having authority only in times of crises or great need, rather than in any official duty of secular oversight of church affairs.[9]

7 Estes, in his *Peace, Order, and the Glory of God*, argues that Luther later turns to the prince as a *cura religionis* with regularized oversight of the clergy.

8 LW 49: 130–38; WA BR 3: 594–6.

9 WA 53: 255. See the seminal article on the subject by Spitz, "Luther's Ecclesiology and His Concept of the Prince as *Notbischof*."

In fact, unlike his colleagues and fellow reformers (as we shall see in the next chapter), Luther guarded against the incursion of secular government into ecclesial affairs lest any emergency leadership be transformed or ossified into an institutionalized control over the church by government. By the late 1530s, Luther was greatly worried that secular leadership, which a decade earlier could be credited for saving the cause of reform, was now threatening it by placing political interests above spiritual ones in the oversight of the evangelical church. Luther made his worries explicit in his sermons on the Gospel of John, first preached to the *Stadtkirche* in Wittenberg, during the long absence of its pastor Johannes Bugenhagen (who helped lead evangelical reform in Denmark).[10] These sermons were later redacted into an extensive commentary on the first four chapters.

While commenting on Jesus's cleansing of the temple (John 2:13–25), Luther recalled the central importance of the two kingdoms (he used the word *Regiment* here) for the survival of the gospel and the well-being of the temporal (*weltliche*) world: these could not be confused without grave spiritual and temporal consequences. "But I exhort you who are one day to instruct consciences in the Christian Church," Luther insisted, "to take heed that you abide by the distinction between the two realms."[11] He wrote: "As soon as a prince says: 'Give ear to me, pastor, and teach this or that! Do not chide and rebuke in this way!' the two spheres are confused. And again, it is wrong for a pastor to say: 'Listen, government or judge, I want you to administer justice as I wish!' But I must say: 'You have your own powers, laws, practice, and usage; therefore do not administer justice according to my opinion, will, or books but according to your own laws.'"[12] But whereas evangelical reform began by preaching against the church's (and, in particular, the pope's) claims of authority over the temporal kingdom, now the threat to the distinction was coming from the secular authorities as they began to assume control over their territorial churches:

10 See the introduction in LW 22: ix–xi.

11 In prefacing his remarks with the exhortation to "instruct consciences," his teaching here was apparently directed not to the congregation overall but to students who would go on to lead the church as pastors. See LW 22: 226, note 18.

12 LW 22: 226; WA 45: 736.

Now the tables are being turned, for the fisted office is being transformed into an oral office. Secular officials now want to administer the spiritual office, control the pulpit and the church, and prescribe that I preach to the liking of the prince. Under such conditions, let the devil take my place and preach! For they are converting the sword of the Spirit and of the mouth into scourges and whips; they are expelling from the church, not the buyers and sellers but the true teachers and preachers! This practice is rampant today. Stern edicts and mandates are nailed to all the church doors, ordering the laity to receive Holy Communion only in one kind and commanding the clergy to preach what pleases them. Moreover, the civil authorities can venture to be so insolent with their counsel and command because they reflect the will of kings, princes, and lords.[13]

Here Luther distinguished himself from his colleagues: he was a steadfast critic of the emerging "territorial churches" of the Reformation. Moreover, lest his objections in his commentary be considered a defence only of the Word (which was obviously paramount), Luther repeatedly insisted also on the separation of kingdoms as essential to the health of governments. Here was also a prime example of Luther's *anti*-authoritarianism (against the abundant accusations of the contrary): the separation of the kingdoms and the concomitant freedom of the Word meant that secular government was *limited* in its scope and powers and, moreover – as this very admonishment had shown – subject to the prophetic condemnations by the true preaching of the Word. Precisely at issue here in this commentary was the freedom of preachers and pastors to call wayward temporal powers to account for suppressing the gospel and shirking the duties that God had bound to their offices. Yet Luther had himself advocated for government oversight of preaching, even if it was for him a temporary measure. How the prophetic role of preachers was to work under the very authorities they were at times to denounce, Luther left unexplained.

Policing Preaching

Nevertheless, aside from provisional leadership over the church, Luther did consider the policing of preaching a legitimate exercise

13 LW 22: 227; WA 45: 737.

of temporal government's power and authority, at least in ensuring that only commissioned preachers – those with demonstrated callings and pastoral charges – were permitted to preach in a given temporal jurisdiction. Two writings in particular exemplify this notion of the policing power of temporal government: *Against the Heavenly Prophets in the Matter of Images and Sacraments* (1525) and *Infiltrating the Clandestine Preachers* (1532). In *Against the Heavenly Prophets*, Luther took to task the civil disobedience of his one-time colleague and friend turned radical reformer, Andreas Karlstadt.[14] At the time, just before the Peasants' War in 1525, Luther was certainly beginning to see profound theological differences between his thinking and Karlstadt's, and Luther suspected that Karlstadt's preaching would stir up revolt much as Thomas Müntzer's preaching was doing elsewhere.[15] To be sure, even though he was an iconoclast and railed against both the Eucharist and infant baptism, Karlstadt had renounced violence for the sake of reform; yet, in Luther's thinking, he had nevertheless disregarded temporal authority by leaving his commissioned post at the University of Wittenberg and assuming an already commissioned pastorate at Orlamünde, both without the knowledge or approval of the prince.[16] Similarly, in his *Infiltrating the Clandestine Preachers* (1532), an open letter to Eberhard von der Tannen (a magistrate at the Wartburg), Luther called on "magistrates, cities, and princes" to be vigilant against secret itinerant preachers – radical reformers – who were appearing all over evangelical lands.[17]

In both of these texts, rather than contradicting his two kingdoms teaching, Luther very clearly believed he was *preserving* the distinction between temporal and spiritual matters. In *Infiltrating the Clandestine Preachers* he was emphatic that the temporal government's policing of secret preaching would preserve the temporal order from revolt and sedition as well as securing the place for the free preaching and teaching of the Word. In both treatises, Luther offered a similar criticism of clandestine preaching: any proclaimer of the Word who could not publicly account for himself – that is, account for his divine

14 See Brecht, *Martin Luther: Shaping and Defining the Reformation*, 157–72.
15 See LW 40: 102–4, 108–115; WA 18: 85–8, 91–9.
16 Brecht, *Martin Luther: Shaping and Defining the Reformation*, 166.
17 See LW 40: 383–6; WA 30 III: 518–21.

calling – and who evaded temporal authorities could not be trusted to be an authentic preacher of the Word of God or a good servant of the temporal kingdom. Hence, Luther concluded, such preaching had to be curtailed for the sake of both the true teaching of the Word and the peace of the temporal kingdom.

Policing Subjects: Blasphemy and the Jews

Luther considered blasphemy a crime punishable by the temporal authorities. In fact, when the topic arose in his works, he treated its status as a public crime; there was no hint of controversy about this position, and thus he offered few additional reflections. Luther assumed that blasphemy was a crime punishable by law, and virtually everyone else in his era believed the same; he was doing nothing new by assigning it to the jurisdiction of temporal authorities as a serious transgression of the outer nature of humanity.[18] At first glance, the policing of blasphemy by government may appear to be a violation of the separation of Luther's two kingdoms, but such a conclusion betrays a misunderstanding of what the separation meant for him: rather than separating "religion" from political matters, a distinction made in much later and different contexts than in sixteenth-century Germany, Luther's two kingdoms separated the saving Word from the sundry means by which God brought order to the world. Blasphemy had nothing to do with salvation; rather, it was concerned with wayward outward conduct and was thus subject to temporal laws, even if the transgression was directed primarily against God.

Moreover, Luther believed – again, typically for his age – that blasphemy *did* threaten the temporal kingdom and thus harm neighbours. At the very least, for Luther it was a public vice legitimately suppressed, like Germany's notorious alcohol abuse: in *To the Christian Nobility* he listed it among the harmful evils accompanying drinking that Germans had to curb.[19] At the worst, it was a denial of God, or a heretical denial of His power or salvation, and thus not only a speech crime like slander but also an attempt to "defame the name of

18 In the *Large Catechism* of 1529, in his instruction on the Second Commandment (prohibiting taking the name of God in vain), Luther wrote that the "misuse of the holy name [was] the greatest sin that can be committed outwardly"; BC, 393.

19 LW 44: 214; WA 6: 466.

God and rob [a] neighbour of [God's] honour in the eyes of the world."[20] Thus, it could not be tolerated without disastrous effects on the public order, he believed. Internal belief was always to be free from external punishment, Luther wrote, but once uttered or taught, it crossed into the temporal jurisdiction.

Luther's treatment of blasphemy underscores a very difficult problem for distinguishing between the two kingdoms when it came to the duties of temporal government toward heretics and non-Christians. The spiritual kingdom was the realm of the Word, yet Luther counselled that any *public* and *outward* denial of that Word – for example, the *publicly advocated* denial of salvation through Jesus – would be subject to the laws and punishments of the temporal government. Thus, aside from whether they ever publicly spoke blasphemous words against Jesus, and aside from the hideously false but persistent accusations of "blood libel" against them, the Jews, who were so often required to be outwardly identifiable in medieval Europe (by, for instance, yellow badges), could be seen under Luther's treatment – by their mere *existence* – as threats to the public order. Indeed, Luther did consider Jews, merely as Jews, to pose a grave public threat, and, at least in his late polemic *On the Jews and Their Lies* (1543), he advocated for a litany of horrifying measures, including pogroms and the burning of synagogues, against them.[21] For Luther, temporal governments were to adopt these measures to protect the lives and property of their subjects.

Luther's treatment of the Jews has been a matter of significant scholarly controversy, particularly in the aftermath of National Socialist tyranny and the systematic mass murder of Jews in the Holocaust. For his violent polemics against the Jews *and* his political views, Luther has at times been considered, in various attempts to understand the causes and roots of National Socialist politics and its anti-Semitic hatred, as a forefather of both the Holocaust and German authoritarianism and totalitarianism.[22] Because Luther's own anti-Semitism was

20 LW 13: 61; WA 31 I: 208.

21 LW 47: 268; WA 53: 522.

22 See for example, McGovern, *From Luther to Hitler*. Shirer's *The Rise and Fall of the Third Reich*, a popular history of National Socialism, attributed the willingness of German Protestants to accept Nazism to the influence of Luther's anti-Semitism and authoritarianism (236). Siemon-Netto's *The Fabricated Luther* effectively critiques Shirer's argument.

present throughout his writings,[23] and not only in a few late-career, angry polemics, as can sometimes be supposed,[24] a much more particularized question remains about his overall thinking and theology: was Luther's anti-Semitism an essential part of, or a necessary conclusion to, his theology of *sola fides* and his biblical interpretations?[25]

In this current study, justice cannot possibly be done to the question of the place of Luther's anti-Semitism in his overall thought. Insofar as understanding Luther's *political* thought is concerned, it suffices to affirm that Luther was clearly anti-Semitic and based his hatred of Jews on theological grounds – that is, on their rejection of Christ and the saving Word – and that for the sake of public order he assigned to temporal government the duty of policing any outward and external displays of that rejection. In this respect, the Jews were the extreme case in a broad collection of problematic subjects whose expression of beliefs, in Luther's view, threatened the worldly order (to say nothing of the spiritual). "Papists" and radicals – such as Müntzer and Karlstadt, in Luther's opinion – were subject to temporal government for the same reasons: a disturbance of the temporal order by the outward declarations of their beliefs. Luther's political view of Jews in his late polemical works put them in the impossible position, short of converting, of keeping their spiritual freedom to be Jews *inwardly* without any outward manifestations that would be subject to government sanction.

In addition to its well-deserved attention in other fields of inquiry, Luther's treatment of Jews, particularly their political treatment in *On the Jews and Their Lies,* deserves more attention for its political significance than it has received to date. First, it demonstrates how far Luther's conception of the separation of the two kingdoms was from what is sometimes now considered an early ancestor of the "separation of church and state" or the relegation of "religious" ends out of the public sphere and into private life. Luther's two kingdoms, as the policing of Jewish subjects shows, worked in tandem for the *common*

23 See *Martin Luther, the Bible, and the Jewish People,* ed. Schramm and Stjerna, which collects many examples of Luther's thoughts on the Jews, as well as his obvious anti-Semitic comments, into one volume.

24 See Barth's criticism of attempts to bracket off Luther's anti-Semitism from overall considerations of his theology in *The Theology of Martin Luther,* 29–39.

25 Gritcsh's *Martin Luther's Anti-Semitism* argues that the anti-Semitism is inconsistent with the core of his theology and his reading of Paul.

end of godly rule over body and soul. That Jews and "papists" were theological transgressors did not mean that temporal government had no jurisdiction over their transgressions: on the contrary, the theologies of Jews and "papists" were subject to temporal punishment the moment their ideas were taught and promulgated, since this made them outward acts. For Luther, the distinction of kingdoms was one within the complete reign of God over the lives of human beings in body and spirit. Keeping the jurisdictions distinct within that reign was Luther's concern, and that balance of kingdoms was to him furthered by curtailing any public plurality of inner belief by the temporal authority.

Second, Luther's treatment of Jews and other theologically dissenting subjects assumed that pluralities were dangerous and ungovernable and that temporal authorities were wise to curtail them as much as possible. As with his anti-Semitism and his views on blasphemy, Luther was by no means alone in his era: much of sixteenth-century politics, at least in the Holy Roman Empire and the confessional conflicts that would in part lead to the Thirty Years War, accepted the veracity of this assumption. Significant new historical evidence suggests that such an assumption was beginning to be seriously challenged by the middle of the century, especially in confessionally mixed cities (at least for a time) such as Augsburg,[26] and of course in the French crises in the latter part of the century.[27] In the seventeenth century, in the Peace of Westphalia (1648) for example, the rights of dissenting subjects – if then only limited to Reformed, Lutheran, and Catholic confessions – were beginning to be guaranteed in laws and treaties. At the very least, Luther's views on the policing of subjects, grounded in his two kingdoms, demonstrate how far he was from not only modern liberal pluralism but even from any modest political toleration of Jews and other nonconformists from prevailing majorities. Luther's position on the policing of subjects pointed straight toward a territorial church in which the boundaries between kingdoms that he deemed so essential could be blurred and confused.

26 Creasman, *Censorship and Civic Order in Reformation Germany, 1517–1648.*

27 See Witte, *The Reformation of Rights.*

FOSTERING GOOD SUBJECTS

Beyond maintaining order by policing subjects and preaching, and in addition to the usual rule of law and execution of punishments, Luther argued that the divine purpose of temporal government was also fulfilled by fostering good, law-abiding, procreating, and prosperous subjects through a number of means available to it. Although he never gave any holistic, systematic account of what may be called this constructive purpose, throughout his career in various treatises and polemics Luther argued that temporal government was responsible for educating its subjects, upholding reasonable laws concerning marriages, and assuming a leading role for poor relief. Again, though much authority was given over to government from what had been the prerogatives of the medieval Latin church, Luther believed he was neither aggrandizing secular authority beyond its divinely ordained affairs nor violating the separation of the two kingdoms; rather, he believed he was distinguishing secular authority from the freedom in the gospel and thus restoring it to its rightful place as the cause of worldly order.

Education and Temporal Government

Temporal government made good subjects by educating them: of the ways Luther accounted for the constructive duties of the worldly kingdom, his articulation of its role in education was perhaps his most impassioned and clearest. He devoted two crucial treatises to the matter: *To the Councilmen of All Cities in Germany That They Establish and Maintain Christian Schools* (1524)[28] and *A Sermon on Keeping Children in School* (1530).[29] Although these treatises were not exclusively about education and the temporal kingdom – employment, class ascendency, and prosperity were also in the mix – his appeals were ultimately directed toward the welfare of the two kingdoms: education, Luther insisted, greatly benefited both the political order and the reception of the gospel. It was thus imperative, Luther believed, that members of temporal government, from the prince down to the local

28 LW 45: 339–78; WA 15: 27–53.
29 LW 46: 207–58; WA 30 II: 517–88.

magistrates, did everything in their power to uphold and sponsor the education of their subjects, from primary schools to universities.[30]

The historical context of Luther's defence of education must be understood: in short, the German Reformation had brought about an immense crisis in education. Luther's part in that crisis began when he scathingly criticized many of the university teachers of his day. From the earliest stage of the indulgences controversy, Luther had attacked the "schoolmen" (the latter-day scholastics of Europe's universities and the prominent orders, especially the Order of Preachers or "Dominicans") for their theology and study of the Bible. For Luther, the work of the schoolmen was, at best, a useless distraction or, at worst, posed a demonic threat to souls with false doctrine and unbiblical teachings. It is of little surprise, therefore, that among Luther's calls for reform in the early Reformation was a wholesale reform of universities. His bold treatise *To the Christian Nobility* (1520) included this as a major part of programmatic reform.[31]

Owing to his theology that emphasized the "priesthood of all believers" and the consequent belief in the divine calling of *all* legitimate walks of life, Luther also called for the dissolution of monasteries. With this ambitious and far-reaching policy, an enormously important and potentially disastrous effect on education soon arose, for monasteries were among the primary means of educating the young. Most educated children in Luther's age were taught in a school affiliated with a monastery or cathedral (though perhaps in a school affiliated with a burger guild or parish). This crucial role and tradition held by monasteries and cathedrals in the Latin West dated at least to the twelfth century's "renaissance," and even to the educational and church reforms led by Alcuin of York (c. 735–804) in the Carolingian Renaissance. By both dissolving monasteries and reordering the universities, German evangelical reform was compelled to rebuild the entire educational system, from primary school to doctoral studies.[32]

30 For an account of Luther's lifelong preoccupation with education, see Harran, *Martin Luther*.

31 LW 44: 200–4; WA 6: 457–60.

32 See Kittelson, "Luther as Educational Reformer."

As if this task were not large enough, Luther also had to face a crisis in the value of education among ordinary Germans.[33] In part, the crisis had been inadvertently precipitated by his own reforms: with doctrines such as the priesthood of all believers and the reform of church offices, a good education for ministerial callings and high clerical offices now appeared to be unnecessary. In addition, what Luther had called the barbarous materialism of the German people was tempting many to neglect the education of their children in favour of the exploding commerce in goods and trades brought about by the expansion of the Holy Roman Empire, the growth of European monarchies, and the exploration of the New World.[34] Germany was subject to an acute demand for manufactured goods and thus skilled tradesmen and developed industry. Mining was one such trade, and Luther knew this world well: he was the son of a successful leaseholder of copper mines in Mansfeld, one of the premier mining territories of Germany.[35] Thus, with the dissolution of the monasteries and the economic demands of the age, education was facing a severe crisis.

LUTHER AND GERMAN EDUCATION IN THE CITIES

To the Councilmen of All Cities of Germany That They Establish and Maintain Christian Schools was Luther's first response to the crisis in education. It was written early in the winter of 1524, after his secret hiding at the Wartburg but before the Peasants' War of 1525. It is noteworthy that Luther began the work by writing to the "councilmen" (*Radherrn*) of the cities to establish and thereafter maintain schools. The treatise is not dedicated to a prince and his courtiers or addressed to the German nobility, but is directed instead to local civic authorities. Although princes were great allies in the cause of educational reform – Luther's own prince had only recently founded the University of Wittenberg when he was brought in as a professor in 1508 – Luther's reasons for leaving them aside were made abundantly clear: princes had shirked their duty to foster education among their subjects in favour of debauchery and licentiousness. They had abandoned this responsibility to their subjects for the amusements of courtly life,

33 See the introduction to the first treatise, LW 44: 341–3.

34 Brecht, *Martin Luther: Shaping and Defining the Reformation*, 139.

35 Brecht, *Martin Luther: His Road to Reformation*, 3–6.

such as sleigh rides and drinking; thus, he acerbically noted that they were too "burdened with the high and important functions in cellar, kitchen, and bedroom."[36] Effective change in education would have to come from magistrates of lower rank in the temporal order.

In his works, Luther's criticism of princes and their courts was commonplace. In his 1520 treatise *To the Christian Nobility of the German Nation,* for instance, the German princes' failure to maintain the laws and institutions of the temporal order was among the chief causes of a moribund church and a rotting social order. Furthermore, the princely neglect of duties toward the public good was a recurring theme for Luther: from his seminal political treatise *Temporal Authority: To What Extent It Should Be Obeyed* to his last biblical lectures on Genesis, Luther forcefully denounced the princes who abused the temporal kingdom. "A Christian prince," he once observed, "is a rare prize in heaven."[37]

In the treatise, Luther also blasted the neglect of the household as another great failing of the temporal order. Conventionally in sixteenth-century Europe, responsibility for the education of the young would have been the exclusive province of parents. For Luther, parents had also shirked their divine and natural duties to educate their children. He perceived several reasons for this colossal failure.[38] First, he believed that many parents were indecent; even if they were able parents, they would nevertheless prefer, Luther argued, to let their child be left alone like the progeny of an ostrich (i.e., laid in the dust to be trampled upon, as in Job 39:14).[39] Second, most parents were simply unfit and ignorant: since they themselves had been educated only to "care for their bellies," they were ignorant of the benefit and importance of an education beyond making money and enjoying bodily pleasure and luxury.[40] Finally, Luther concluded that almost all parents (regardless of their morals or knowledge) lacked the opportunity to properly educate their children, given their other duties in the household and their obligations beyond it. Because the costs of private tutorship (the typical mode of education for the children

36 LW 45: 368; WA 15: 45.
37 LW 45: 120; WA 11: 273.
38 LW 45: 354–5; WA 15: 33–4.
39 LW 45: 355; WA 15: 34.
40 Ibid.

of nobility) would be far too burdensome for the common family or for the guardians of orphans, "necessity compels us," Luther wrote, "therefore to engage public schoolteachers for the children."[41] Thus, with both princes and parents unable or unfit to take responsibility, Luther appealed to the city leaders as the only possible effective actors in the temporal kingdom.

Luther considered the renewal of the church and the reception of the gospel as paramount, and widespread ignorance directly hindered them. An ignorant people was susceptible to the spiritual darkness that in his view had plagued Germany; for him, not only had a tyrannical and apostate church flourished because of this ignorance, but vain superstitions and pagan practices had flourished as well. Education also shaped the church's leaders. "There is a vast difference," Luther wrote, "between a simple preacher of the faith and a person who expounds Scripture."[42] Interpreting scripture required an education in the ancient languages and the rigour of the liberal arts, lest great errors enter and the faith either decays or "is thus held up for ridicule."[43] In Luther's view, this is precisely what had happened in the Middle Ages that preceded him – the loss of Hebrew, Greek, and classical Latin had corrupted the understanding of the Word and polluted the church and universities with all sorts of fancies, wayward doctrines, and interpretations, leaving places of learning as wicked dens of ignorance and a church bereft of the gospel: "As proof and warning of this, let us take the deplorable and dreadful example of the universities and monasteries, in which men have not only unlearned the gospel, but have in addition so corrupted the Latin and German languages that the miserable folk have been fairly turned into beasts, unable to speak or write correct German or Latin, and have wellnigh lost their natural reason to boot."[44] Thus, for Luther the health of the spiritual kingdom necessitated the revival of a robust education.

However, Luther also appealed to the *Radherrn* to establish and maintain schools on the basis of a political argument: in sum, that the greater well-being of the temporal kingdom was at stake, since it

41 Ibid.

42 LW 45: 363; WA 15: 40.

43 LW 45: 362; WA 15: 39.

44 LW 45: 360; WA 15: 38.

would not survive without educated subjects. In Luther's day, it was commonsensical that resources ought to be given over for the sake of common defences, such as city walls and the accumulation of money and food supplies. This was especially true for cities within such a politically complex and often conflicted entity as the Holy Roman Empire, with ducal cities, independent commercial cities (such as those of the Hanseatic League), and bishopric cities. But such defensive measures were detrimental, even fatal, if ignorant men led the city. For "a city's best and greatest welfare, safety, and strength," Luther argued, "consist rather in having many able, learned, wise, honourable, and well-educated citizens."[45]

Luther argued that the pagans had much to teach his contemporary Germans about the political importance of education. He pointed to the greatness of Rome and the city-states of ancient Greece: many were models of civic spiritedness formed by good education, and hence were models of the temporal kingdom well understood and in good health.[46] Thus, for Luther, pagan political wisdom was in fact bona fide wisdom and proper to emulate. At the very least, he believed that the ancients needed to be read; for Luther, the histories and political philosophies of the ancients constituted an essential part of the desperately needed curriculum to prepare German men – and women[47] – to become citizens capable of governing and being governed. For Luther, the temporal kingdom's sponsorship of education would thereby also redeem the political reputation of the Germans and rescue them from a future of rule by louts and boors. Unless German temporal authorities educated their subjects, they would deserve both the poor governments and the stereotypes that the Italians (for example) had imposed on them. Since "nothing is known in other lands about us Germans," Luther wrote, "we must be content to have the rest of the world refer to us as German beasts who know only how to fight, gorge, and guzzle."[48]

Moreover, a flourishing temporal kingdom had to invest in good teachers and educational infrastructure. One of the most striking examples of this in the treatise is his insistence on founding new and

45 LW 45: 356; WA 15: 34.
46 LW 45: 356; WA 15: 35, LW 45: 368; WA 15: 45.
47 LW 45: 370; WA 15: 47
48 LW 45: 77; WA 15: 52.

expanding existing public libraries. With respect to the revival of liberal arts and the study of classical and biblical languages, Luther argued that cities ought to found libraries and equip them not with only good textbooks and primers – instead of the contemporary ones he excoriated for their poor Latin and unchristian theology – but also with great works of literature and poetry from ancient Greece and Rome. But these libraries ought to stock books in the vernacular as well.[49] Even though this was in the age of the printing press, such a course would be incredibly expensive. Luther thereby encouraged the cities that were benefiting from the explosion of commerce to reinvest – through city taxes and tariffs – in local repositories of the best of Christian and pagan knowledge.

SERMON ON KEEPING CHILDREN IN SCHOOL

When Luther composed his *Sermon on Keeping Children in School* in 1530, he was in retreat at the fortress of Coburg during the Diet of Augsburg and thus, like many of his fellow evangelical reformers, was under an enormous amount of pressure and anxiety over the coming conflict.[50] Therefore, for Luther to have devoted time to composing this text at this critical juncture in the Reformation speaks to how important the cause was to him.[51] In fact, in a contemporary letter to Philip Melanchthon at the diet, Luther joked about the verbosity that the subject was provoking in him,[52] and he prefaced this "sermon" with the admission that "it [had] almost become a book" and that he had "forcibly restrained [himself] to keep it from becoming altogether too big, so rich and full is this subject."[53]

Though not as deadly as the great confessional divide that was emerging, the educational crisis precipitating this treatise was for Luther no less grave than at the time of the previous treatise, for it spelled certain doom for the reform movement if the current deplorable conditions of schools and student enrolments were not reversed. At the University of Wittenberg the numbers of matriculating students were telling: in 1520 it had reached a peak of over five hundred

49 Ibid.

50 Brecht, *Martin Luther: Shaping and Defining the Reformation*, 369–79.

51 Ibid., 381–2.

52 WA BR 5: 439.

53 LW 46: 213; WA 30 II: 517.

students, but by the end of the decade the university would average only around two hundred students.[54] Moreover, as a result of the growing confessional divide, the number of students from Catholic lands had bottomed out.[55] Yet just as the university was becoming a centre of the Lutheran confession, elementary school enrolments in Protestant territories were sharply declining; in fact, some schools had been abandoned entirely, as were some universities, such as Leipzig and even Erfurt, where Luther had been a student.[56] The University of Wittenberg could barely enrol enough students to survive. In response to this dire situation, Luther wrote *A Sermon on Keeping Children in School* and proposed "to take up the question of what is at stake in this matter in the way of gains and losses, first those that are spiritual or eternal, and then those that are temporal or worldly."[57] Education could maintain the two kingdoms.

The spiritual kingdom, by which Luther meant here the kingdom composed of the "office of preaching and the service of the word and sacraments and which imparts the Spirit and salvation," was a divine kingdom of such great dignity and honour that even some of the best of the church fathers, Luther noted, greatly avoided it.[58] But with the massive decline in educated subjects, Luther then asked, "By whom shall it be maintained?" Only the properly educated could possibly begin to serve the role as pastor and preacher. Luther had no time for the radical reformers who had dismissed education as the purview of the upper classes, enjoyed only to maintain their societal privileges rather than to strengthen God's ministry. For Luther, the gains affected by educating future preachers and teachers in the liberal arts were beyond measure: the care of souls, the preaching and teaching of the Word, and the salvation of God were beyond any tabulation, and these, by divine purpose and sanction, depended on the educated. The losses, by contrast, would be apocalyptic. Thus, Luther asked, "Ought you not leap for joy that with your money you are privileged to accomplish something so great in the sight of God?"[59]

54 Schwiebert, *Luther and His Times*, 604–6.
55 Ibid., 606.
56 Ibid., 607.
57 LW 46: 219; WA 30 II: 522–3.
58 LW 46: 220–1; WA 30 II: 528–9.
59 LW 46: 225; WA 30 II: 535.

Luther's appeal to the health of the spiritual kingdom also had a compelling corollary for the prospective students and parents who would be more convinced by their "bellies": the service of the spiritual kingdom offered liberation from livelihoods dependent on commercial enterprise. In the midst of the crisis in education, heightened in part by the effects of reform and the profits wielded by goods and manufacturing, a great shortage of pastors in parishes and teachers in church schools was already being felt: "[H]is living is ready for him before he needs it; he does not have to scrape it together for himself!"[60] Luther estimated that there were four thousand educated ministerial positions in his principality of Saxony, but scarcely that many students in all its schools. With vacancies due to mortality alone – aside from the upheaval of reform – Saxony was very quickly headed toward an enormous shortage of pastors, preachers, sacristans, and teachers.

Yet again, however, Luther turned his attention to the temporal kingdom: unequivocally, he argued, its health utterly depended on having educated subjects. It behoved government, therefore, to educate. *A Sermon on Keeping Children in School* affirmed that one of temporal government's most essential roles was to "make men out of wild beasts and to prevent men from becoming wild beasts."[61] In a manner typical of his accounts of temporal authority throughout his career, Luther affirmed government as the protector of life and property. Lest anyone think that temporal affairs were ruled only by the use of force, Luther emphatically argued that reason and the rule of law upheld temporal authority. Thus, Luther gave high praise for the recent introduction of imperial law (which was based on ancient Roman law via the Code of Justinian), precisely because it was more reasonable and effective in the securing of property and persons.[62]

By emphasizing the importance of the rule of law over force in the temporal kingdom, Luther then concluded that its health depended on the preservation of law by jurists and scholars. Although Luther's

60 LW 46: 234; WA 30 II: 549.

61 LW 46: 237; WA 30 II: 555.

62 LW 46: 239; WA 30 II: 557. In 1520, however, in his *To the Christian Nobility of the German Nation* (LW 44: 203), Luther rejected Roman law for superseding German customary laws. What precisely had led Luther to change his mind is not clear. He also praises the natural law and rule of law – which was Roman law – at length in his *Commentary on Psalm 101* (1534).

conception of the actual bearer of political authority did not stray fundamentally from the feudal rule of hereditary principalities and duchies, here in this treatise he showed that he had given the mechanisms of political power and authority more thought than is sometimes supposed. In this treatise, he emphasized the essential importance of liberal arts education for the protection of person and property. Without schools and universities to train jurists and lawyers, without even scribes to assist all nobles who ruled, the temporal estate would fall and ordered civilization cease: "You would have to be a gross, ungrateful clod, worthy of being numbered among the beasts, if you should see that your son could become a man to help the emperor preserve his empire, sword, and crown; to help the prince rule his principality; to counsel and help cities and lands; to help protect so many men's bodies, wives, children, property, and honour – and yet would not risk enough on it to let him study and come to such a position."[63] Once again, as in the earlier work on education, Luther appealed to career prospects: just as the school crisis was creating a shortage of capable pastors, so too was a shortage of clerks, lawyers, and scribes beginning to affect Germany. Princes needed chancellors and jurists, cities needed scribes, and "there [was] not a nobleman who [did] not need a clerk."[64] Meaningful and prosperous employment in the service of the temporal kingdom awaited the well educated. Luther also noted that teaching the liberal arts brought employment opportunities, as did the study of medicine, all of which were being neglected in the Reformation crisis of German schools, despite the good prospects for "honestly gotten wealth."[65]

Luther's sermon also appealed to honour by taking on the common notions that good education made one soft and reluctant in the face of difficult work. He countered that the most honourable task, what helped government fulfill its divinely ordered role the most, was preserving the rule of law and an ordered civilization, which came in the end not by the use of the sword but by the exercise of reason. Thus, the highest honour was due to men of high education who served the temporal kingdom. The "swagger" of knights and armoured soldiers came from empty boasts: though there was without

63 LW 46: 241; WA 30 II: 561.
64 LW 46: 244; WA 30 II: 565.
65 LW 46: 244; WA 30 II: 567.

a doubt a role in the temporal estate for those who wielded the sword, and they too had a divine calling for Luther, the most honourable work remained with the scholars who quietly maintained the reasonable order of the world. They were the treasures of the temporal kingdom: even the "businessmen" in the absence of them would "be glad to dig twenty feet into the earth with their bare hands just to get a scholar,"[66] for no business would ever take place without the temporal government, and temporal government could not survive without educated subjects.

THE POLITICAL SIGNIFICANCE OF LUTHER'S WRITINGS ON EDUCATION

The enormous challenges in education that had inspired Luther's two treatises were met with some degree of success and improvement over the following decades. The number of schools increased, and they continued to do so in Lutheran territories into the following century. Literacy (especially in Latin) grew, and general schooling among both boys and girls increased. Wittenberg was a fine example: under the direction of Luther and Melanchthon, boys' and girls' schools were opened in the city and began to flourish. Throughout the Lutheran territories, education became systematized under the oversight of magistrates and superintendents of the cities and principalities. Universities grew once again: for instance, by the 1530s and 1540s the University of Wittenberg had nearly tripled its average matriculation from its low in the 1520s.[67] Of course, these limited successes did not result simply from the publication of Luther's treatises, but his apology for education must be recognized as an essential component of his evangelical reform.

These texts also ought to be considered as an integral part of his political thought, for his appeals for education were intimately connected to his conception of the two kingdoms. For Luther, education, particularly higher education in the liberal arts, was vital to the temporal kingdom. Educated Germans made for subjects who would best understand the duties and purposes of government. For Luther, the long neglect of the temporal kingdom by the passing age, the upheaval of early Reformation, and now the crisis of education all

66 LW 46: 251; WA 30 II: 578.
67 Schwiebert, *Luther and His Times*, 607.

threatened its stability and health and thus the protection of person and property, the rule of law, and the spreading of the gospel.

Luther's appeal for education for the sake of the temporal kingdom is an underappreciated indication of the "humanist" character of his political thought. Given his push for stable regimes for the rule of law, the protection of person and property, and the education of subjects and citizens in the liberal arts and the classics, Luther's writings on education are certainly in a general humanist mode. However, unlike the humanist-inspired civic republicanism of the Italian Renaissance, Luther showed little concern for ancient republicanism and "maintaining the state" – issues that would make Niccolò Machiavelli most famous. He was content to argue for the benefits of education for the well-being of the temporal kingdom without offering extensive treatments on civic virtue or the best regime.

Luther's advocacy of education is perhaps best seen as a specific application of his two kingdoms teaching. Since this teaching was an ontological treatment of humanity in relation to one another and to God, other philosophic questions for him paled in importance; the kingdoms were derived from the very basic modes of existence for all of human life. The decay of education threatened both kingdoms: the spreading of the gospel and the upholding of the rule of law would be severely limited by an ignorant and illiterate populace. Preoccupations with other philosophic questions, such as the best regime, did not help relieve the educational crisis in Germany that threatened both law and gospel alike.

Aiding the Poor

In *To the Christian Nobility* in 1520, Luther had argued that the support of the poor ought to be the responsibility of each city.[68] Of course, with the wholesale reforms that were soon to come, with all of the accompanying social and economic upheavals, the church, at least as Luther envisioned it, was going to be in no position to continue its central role in benefiting the poor, sick, and destitute, as it had in the late Middle Ages. In turning to cities to support those worst off, Luther envisioned the institution of what he later endorsed

68 LW 44: 189–90; WA 6: 450–1.

as "common chests," which, despite its simple name, would take on the complex task of not only providing for the poor but also managing church finances (including pay for pastors and sacristans), hospitals, schools, and all local matters of benefices and property bequests to monasteries and orders made obsolete by the evangelical church. In his endorsement of the plan for a common chest by the congregation in Leisnig in his preface to the publication of their proposals,[69] Luther approved of a plan that appeared genuinely communal, thus approximating the practice of the early apostles (based on the example of Acts 4:32–37), since its directors were to be made up of a wide array of local walks of life and were thus able to properly discern the community's needs and provide money accordingly.

As such, the plan for the common chest was not precisely an organ of the temporal government, though it certainly dealt with the temporal kingdom's matters of wealth, property, bodily health, and so on. In Luther's thinking on the matter, at least in the few times he treated it, it was the temporal government's ability to outlaw certain practices that would make this common chest system work. In particular, as was already clear in *To the Christian Nobility*, Luther argued that temporal government had to abolish all forms of begging, curb the gain of wealth, and prohibit unjust practices such as usury.

To the modern eye. Luther's knowledge of economics in his treatise *Trade and Usury*[70] may appear quaint, even though the work is a fascinating piece of economic history. In his distrust of commercial trade, and especially in his rejection of usury (which he defined simply as the charging of interest), Luther was part of a long and overwhelming tradition of economic thought that was only beginning to wane as commerce and industry grew to overtake feudalism. But, as always, Luther approached his topics first as a pastor of the Word, and so even if his economic theories were questionable, his pastoral theology was much more compelling: wealth and money making, Luther warned, can be dangerous to the soul (and so subject to his spiritual jurisdiction) *and* dangerous to the public order. The curbing of greed was not only a task for the counsellors of conscience: by assigning these responsibilities to the temporal government, Luther also considered it a matter for the outer man, subject

69 LW 45: 169–76; WA 12: 11–30.

70 LW 45: 231–73; WA 15: 293–313, 321–2.

to the laws and judgments of authorities, for the sake of making good subjects of the worldly realm.[71]

The abolition of beggary was also the responsibility of temporal authority, for much like his rejection of marriage canons, Luther saw its toleration as a pernicious confusion of the two kingdoms, resulting in a view of justification by worldly actions rather than divine grace. From the support of mendicant orders (orders that essentially relied on donations for sustenance), ordinary people had been duped, Luther argued, into believing that their charity had some effect on their justification before God; meanwhile, those very orders themselves, he thought, were fooled into thinking that their vows of poverty were in some way more holy and blessed in the eyes of God. For Luther, the prohibition of beggary (of any type) made the temporal government take poverty back into its jurisdiction and out of the spiritual kingdom. Poverty would cease to be seen as an outward sign of inward spiritual grace and remain an outward sign of worldly misfortune. In this way, temporal government's prohibition on beggary would reveal the truly poor and destitute, such that cities could aid them with the surpluses committed to the common chest, as was done in the early church of the apostles.

Marriage

In his *Sermon on the Estate of Marriage* (1519), Luther had understood matrimony, fairly typically for the late Middle Ages, as an institution established by God for the sake of curbing sins of the flesh (resulting from the Fall) for those who could not be celibate; he had even called it a "hospital for incurables."[72] By 1520, however, major changes in his thinking began to take place: in *The Babylonian Captivity of the Church,* he began to publicly denounce all canon law concerning marriage,[73] and by 1522 he had published *The Estate of Marriage,* which now emphasized the institution and the conjugal relationship as a manifestation of God's ordinance to be fruitful and multiply (Genesis 1:28), and thus *not* an inferior status to celibacy.[74] By 1525, Luther was

71 LW 45: 246–7; WA 15: 293–4.
72 LW 44: 9; WA 2: 167.
73 LW 36: 92–106; WA 6: 550–60.
74 LW 45: 11–49; WA 10 II: 275–304.

himself married to Katherine von Bora, a former nun, with whom he would have six children (two of whom died in childhood) and raise four more orphaned relatives. Luther's praise of marriage as a godly institution continued throughout his life and would come to be seen by him, as the *Book of Concord* would describe it, as a way of life so important that it was before and above *any* other, including that of emperor, prince, or bishop.[75] Moreover, from the publication of *The Babylonian Captivity of the Church* to the end of his life – though with the significant exception of his *Lectures on Genesis*, in which he named marriage as another "estate" *apart* from temporal authority[76] – Luther would insist that marriage was a matter for the temporal kingdom, and thus its regulation fell under the jurisdiction of the secular authorities rather than under the clergy as a sacrament.

One of Luther's clearest statements on the issue came in his treatise *On Marriage Matters* in 1530.[77] Just as the Reformation had brought upheaval to education, so too did it raise profound problems for marriage: the rejection of canon law by evangelical reformers meant that both temporal authorities (who had been subservient to the church canons on marriage) and the clergy were left confused as to what constituted the essential elements of a proper marriage.[78] Luther's treatise, therefore, was timely in that it addressed this pressing problem, but he nevertheless refused to author new laws on marriage, and attempted only to settle "troubled consciences." This role

75 BC 414; Janz, *Westminster Handbook to Martin Luther*, 90–1.

76 Why were there three "estates" (sometimes also "hierarchies" and "orders") in his lectures on Genesis, as well as in his *Confession Concerning Christ's Supper* (LW 37: 364; WA 26: 504) and *On the Councils and the Church* (LW 41: 177; WA 50: 652)? How did they relate to the "two kingdoms?" Luther explained the "estates" as the most important and distinct orders (for he hints that there were many more than three) of God's creation, none of which had any significant power over the other two. These were primordial and foundational orders of creation, associations written into nature by God for the benefit of humanity. The two kingdoms were the two realms of human existence, corresponding to law and gospel and to the governments over them. Luther's "estate" or "order" of marriage emphasized its universality in all human life and experience. But as far as the two kingdoms teaching was concerned, temporal government, Luther argued, was best suited to regulate marriage because it was an outward and bodily matter. See Lohse, *Martin Luther's Theology*, 245–7. See also Maxfield, *Luther's Lectures on Genesis and the Formation of Evangelical Identity*, 98–119.

77 LW 46: 259–320; WA 30 III: 205–48.

78 Witte convincingly argues that this upheaval in marriage law in Lutheranism spurned a major revolution in the institution of marriage; see *From Sacrament to Contract*, 113–58.

of legislating on marriage, in Luther's view, was the exclusive prerogative of the temporal authorities:

Here I want to close and leave this matter for now, and, as I did above, advise my dear brothers, the pastors and clergy, to refuse to deal with marriage matters as worldly affairs covered by temporal laws and to divest themselves of them as much as they can. Let the authorities and officials deal with them, except where their pastoral advice is needed in matters of conscience, as for example when some marriage matters should come up in which the officials and jurists had entangled and confused the consciences, or else perhaps a marriage had been consummated contrary to law, so that the clergy should exercise their office in such a case and comfort consciences and not leave them stuck fast in doubt and error.[79]

Luther was perhaps even more blunt about the jurisdiction of temporal government in his *Lectures on the Sermon on the Mount* (1532): "What is the proper procedure for us nowadays in matters of marriage and divorce? I have said that this should be left to the lawyers and made subject to the secular government. For marriage is a rather secular and outward thing, having to do with wife and children, house and home, and with other matters that belong to the realm of the government, all of which have been completely subjected to reason (Gen. 1:28). Therefore we should not tamper with what the government and wise men decide and prescribe with regard to these questions on the basis of the laws and of reason."[80]

Yet Luther argued that he was entirely justified to intervene when the temporal kingdom neglected or abused its responsibilities concerning marriage: this was his steadfast position, for example, in the sermon he preached regarding Matthew 2:1–12, on the feast of the Epiphany, 6 January 1544, in Wittenberg.[81] Luther took the opportunity to denounce the two jurists of Wittenberg's consistory, a committee of four (the two jurists and two theologians from the university) that oversaw marriage matters and general church life, for their decision in the marital dispute of university student Kaspar Beyer. Beyer had been secretly engaged in the summer of 1541 to a woman from Torgau, contingent on her father's future approval, only to become

79 LW 46: 317–8; WA 30 III: 246.
80 LW 21: 93; WA 32: 376–7.
81 LW 58: 56–70; WA 49: 294–307.

publicly engaged the next summer to a woman from Wittenberg (who also happened to be an orphan under the guardianship of Melanchthon).[82] Canon law recognized a clandestine betrothal, with or without parental approval, as a legitimate (and thus indissoluble) marriage.[83] The Wittenberg jurists, in upholding the first engagement as a legal marriage, were thus (in Luther's view) bringing back the "government of a tyrant" – the pope – into the temporal kingdom.[84]

Luther's sermon was scathing toward the consistory's decision, and he promised that by his condemnation "they shall leave me in peace with this [spiritual] government and not meddle in the kingdom of Christ or confuse or torment consciences."[85] Luther's harsh reaction, therefore, arose from his zeal to defend and distinguish the kingdoms, which he considered threatened because civil authority had taken an ostensibly spiritual law (canon law) to deal with a properly civil matter. Again, as in several other matters considered earlier in this chapter, Luther's own opinion and actions might be seen (at least from a certain angle) as a breach of the two kingdoms distinction: here was Luther, a pastor and theologian, calling out jurists for failing their temporal duties on a matter that was their own due concern. But again, his words and actions were directed at keeping the kingdoms distinct, as, he argued, God had intended them to be. The jurists were making trouble for the Christian conscience: this was the territory of the pastor, and Luther was not about to let the princes and their magistrates invade it and shirk their own duties.

CONCLUSION

In all his writings on the two kingdoms, and in all of the ways in which the evangelical reform changed the church and temporal government, Luther insisted that the kingdoms be kept separate yet also work in tandem to bring the complementary divine gifts of salvation

82 See Estes's helpful introduction to both the historical context and the sermon, LW 58: 53–6.

83 In fact, Luther had written on secret betrothals and parental consent in his 1524 publication *That Parents Should Neither Compel Nor Hinder The Marriage Of Their Children, And That Children Should Not Become Engaged Without Their Parents' Consent*, LW 45: 385–92; WA 15: 163–9.

84 LW 58: 58; WA 49: 297.

85 LW 58: 59; WA 49: 298.

by grace and worldly order to humanity. Thus, he could write about the duties of temporal authority; insert himself into the practical affairs and controversies of the Reformation, such as policing subjects, overseeing the church in emergencies, aiding the poor, educating the people, and fostering marriage; and still maintain, with some consistency, that he was not confusing them. Far from it: the Bible and good reason affirmed it, he believed, and as a pastor and preacher he insisted on retaining the prophetic ability to call temporal government to account for its failings, even if he was first to admit that these same duties were outside of his jurisdiction. As his fiery denunciations of temporal authorities in, for example, his sermons on John's Gospel or on the Epiphany show, Luther took it upon himself to censure and decry any representative of the temporal kingdom who sought to aggrandize their power by, say, invading conscience, the inner soul, or even regularized church oversight. In this way, contrary to common appropriations of his political thought, Luther was, at least in sixteenth-century terms, an advocate of limited government, by holding it to account, via the pulpit and the pen, for carrying out its God-given duties.

But, despite Luther's best efforts, the difficulties in defining the boundaries between the kingdoms, and assigning the precise duties of the spiritual and temporal governments, continued throughout his lifetime and beyond. In fact, his followers would overturn some of the most contentious issues for Luther – such as his insistence upon only emergency government oversight of the church – and still maintain that they were being true to his two kingdoms teaching.

6

Luther and the Political Thought of the Reformation

THE REFORMATION BEGAN, so the current account of it goes, with the publication of Luther's Ninety-Five Theses and the ensuing debate over the efficacy of indulgences and the authority of the pope. Of course, a critical reflection on what marks the beginning of this era betrays the historical assumptions of our own time, as well as the complexity of Luther's. Only in retrospect – if public commemorations of the Reformation in Lutheran Germany are a good indication, centuries after the event[1] – could something as mundane as a call to academic debate over indulgences from a hitherto unknown doctor at an upstart university be considered something of, in the words of G.W.F. Hegel, "world-historical" importance. Luther's own mature reflections on his early career instead placed emphasis on his "discovery" of *sola fides*, well before the publication of his theses, and on the debates over papal authority in 1518–19. Nevertheless, Luther's role as a seminal figure of the Reformation, even if that role is qualified as a prophet, arch-heretic, modern founder, and so on, has been nearly universally agreed upon across confessions, over the centuries, and among various academic disciplines.

A study of Luther's political thought must therefore account for its place in Reformation political thought in general, especially since his political thought was for him so closely connected to his theology and interpretation of the Bible, which had launched programmatic

1 Howard sketched the commemorations of 1517 through the centuries, showing that the importance of the Ninety-Five Theses – including the popular image of Luther nailing the theses to the castle church door – was a relatively late (eighteenth-century) phenomenon; "Reformation Commemorations: Then and Now."

church reform in the first place. It is a contention of this chapter, with its brief comparisons and contrasts to other major reformers, movements, and thinkers of the era, that Luther's political thought was seminal and unique in the Reformation in that it so strongly and clearly emphasized the divine origins and purpose of temporal government, grounded it in his law and gospel theology and inner and outer ontology, and elevated service to the political order as service to God. Luther boasted several times that this emphasis was his crucial contribution to the understanding of temporal government through the ages; this chapter merely takes Luther seriously at his word by briefly comparing his ideas with Reformation-era political thought. Thus, this chapter accounts for several significant convergences and divergences between Reformation political ideas and Luther's political thought.

One striking area of common ground across Reformation political thought was a preoccupation with the nature and extent of political authority over the church and the promotion of the faith (however it was defined in a given confession). Since the support of secular authorities was a crucial and often deciding factor in what kind of church reform would gain a foothold in a given territory, a major political effect of the Reformation across Europe (Protestant or Catholic) was the consolidation and centralization of secular powers and the establishment of territorial and national churches. Though with very different political and ecclesiastical consequences, similar debates over political control over the church raged in, for instance, the Holy Roman Empire, France, and England.

Yet there were also key political differences among Reformation confessions. The Church of England, or at least the prevailing Elizabethan version of it, in which ecclesial and temporal powers were united under the authority of the crown, could scarcely be contrasted more from the wholesale rejection of political power by the Mennonites. Moreover, even within confessions, differences in political thought were sometimes hotly contested or else radically shifted as events and circumstances changed. John Calvin unequivocally forbade revolution, yet in the midst of the French civil war, particularly in the aftermath of the St Bartholomew's Day Massacre (beginning on 23 August 1572), the Huguenots developed a doctrine of armed resistance to tyrannies that threatened the Reformed faith. In German lands, evangelical reformers claimed to be faithful to

Luther's two kingdoms teaching; yet they approved of and developed the regular exercise of civil authority over church affairs.

LUTHER AND THE POLITICAL THOUGHT OF GERMAN EVANGELICAL REFORM

The centrality and influence of Luther's political thought and two kingdoms teaching in German evangelical thought are attested to by Article XVI of the Augsburg Confession, "Concerning Public Order and Secular Government," and Melanchthon's defence of the article in his *Apology of the Augsburg Confession.* The article reads: "All political authority, orderly government, laws, and good order in the world are created and instituted by God and that Christians may without sin exercise political authority."[2] Defending the article in the aftermath of the Diet of Augsburg of 1530, Melanchthon wrote that "the distinction between Christ's kingdom and the civil realm has been helpfully explained in the writings of our theologians." Luther's *Temporal Authority,* to which Melanchthon was undoubtedly alluding, was beginning to be considered a definitive statement on the status of political government and service by German evangelical reformers.

Despite the formative influence of his two kingdoms teaching, many evangelical reformers disagreed with Luther's insistence that the secular authority could govern only over church affairs on a temporary or emergency basis. Many leaders, including some of the most prominent of Luther's own generation, argued that secular government had a regular duty to ensure that the true religion was not only firmly established but also continually maintained in a given territory. Yet even with this departure from Luther's political thought, these same reformers claimed to uphold some version of Luther's two kingdoms teaching and considered a normalized government oversight of the church as a faithful application of it. The justification was simply that the institutional church, far from being merely the embodiment of the spiritual realm, straddled both the spiritual and the secular kingdoms. Apart from the Word and sacraments, insofar as the evangelical church was involved in good morals and discipline, and even in the administration and oversight of its clergy, these

2 BC 48.

reformers believed that it clearly fell under the jurisdiction and authority of the secular government.

In fact, it was Melanchthon himself, as well as other prominent reformers such as Johannes Brenz, who championed this development of reformation thought on secular government.[3] In Melanchthon's view, the secular magistrate was the *praecipuum membrum* – "the foremost member" – of the church and therefore had the duty, through all forms of external discipline, to preserve and maintain a Christian society in all its public observances. More than the maintenance of external peace, under this more expansive view the secular government took on the role of guardian of all public observances of the duties demanded by the Decalogue. Thus, the jurisdictions of magistrates included not only the relationships between neighbours, that is, the "second table" of commandments, but also the "first table," or the commandments regarding humankind's relationship to God.[4] Since these commandments prohibited idolatry, forbade blasphemy, and instituted the Sabbath day of rest, it meant that magisterial authority was duty bound to ensure the proper worship of God in its jurisdiction, and that in their actions and public forms, subjects were to be policed to ensure conformity to the moral and ecclesial order. Since this development of the magisterial role in morality and worship became dominant in Protestant Germany (though notably elsewhere and across confessional divides as well), it has also been considered the beginning of the *landesherrliche Kirchenregiment*, or the territorial church of the magisterial Reformation.

With this development away from Luther's particular teaching on the matter, political thought in the German Reformation shifted toward a view that saw the ends and purposes of church and secular government as much more intricately connected and overlapping in

3 See Estes, *Peace, Order and the Glory of God*. For an overview of the importance of Melanchthon's political thought, see Wengert, "Philip Melanchthon and a Christian *Politics*."

4 Following the Vulgate's numbering (instead of the Hebrew Bible's), German evangelicals considered the first three commandments as the "first table," or the commandments directed toward God – that is, the commandments prohibiting worship of other gods and blasphemy, and instituting the Sabbath rest. Reformed theologians, such as Huldrych Zwingli, considered the prohibition of images as a fourth first table commandment and reduced the last two of the traditional second table – one prohibiting coveting of a neighbour's property and another prohibiting the coveting of a neighbour's wife – into one final commandment.

the final goal of godly worship and temporal order. Like Luther himself, this shift echoed the medieval idea of Christendom, in which all offices of authority worked together for the common whole of an ordered Christian civilization, but it also bore the marks of Christian humanism, particularly of the sort exemplified by Erasmus, which sought to renew the ideal of a Christian commonwealth by, among other things, reinvigorating Christian thought and practice in the wielding of political power. In both the medieval echo of Christendom and the humanist revival of Christian ethics, political thought in the German Reformation moved toward a specifically Christian politics. Again, there was a departure from Luther: although he readily admitted that Christian princes were likely best, and that in fact such a prince was a rarity, he nevertheless acknowledged that some of the best wisdom and exemplary practices regarding the temporal order were to be found among the pagans. For Luther, a good government was not necessarily a Christian one; even the Bible taught this lesson. In this regard, Luther's views were not necessarily in direct contradiction to the political ideas of Melanchthon, Brenz, and others, especially since most of these same reformers readily acknowledged, for instance, the political wisdom found in the ancient Greeks;[5] nevertheless, a considerable tension remained between Luther's political thought and the view of other reformers that the duties of secular authorities necessarily demanded maintenance of the true religion in their jurisdictions.

Yet there was still a great congruence between Luther's political thought and contemporaries such as Melanchthon and Brenz: their agreement and unwavering insistence on political service as a godly calling. Luther's two kingdoms teaching began with his attempt to reconcile the apostolic teaching to honour and serve government with the injunctions of Jesus to "turn the other cheek" and to love one's enemies. Luther believed that his two kingdoms doctrine resolved this tension, and that it further underscored the divine gift of temporal government and the divine calling it was to serve and honour. This was, after all, the foremost reason that he boasted that his political teaching was the most important since the apostles or Augustine. Melanchthon and Brenz were wholly in agreement with

5 Wengert, "Philip Melanchthon and a Christian *Politics*," 49–54.

this elevation of political service;[6] even the concept of the *praecipuum membrum*, despite its differences with Luther's "emergency bishops," nevertheless attests to their unwavering agreement with him that the political office was "the most precious jewel on earth" and that the medieval legacy of relegating it to beneath the authority of the papacy and the church in general – however true that actually was in medieval thought and practice – had been a disastrous abuse of God's gift.

Luther's influence on evangelical political thought is perhaps best understood through this teaching and the way in which the two kingdoms doctrine buttressed it as one that rested on strong and stable biblical support. The enduring effects of Luther's view that political authority was divinely instituted and a high calling can been seen through Lutheran Germany's immensely important, though seldom fully acknowledged or appreciated, legal revolution.[7] For the Lutheran reformers, since God ruled the temporal kingdom primarily through the rule of law, *all* positive law – whether it was directed to criminal, moral, commercial, ecclesial, or societal ends – was the embodiment of divine command and the gift of worldly order. Thus, a great legal transformation occurred in Lutheran lands to consolidate and refound the rule of law on a coherent system of positive civil law based on legal norms gleaned from the Western legal tradition (including natural law, Roman law, and canon law), as well as from the Bible.

The engine of this legal revolution was the enactment of *Ordnungen* and *Kirchenrechte*, or the statutes and church laws, in the numerous Protestant territories throughout the empire.[8] These laws and statutes governed the institutional churches, marriage and family life, moral and criminal codes, schools and education, and services to the poor, widowed, homeless, orphaned, and unemployed. Because these Reformation ordinances covered so much, they beckoned reconsideration of the principles and philosophies of law that undergirded them.

Thus, a broad-based, evangelical legal philosophy was developed that emphasized the unity of *all* law under a "common law." The

6 Ibid., 55.

7 The scholarship of Berman, *Law and Revolution II*, Witte Jr., *Law and Protestantism*, and Mäkinen, *Lutheran Reformation and Law*, has been outstanding on this topic.

8 Witte, *Law and Protestantism*, 177–96.

principles of this Lutheran common law were derived from canon law (despite Luther's initial and vehement rejection of it as a tool of papal tyranny), from Roman law (or the Code of Justinian), and from feudal, mercantile, and urban law. German evangelical reform thereby developed legal studies to accompany its broad legal philosophy. Melanchthon was formative for this movement, for several of his students from Wittenberg, such as Johannes Eisenberg, subsequently went on to make their own great marks on this legal revolution.[9] In fact, Eisenberg would become the first professor of law at Marburg's new evangelical university, and he was soon joined by another great legal mind, Johann Oldendorp, making the school one of the key intellectual centres of this legal movement.[10]

Behind it all were Luther's two kingdoms and the divine calling of service to secular government. Although Melanchthon, Eisenberg, and Oldendorp stressed the co-operation of the kingdoms rather than their separation, each nevertheless clearly acknowledged the seminal place that Luther's two kingdoms held for their own thinking about law and theology. The very possibility of such a legal movement was predicated on Luther's elevation of service to secular government and the devastating theological critique he had brought to canon law beforehand. Just as Luther restored political service as a godly service, worthy of utmost honour and respect, but did not counsel unlimited obedience to political powers, so too did the Lutheran jurists encourage a strong and effective government over Germans, but one bound by laws. The accusations of "absolutism" in Luther's political thought make even less sense for the political and legal minds he had influenced in his own sixteenth-century Germany: rather than government by absolutist fiat and caprice, German Protestant territories moved toward the rule of principled and universal law, grounded in the Bible and in sundry aspects of traditional legal thought and practice. Under this law, no human being – prince or pauper or pastor – could claim outright exemption.[11]

9 Ibid., 140–54.

10 Ibid., 154–68.

11 Ibid., 173. Witte argues that "the Lutheran jurists' arguments for enhancing the power and prestige of the political office also paradoxically put additional safeguards on it."

LUTHER AND REFORMED POLITICAL THOUGHT

The "Reformed" churches, the more accurate and representative term for what have been popularly called "Calvinist" churches, came to have an enormous impact on Western Christianity, particularly in France, Switzerland, Germany, the Low Countries, England, Scotland, and eventually America. Among the problems with the term "Calvinism" is the implication that this particular reform movement began with John Calvin in Geneva. In fact, much of the programmatic reform Calvin helped institute in Geneva had already been developing for decades in various cities. Under the reforming leadership of humanist preacher Huldrych Zwingli, Zurich became the first centre of the Reformed movement. Zwingli met an early and violent death defending his city in the Battle of Kappel in October of 1531. His successor as Antistes (the head of the synodical Swiss emerging protestant church) and another great reformer and theologian in his own right, Heinrich Bullinger, greatly helped teach and spread the Reformed movement across Europe.

A reading of Zwingli's *On Divine and Human Righteousness*[12] (1523) gives the impression that his political thought had much in common with Luther's and may even have been influenced by *Temporal Authority*, which had been published a mere six months beforehand.[13] There was at least one similar overarching purpose to both writings: to distinguish and defend the political side of their respective programmatic reforms from the radical reformers who either threatened outright revolution or rejected all political service as inherently sinful.[14] But in fact Zwingli's political thought was more clearly distinguishable from Luther's.[15] There were no two kingdoms or inner and outer ontology in Zwingli's thinking. Thus, there was no distinction between Christian faith in the spiritual realm and political service in the secular one. Zwingli's view, rather, was that moral law and the gospel were under *one covenant* that governed all members of the community, be they magistrates, pastors, or the people. Zwingli's city

12 An English translation can be found in Furcha and Pipkin, *Selected Writings of Huldrych Zwingli.*

13 Walton, *Zwingli's Theocracy*, 168.

14 Potter, *Zwingli*, 250.

15 Walton, *Zwingli's Theocracy*, 167–70.

therefore resembled a Christian version of the people of Israel in the Old Testament: living under one law that regulated civil, spiritual, and cultic matters and was administered and presided over by both civil and priestly offices. Zwingli's polity was an integrated Christian commonwealth, and that basic idea would prove highly influential in Reformed political thought, even if his own ideas of civil control over church discipline (such as excommunication) would be rejected by Calvin and subsequent Reformed thought and practice.[16]

Zwingli's political thought was also very rooted in his Swiss context: approving of magisterial authority over the church (unlike Luther), he sought to uphold the de facto ecclesial autonomy the Swiss cantons had been wielding long before the Reformation. Moreover, Zwingli's view of a covenantal community fit closely into the prevailing Swiss context of small city republics governed by aristocracies of merit, and hence his efforts to reform Zurich in the 1520s were always closely in tandem with the efforts of the city's magistrates. Zwingli's emphasis on the covenantal community was accompanied not only by his strong stance against mercenary service (influenced in part by Erasmus and in part by geopolitical events)[17] but also by a strong stance on the justice of taking up arms in defence of one's commonwealth. Zwingli's own willingness to take up arms in a battle to defend an emerging alliance of reformed cities cost him his life in 1531.

Although John Calvin would become one of Protestantism's most important and influential theologians, his political thought, at least insofar as it was distinguishable from that of Zwingli or the German evangelical reformers, did not represent a radical new shift in political thought and practice from what Protestant reform had already achieved in the decades before Calvin's rise to prominence. On the question of magisterial authority wielded over ecclesiastical affairs, for example, Calvin's thought coincided with that of reformers such as Melanchthon and Brenz: magistrates were to work in cooperation with church leadership for the common cause of a temporally and spiritually ordered Christian society. In contrast to Zwingli, however, Calvin insisted on a separate ecclesiastical court to deal with church discipline, even if this discipline was to be exerted in tandem with the punishments given out by the civil authorities. Both Calvin's political

16 See Baker, "Church Discipline or Civil Punishment."

17 Walton, *Zwingli's Theocracy*, 32; 50–9.

vision, as transmitted through many editions of his *Institutes of the Christian Religion*, and his practical influence in making Geneva a model of a gospel-centred community were directed toward rendering his city a complete "Christian polity" in which the demands of the gospel, the moral law of the Bible, and the purity of Reformed worship permeated the government, church, and people, making them an ordered, godly, and peaceful whole.[18]

The "Civil Government" section of the *Institutes*, of any edition, appeared quite reconcilable to Luther's political thought and his two kingdoms teaching. In the widest of terms, this was true: like Luther, Calvin affirmed the divine gift of government, the duties Christians had to honour and obey it, and the abilities Christians had to serve it without endangering their souls or violating their consciences. But there were also great contrasts between these two seminal Protestant thinkers; in fact, Calvin's own core theology put him at odds with the theological underpinnings of Luther's two kingdoms. Calvin's theology did not contain a theological dialectic of law and gospel like Luther's; rather, Calvin's thought emphasized the "law" in the "third use," or as a guide for living in the light of the gospel. Not only did that mean that Calvin did *not* emphasize a strict separation of the kingdoms, but he had hardly argued that there were separate kingdoms at all. For Calvin's theology, biblical laws and morality were much more singularly integrated into thankfully receiving and living the gospel. Hence, *both* the political and ecclesial authorities were concerned not only with public morality and its strict enforcement but also with understanding and applying the biblical imperatives behind it. Calvin's "Christian polity" precluded the clear separation of spiritual and temporal authorities that Luther insisted was essential to the reception of the gospel and to the health of secular government.[19]

Calvinism is often associated with the right of resistance, opposition to monarchy, and support for republicanism. Insofar as this was true, none of these ideas can be justifiably argued to have begun in Calvin's political thought. On the matter of resistance, Calvin's teaching resembled Luther's: tyranny was to be obeyed and endured

18 Here I borrow the phrase from Höpfl in his classic study of Calvin's political thought, *The Christian Polity of John Calvin*, the most detailed and informative study on the matter to date.

19 Ibid., 24–31.

by Christians, though resistance to it could legitimately come from lesser magistrates, as it was their duty to protect their subjects. Yet Luther's teaching on resistance had been articulated and published years before Calvin had even begun to write the *Institutes*, remained central in evangelical political thought, and was subsequently expanded and developed as tensions and conflicts grew in the empire. On the forms of government, Calvin himself articulated few preferences until his 1543 edition of the *Institutes* identified aristocracy as the preferable form, but this claim was not without its nuances and caveats, and it was not a clear indication (nor was there ever one) that he was, or was becoming, anti-monarchical.[20] His epistle dedicatory of the *Institutes* to Francis I, first written in 1535, but which continued to be appended in later editions despite the failure to secure favour for reform from the French crown, can in no serious way be considered an early critique of monarchy. First, on the surface, Calvin's letter to Francis was an effort to defend the overall cause of reform against accusations of sedition and rebellion, in the wake of the Affair of the Placards in October 1534. Second, it was likely also intended to warn German evangelical princes, whom Francis I had been courting for an alliance against the Hapsburgs, that the French crown was persecuting their evangelical brethren (even calling them "Lutherans") for rebellion and anarchy, even though these French reformers, as Calvin – as one of them – insisted, had been counselling political obedience and peace.[21] An anti-monarchical position would have undermined both key purposes.

It was the successors of Calvin in the Reformed movement who became more closely committed to resistance and either limited monarchy or outright republicanism. This development followed closely the grave misfortunes of Protestantism in the middle of the century: resistance theory grew when Protestants all over Europe were being threatened with violent suppression and eradication.[22] After decades of escalating persecution, French Huguenots were embroiled in a prolonged period of civil war against the militantly Catholic Guises, which included the decisive event for spurning

20 Calvin, *Institutes*, IV.20.8. Höpfl, *Christian Polity of John Calvin*, 153–5.

21 See Battles's "Introduction" to Calvin, *Institutes*, xvii-xxi, xxxix-xl.

22 See Skinner, *Foundations of Political Thought, Volume* 2, 189–91, for a succinct introduction to this context.

Protestant resistance theory, the St Bartholomew's Day Massacre of 1572. Thereafter, there appeared several important works of primarily, though not exclusively, French Reformed resistance and anti-absolutist theory, each significantly departing from Calvin's counsel for obedience within a decade after his death: François Hotman's *Francogallia* (1573), Theodore Beza's *The Right of Magistrates Over Their Subjects* (1574), Philippe du Plessis Mornay's *Defense of Liberty Against Tyrants* (1579), and George Buchanan's *The Right of the Kingdom in Scotland* (1579).

Yet even this development of Reformed resistance theory in the late sixteenth century, decades after Luther's death, was by no means independent of his seminal influence on the matter. The Lutheran armed defence of the city of Magdeburg against the empire and its attempt to eradicate Protestantism (after Catholic victory in the First Schmalkaldic War in 1547) became a crucial example for resistance theory. With the very survival of evangelical reform at stake, a group of "Gnesio-Lutherans" in Magdeburg defended by force – even enduring a long siege – its adherence to the Augsburg Confession, as it understood it, against the forceful Catholic terms of the Augsburg Interim, and then after the threats to the faith in the Leipzig Interim.[23] Although Magdeburg's siege at first appeared to be the beginning of the end of evangelical reform in 1547, the resistance helped reignite the conflict and ultimately led to imperial concessions to the Protestants in the famous Peace of Augsburg in 1555.

Magdeburg's resistance to the empire, as *The Magdeburg Confession* showed, was firmly based on Luther's two kingdoms teaching and the doctrine of resistance he had first articulated with his colleagues at Torgau in October 1530 and later published in his treatise *Dr Martin Luther's Warning to His Dear German People* (March 1531).[24] In fact, *The Magdeburg Confession* echoed Luther's treatise in both arguments and form: it was similarly divided into three sections (a précis of the events, a summary of the theological issues, and a dire warning), and

23 This period of Lutheran history and the conflict between the "Gnesio-Lutherans" ("true" Lutherans) and the "Philippists," the followers of Philip Melanchthon in search of compromises with Catholic authorities, is fascinating but complex. See one of the most recent, helpful, and insightful accounts of the conflict and the general period leading up to the *Book of Concord*: Arand, Kolb, and Nettleship, *Lutheran Confessions*.

24 See Whitford's succinct treatment of Luther's influence on *The Magdeburg Confession* in his *Tyranny and Resistance*.

it similarly defended the city's resistance on the basis of natural law, positive law, and the proclamation of the gospel.[25] Thus, it presented resistance as a matter of ensuring the separation of the two kingdoms, thus ensuring spiritual health in grace and temporal order. The resistance of evangelical pastors against the Interim was for the sake of the gospel; the resistance of the "inferior magistrates" against their imperial superiors was for the sake of the temporal kingdom and the good order God had ordained through the imperial law and constitution, which were now, they argued, being usurped. Luther's political thought was not only influential for Magdeburg: it was foundational. His two kingdoms, his law and gospel theology, and his basic restoration of temporal government to high honour and divine purpose – and all of these with his rich biblical corroborations – had enabled besieged evangelicals not only to survive against grave imperial threats but also enshrine their position in official imperial recognition.

After Magdeburg, but before the St Bartholomew's Day Massacre, several radical voices in Reformed political thought departed from Calvin's insistence on obedience. Three Marian exiles, John Knox (c. 1513–1572), John Ponet (c. 1516–1556), and Christopher Goodman (c. 1520–1603), were perhaps among the most noteworthy, and this radical turn in Reformed political thought has been noted for its general position that tyranny by definition could *not* be ordained by God, and that resistance and revolution were *not* just confined to the "inferior magistrates."[26] But the general Reformed view on the matter, if important continental leaders like Beza are considered, followed Luther and the Lutheran justifications for resistance. Even with the emergence of the resistance theories as a response to the French crises, several decades after Magdeburg the Lutheran justifications of resistance, and the city that symbolized it, were still held in high esteem. Beza's own *The Rights of the Magistrates* was first published anonymously, claiming itself – in its very title – to be a reprinted work from Magdeburg during the crisis.[27] Luther's political thought, even when subsequent reformers like Beza developed their own, was still seen as an authoritative source for

25 Ibid., 78.

26 Skinner, *Foundations of Modern Political Thought*, vol. 2, 225–38.

27 See Whitford, *Tyranny and Resistance*, 61.

understanding secular government's divinely ordained place in a world revolutionized by the restoration of the gospel.

LUTHER AND THE POLITICAL THOUGHT OF THE RADICAL REFORMATION

In many of the centres of emerging reform in the 1520s, such as Zurich and Wittenberg, especially after galvanizing events such as Luther's condemnation at the Diet of Worms, evangelical preachers appeared and began to gain popular followings that spread quickly to other cities and throughout the countryside. Since the mantras of the early Reformation were at once so compelling and so simple, yet also so ill-defined (such as, for example, "the priesthood of all believers"), an inevitable difference of doctrine and teaching developed between these centres of reform and the diffuse preaching of the gospel that was beginning to shake up church and temporal order. This challenge over what constituted true doctrine was a particularly acute problem for reformers who had successfully sought the support of local magistrates. In Zurich, for example, several of Zwingli's original followers split with him over the issue of infant baptism; these "Anabaptists," or "re-baptizers," as the Swiss Brethren were at first pejoratively called, became enemies of both the Zwinglian church and the town of Zurich. The Anabaptists were among the first groups of the Radical Reformation, a collection of loosely interrelated, generally outlawed, and persecuted movements of dissent against the Church of Rome *and* the magisterial Protestants.[28]

Since the Radical Reformation was so dispersed and varied in place and in matters of faith (and their faith was so inextricably woven with their political visions anyhow), there was no single, definitive core of radical political thought. There was also little treatment of political matters as such, in the way that Luther had focused on the nature of government in his treatise *Temporal Authority*. Instead, the radicals tended to concentrate on teaching how to best live a simple, pure, and biblically based Christian life.[29] The political questions that arose were how they, as the true and pure Christians, were to regard

28 The best source on the Radical Reformation remains Williams, *The Radical Reformation*. See also his brief overview, "The Radical Reformation."

29 See Baylor, *The Radical Reformation*, xvii.

secular authority in general and that authority's use of force in upholding law and order in particular.

Of course, Luther had abundantly answered those questions: government was to be obeyed, and service to temporal power, including coercion for the sake of a just cause, was not to be shunned by Christians. In this basic position, Luther and the evangelical Germans aligned themselves with many contemporary Catholics and Protestants, as well as most of the inherited Christian tradition. In stark and nearly unanimous contrast – the one major exception being the Anabaptist Balthasar Hubmaier (1480–1528)[30] – radical reformers taught that since the world outside their Christian community was corrupt and godless, they could only conclude that all temporal government was demonic and thus could not be served and obeyed by Christians. Two antithetical responses to these conclusions developed among radical groups. Some radical reformers, such as Thomas Müntzer and the leaders of the Peasants' War, or the revolutionaries who attempted to establish a millenarian regime in Münster (1534–35), sought to bring about an apocalyptic revolution of the entire political and ecclesial order and to refound all authority on the basis of their understanding of biblical revelation. Other radical reformers, such as Menno Simmons (1496–1561), sought to withdraw from the corrupted and condemned world altogether by living in separated and isolated communities and renouncing all forms of coercion. In the aftermath of the Peasants' War, radical reformers were considered by Catholics and Protestants alike to be not only heretical but also politically dangerous and subversive. The events at Münster seemed only to confirm it. Thereafter, the radical reformers tended to advocate peaceful withdrawal, though even then the survival of their communities depended on the permission of a temporal power that tolerated their settlement.

Luther's experience of Radical Reformation political thought, as chapter 3 has shown, was foremost of the revolutionary variety. As has been seen, Luther wrote extensively against the Peasants' War and Müntzer, and countered the radical revolution with his two kingdoms teaching and his unwavering stance that temporal authority was ordained by God and fit for obedience and service by all Christians. In

30 See Hubmaier's *On the Sword*, in Baylor, op. cit., 181–209.

the decades after the Peasants' War, Luther tended to associate all radicals with Müntzer and the Anabaptists, even if certain radicals such as the Mennonites, or Michael Sattler (1490–1527) and *The Schleitheim Articles*, presented very different perspectives on the political order.[31] For Luther, these radical sectarians, insofar as he knew of them, were lumped together not because they presented the same revolutionary and seditious dangers to the temporal order, but primarily because they threatened the gospel. The sedition and criminality of radical groups were indeed a grave threat, subject to the persecutions and punishments of the temporal powers, as Luther had made clear on many occasions, including by signing on to the 1536 statement to Prince Philip of Hesse by the Wittenberg theologians, *That Secular Authority Is Obliged to Defend Against the Anabaptist with Physical Punishment.*[32] But his primary concern was the spiritual warfare waged by the radical reformers. Luther considered the catastrophe of Münster a prophetic warning against its spiritual corruption; its concomitant political collapse was, for him, a fitting corollary.[33]

LUTHER AND THE POLITICAL THOUGHT OF REFORMATION ENGLAND

The formal establishment by England's King Henry VIII (r. 1509–47) of supreme royal authority over the Church of England in the Act of Supremacy of 1534, though precipitated by the pope's refusal to grant Henry an annulment of his marriage to Catherine of Aragon, was essentially a formality, given the de facto authority Henry had already assumed over the *ecclesia anglicana*. In fact, royal supremacy over the church remained the norm for the rest of the century, and,

31 *The Schleitheim Articles* are found in Baylor, op. cit., 172–80.

32 WA 50:8–15; forthcoming in LW 74. In his commentary on Luther's preface to Justus Menius's (1499–1558) *How Every Christian Should Conduct Himself*, Robert Kolb notes that Luther's position encouraged "moderate punishment with grace" in order that heresy, which was, properly speaking, a spiritual matter, could be overcome with the Word (LW 60: 210–1).

33 Several of Luther's prefaces in the 1530s and 1540s give some insight into his later thinking on the Anabaptists. See especially Luther's prefaces to three of Menius's works against the Anabaptists: *Doctrine and Secret of the Anabaptists* (1530; LW 59; WA 30 II: 211–14), *How Every Christian Should Conduct Himself With Regard to All Doctrine, Good and Bad Alike, According to God's Commandment* (1538; LW 60: 211–3; WA 50: 346–7), and *On the Spirit of the Anabaptists* (1544; LW 60: 333–5; WA 54: 117–8).

save for the famous martyrdom of dissidents Thomas More and John Fisher in 1535, it went largely uncontested. Even the reign of Mary I (1553–58), which brought the Church of England back to the papacy, exercised supremacist-style rule in its very efforts to return the church to Rome. Instead of supremacy, the focus of debate was what form the Church of England ought to take, including its liturgy and doctrine, and what form the episcopacy should take, or whether it was to be abolished. Since royal supremacy remained, the attitudes of each Tudor monarch toward the shape of the church were formative in the direction the English Reformation was to follow.

There is scant evidence that Luther's political ideas had any direct influence on political thought in the English Reformation; it was Reformed political thought that had a much greater impact. Henry VIII and his court had vehemently opposed Luther's original call to reform in the 1520s; the Church of England only began to move toward reform late in Henry's reign, when Luther's own career was waning and, more importantly, the Reformed movement was on the rise. Thus, under the very young and Protestant king Edward VI (r. 1547–53), Thomas Cranmer (1489–1556) and two continental exiles, Martin Bucer (1491–1551) and Peter Martyr Vermigli (1499–1562), began pushing for programmatic reform through royal supremacy. On the one hand, their reform moved toward what would become the typical English emphasis on *commonwealth*, a Reformed-inspired unity of crown, government, and an evangelical universal church. On the other hand, there were also several commonalities with Luther's political thought: as with the separation of the two kingdoms, English bishops were to be stripped of all temporal and secular functions, and as in Vermigli's political thought, temporal authorities were not only sharply distinguished from clergy but were limited by law and constitution, thereby giving some legitimate grounds for disobedience to tyranny.[34] Yet in the "Settlement" under Elizabeth I (r. 1558–1603), under which the crown reasserted its supremacy and the church became decidedly Protestant in doctrine (though still retaining its episcopacy), there was nothing recognizable as Luther's separation of kingdoms. For the Settlement's most prominent defender, Richard Hooker (1554–1600), the monarch was the sole

34 See Kingdon, "The Political Thought of Peter Martyr Vermigli."

head of the commonwealth and thus commander and judge of matters pertaining to body and soul alike.[35]

LUTHER AND CATHOLIC REFORMATION POLITICAL THOUGHT

Catholic political thought of the Reformation period was largely a continuation of medieval and Renaissance political thought and its preoccupations, such as the papalism–conciliarism dispute, even though many Catholic thinkers of the sixteenth century directly responded to Protestant ideas and controversies. Thus, in the general perspective of sixteenth-century history, reform in the Catholic Church is considered in part a Catholic Reformation (and so in continuity with reform movements that occurred *before* the Protestant schism and were generally independent of them) and in part a Counter-Reformation, in direct response to Protestant reforms.[36] Luther's political thought, in this grand panoply of Catholic political thinking, attracted very little attention. However, not only were there significant convergences of Luther's political ideas with several currents of Catholic Reformation political thought, but there were also Counter-Reformation political theories that aimed to counter what were deemed the *political* errors (not to mention the litany of theological ones) of Lutheran and subsequent Protestant thinking.

From the start of the indulgences controversy, Luther's protest had some affinity with conciliarism. At first, this affinity was not a substantial defence of the authority of church councils, but rather was a criticism against what he considered to be illegitimate papal powers, as outlined in the *Disputation on the Power and Efficacy of Indulgences*. With a defence of extreme papalism coming from both Tetzel's theses, published in the spring of 1518, and Prierias's *Dialogue Against the Presumptuous Conclusions of Martin Luther*, published in the summer, the dispute quickly turned into one that centred on papalism rather than indulgences. In his defence, Luther was not a conciliarist: scripture was the final basis of authority. Councils, Luther believed, could

35 Hooker, *The Laws of Ecclesiastical Polity*, III; Skinner, *Foundations of Modern Political Thought*, vol. 2, 107.

36 For the complexities of early modern Catholicism as "Catholic Reformation" and/or "Counter-Reformation," see O'Malley, *Trent and All That*.

also err.[37] But after his meeting with Cardinal Cajetan in Augsburg on 18 November 1518 Luther *did* appeal to the authority of a church council to settle the growing dispute.[38]

Years before the indulgences controversy, Cajetan's papalism had been clearly established in two erudite and careful defences he made in opposition to the antipapal Council of Pisa (1511) while he served as master general of the Dominican order: *On the Comparison of the Authority of the Church and Council* (1511), and his *Apology* (1513). The conflict between the supporters of Pisa (which included the King of France and the Holy Roman emperor) and the papalists under Pope Julius II erupted into a war of words between Cajetan and a professor of theology and conciliarist at the University of Paris, Jacques Almain, who penned his treatise *A Book Concerning the Authority of the Church* – against Cajetan's work – in 1512.[39] Among Cajetan's arguments for papalism was the idea that the authority of the pope was, *unlike* that of temporal powers, the embodiment of a divine command, and so it could not be considered inferior to the corporate church and subject to its constitutional or legal limits, the way temporal authorities were subject to natural law as expressed in constitutional orders.[40] For Cajetan, Luther's denial of papal authority, at least in the form Cajetan understood it, was a denial of *the* authority of the church.

For Luther's part, his appeal to a future council was not based on any developed conciliar theory in the style of Almain, or on any number of the other disparate voices on the conciliarist side in the medieval age. Rather, he had appealed to the central truths of the church, as represented in a council, particularly the church's doctrine of salvation and the authority of scripture. On conciliarism in particular, Luther was henceforth silent until he published a string of treatises that coincided with Pope Paul III's call for a church council in 1536 (though Trent did not open until 1545). Luther's *Against the Council of Constance* (1535), *Disputation on the Power of Councils* (1536), and *On the Councils of the Church* (1539) nevertheless affirmed his original position: councils could err – the Council of Constance's condemnation of Jan Hus was for him proof enough – but insofar as they were

37 WA 1: 656. See Janz, *Westminster Handbook to Martin Luther*, 28–30.

38 WA 2: 34.

39 See these texts in Burns and Izbicki, *Conciliarism and Papalism.*

40 Ibid., xii–xiii.

true church councils, the authority of scripture would have to be clearly affirmed.

Of course, the papalism–conciliarism dispute was foremost a dispute over *ecclesiastical* authority, but as Cajetan's defence of papalism showed, church authority could be defined in distinction to temporal authority. Both Luther's *sola scriptura* and Cajetan's papalism shared the fact that church authority was based not on law or human understanding but on divine grace and revelation. Like Luther's secular kingdom, the basis for temporal authority, Cajetan's *Apology* implied, was natural law and human understanding.

In sixteenth-century Thomistic thinking, emphasis on the natural law basis of political rule, and thus the ability of human beings to live justly according to inherent reason, was a major pillar of their philosophy (following the rich philosophy of law in Thomas Aquinas's *Summa Theologiae*). But this emphasis also served as a major defence of Catholic polemics against Protestant heresies. Hence, in their scholarship the major Dominican theologians of the sixteenth century coupled their battle with heresies with their defence of Thomistic natural law. For example, Domingo de Soto (1495–1560), Charles V's representative for the opening of Trent and founding figure of a major Thomist school based in Salamanca, penned both the anti-Protestant polemic *On Nature and Grace* in 1547 and his *On Justice and Law* in 1553.

Many Thomist theories of the period began to argue that God indirectly gave secular government to mankind through the natural inclinations in human beings to govern and to be governed – by consent – in a political community.[41] Later Jesuit arguments in defence of papal authority, and against Protestant heresies, adopted this as a foundational idea for refuting Protestants and distinguishing the special nature of spiritual authority. Robert Bellarmine (1542–1621), in his *On the Temporal Power of the Pope*, famously distinguished papal power as indirect in civil affairs, but direct from God over the church; secular government, by contrast, came indirectly from God through humanity's "natural instinct to elect for [itself] a magistrate by whom to be governed."[42]

41 Skinner, *Foundations of Modern Political Thought*, vol. 2, 162–3.
42 Bellarmine, *On the Temporal Power of the Pope*, 186–7.

Countering the Lutheran insistence on justification by faith, Thomistic thinking (like de Soto's and, indeed, the statements on justification at the Council of Trent) sought to staunchly defend the ability of humanity to use its indwelling justice and goodness, apprehend the laws of God (both natural and revealed), and organize life (political and ecclesial) accordingly. The general problem of these refutations was that Luther had not in fact denied this ability in the first place: *sola fides* was a teaching about salvation, not about worldly righteousness and justice. Catholic polemics took Luther's justification by faith alone as an antinomian teaching for the whole of human life. Catholic polemicists, therefore, put Luther in the same heretical and rebellious category as the radical reformers, undermining all political authority and basing revelation on his individual interpretations. Luther's two kingdoms and law and gospel teachings, however, so central to his entire theology, abundantly and consistently showed those polemics to offer few convincing refutations and even fewer insights into his true political thought.

In general, despite the acerbic, foul-mouthed, and intemperate arguments between Lutheran and Catholic political thinkers of the sixteenth century, there was a great deal of common ground between them, particularly as both confessions grappled with limiting temporal authority over spiritual affairs and distinguishing what was properly spiritual from what was temporal. Even so, Luther's claim to be the most significant teacher of temporal authority once again breaks through this common ground and distinguishes him from the Catholic political thought of the period.

Luther had elevated temporal authority, which medieval thought had widely considered as subservient to spiritual power, to a calling and godly service. By and large, Catholic political thought of the sixteenth century continued to view both political and ecclesiastical authorities as an ordered hierarchy, reflective of the ordered hierarchy of God's creation and the hierarchy of laws, from human to eternal, that governed over us, punished the vicious, and encouraged the virtuous. Luther's political thought, and indeed his theology, while not altogether denying hierarchical arrangements of government, and certainly not denying the ability to live virtuously, denied any theory that could posit, for example, papal or imperial supremacy on the basis of a natural hierarchy of being. Luther's two kingdoms and his "three estates" unequivocally precluded the claims of clerical authority to have jurisdiction over temporal affairs, including marriage (hence, Luther blasted the canon laws on marriage), and precluded any pretentions civil magistrates had of wielding power over spiritual affairs. Magistrates were supreme in their own affairs, the Word was supreme in the church, and hence Luther denied *any* claims of subservience of one authority to the other. The kingdoms were bound together in this life. This, for Luther, was God's will, as expressed in the Bible and understood by reason.

7

The Significance of Luther's Political Thought

THE APPEALS OF LUTHER'S POLITICAL THOUGHT

Even at the conclusion of this study on Luther's political thought, few will agree that "not since the time of the apostles have the temporal sword and temporal government been so clearly described or so highly praised as by [him]."[1] This study does not aim to validate Luther's hyperbolic boast; the early sixteenth century alone provided many significant thinkers whose contributions to the history of political thought eclipsed Luther's. Niccolò Machiavelli is but one example. Yet this study does show that Luther's contribution to political thought was more significant than has been generally believed.

In several general ways, Luther's political thought appealed to an early modern age that faced an enormous crisis of political and ecclesiastical authority. His two kingdoms teaching possessed a broad explanatory power over not only government but also church, souls, individuals, and communities. Luther's political theory was also a biblical one: in an age that demanded renewal upon biblical meaning, it offered a vision of government that claimed to be sanctioned by a deeply considered examination of scripture that was nevertheless also accessible to the common person. Luther's political thought also elevated the status of political service vis-à-vis dedication and service to the church. Finally, in correlation with the last point, Luther consistently and emphatically praised *all* government as a precious gift

1 LW 46: 95; WA 19: 625.

from God. Each one of these aspects of Luther's political thought strengthened its appeal to a world suffering from the upheavals of reform and counter-reform.

The Explanatory Power of the Two Kingdoms

Luther's two kingdoms undergirded most of his political thinking, as he made clear in treatises such as *Temporal Authority* and *Whether Soldiers, Too, Can Be Saved.* With such a foundation, Luther's political thought grew out of this attempt to explain human existence in its relationships both to God and neighbours. Luther's two kingdoms has been accused of counselling, or at least resulting in, an inescapable and unresolvable ethical dualism between the duties of spiritual life and the duties owed to worldly affairs.[2] However, Luther's two kingdoms, and the political meaning derived from them, sought to *unify* human existence under God's complete governance.[3] There was never any *true* conflict between the demands of government and the freedom of the gospel, since God had ordained both kingdoms. Thus, the two kingdoms doctrine was Luther's guide to reconciling apparent conflict between them brought about by the limits of human understanding or by their sinful abuse.

It has been argued that the Protestant Reformation, including Luther, destroyed the medieval unity between human beings and the cosmos. Through the dominance of Western Christianity and the Roman Church, so the general argument goes, medieval political and social life was understood with reference to God's governance over the whole cosmos and the hierarchy of being he had created. Each station in life, prince or pope or baker, was understood within this cosmic and divine order. In destroying this order, the Protestant Reformation left human beings unmoored from an understanding of their place in God's creation. Jacques Maritain, for example, in his

2 See various treatments of this problem in Lohse, *Martin Luther's Theology*, 320–1; Janz, *Westminster Handbook to Martin Luther*, 50; and Althaus, *Ethics of Martin Luther*, 79–82. Wright provides an excellent overview of the interpretation of Luther's two kingdoms in the nineteenth and twentieth centuries and the supposed ethical problems associated with it in *Martin Luther's Understanding of God's Two Kingdoms*, 17–43.

3 Thus, Luther's two kingdoms doctrine was an ontological treatment of humanity, a theology of human beings that defined human existence in distinct relationships to God and his complete order of life. See Kolb and Arand, *The Genius of Luther's Theology*, 21–128.

Trois Réformateurs: Luther, Descartes, Rousseau, traced the modern collapse of social cohesion to Luther's supposed divorce of faith and reason; thus, Luther greatly contributed to the collapse of a medieval world order.[4] Whatever truth there is in this general argument – and certainly Luther *did* (at the very least) dispute the inherited place of the clergy in that medieval order – any view of him as a harbinger of *anomie* to a once-rooted medieval existence cannot be justified. The two kingdoms doctrine was a case in point: he used the distinction of these realms to resolve ethical and spiritual questions and conflicts – for example, how one could obey the prince to go to war *and* follow the commands of Christ – into an integrated (if nevertheless transitory and paradoxical) existence of being at once already saved and yet still mortal.

Luther's political thought, grounded in his two kingdoms teaching, aimed to aid all Christians in the discernment of their duties to God and neighbour in the often confusing and clashing claims that various worldly authorities demanded of their subjects. By founding temporal government on the universal ontology of inner and outer man, Luther sought to make his political and ethical teaching applicable and comprehensible to princes and lowly subjects alike. Thus, his political thought was meant to appeal to a wide range of people in a plethora of worldly stations and ranks. To the peasant or humble burger, Luther's two kingdoms offered comfort to troubled consciences over the demands that worldly powers sometimes foisted upon them. To the princes, Luther settled consciences over the need to enforce and coerce, versus the Christian ideal of love of neighbour. To the lowly (such as the peasant rebels in 1525), Luther warned against violent revolt; to the princes, he warned against abuse of power. All of this pastoral advice was consistent with the two kingdoms teaching. Moreover, while serving as the starting point for resolving these pastoral challenges, the two kingdoms also served as the guide to complex matters of church reform, even if, as shown earlier, the resolution of these matters for Luther's followers was not in accord with his own point of view on the separation of the kingdoms. Overall, therefore, the two kingdoms idea and the political teaching derived from it had a compelling explanatory power, with

4 Maritain, *Trois Réformateurs.*

wide-ranging applicability, to resolve political questions in the light of the evangelical message of *sola fides*.[5]

Seen in this way, Luther's two kingdoms could be considered to have precisely the opposite purpose and influence that Maritain had argued it had. Rather than promoting an *anomie* that divided reason and faith, the teaching aimed to integrate people of all ranks and standing into the divinely governed modes of inner and outer existence under God's sovereignty. In this light, the two kingdoms was a teaching much more medieval in character than interpretations like Maritain's appreciated. In fact, the interpretation of Luther as a medieval thinker has had its prominent defenders: Heiko Oberman's classic biography *Luther: Man between God and the Devil*, for example, provides an outstanding corrective for any hasty rendering of the reformer as a harbinger of all things modern.[6]

A Biblical Political Theory

Luther's political thought was also appealing because it was based on simple biblical truths that, in his view, could not be explained other than as binding truths for all Christians. Government was instituted by God and thus must be generally honoured and obeyed, as the apostles Peter and Paul had taught about the Roman emperors. But Christians must also heed the pivotal teachings of Jesus to turn the other cheek, love one's enemies, give over one's cloak, and give no resistance to an evildoer. Luther's political thought was an extension of his biblical interpretation that neither the injunctions of the apostles nor the teachings of Jesus could be ignored or rejected.

In our age and context, when the role of the Bible as a general cultural, spiritual, and civilizational loadstone has been removed, the power of Luther's political thought to teach human beings how to live with seemingly clashing biblical imperatives is too easily overlooked. Indeed, in the modern study of the history of political thought, the biblical basis for Luther's political ideas has typically

5 The appeal of the two kingdoms for Christian life extends far beyond the sixteenth century and among Lutherans. See the contemporary American Reformed theologian David VanDrunen's works *Natural Law and the Two Kingdoms* and *Living in God's Two Kingdoms*.

6 Oberman, *Luther: Man between God and the Devil*.

been only superficially understood in lieu of conjectural and tenuous connections between his thinking and a tradition of medieval political thought that he never analyzed or even mentioned. To understand Luther in context, the obvious must not be overlooked: his political thought was informed by an interpretation of the Bible, and as such it was meant to provide teaching and comfort across a wide swath of stations and ranks in sixteenth-century life and society.

In overlooking the biblical basis for his political thought, not only are his rich commentaries neglected as sources of this thinking, but more generally the depth of his biblical political thought – and with it the strength of its appeal – is neglected. Luther found biblical evidence for his political thought throughout the biblical canon, and sometimes in seemingly the oddest of places: Luther's view that the *Song of Songs* was an "encomium" of temporal authority, rather than being dismissed today as simply untrue or at least fanciful, ought to be understood as emblematic of his remarkably biblically grounded political ideas. Similarly, the notion of temporal government as a "holy order" in his *Lectures on Genesis* ought to hold a much more prominent place in its interpretation. Just as the relationship between Abraham and Abimelech modelled for Luther the proper relationship of the spiritual and temporal orders, it also showed that the proper understanding of temporal authority was both biblically revealed and understood by reason. Hence, we also find Luther (in his *Commentary on Psalm 101*) praising pagan political wisdom as true wisdom that complemented the wisdom revealed by the Bible.

The Elevation of Political Service

In 1520, with the publication of *To the Christian Nobility of the German Nation* and *The Babylonian Captivity of the Church*, Luther began a lifelong opposition to the supremacy of clerical status within the Christian community. For well over a millennium, Latin Christianity had privileged clerical life with a special status of vocation for God's work. In Luther's view, this privileged status was the source not only of the clergy's supreme authority, including political authority, over the laity, but also of a pervasive and underlying temptation of a works-based justification in the Christian church. Luther's reform based on *sola fides* aimed at overturning this long-standing view of clerical vocation, replacing it with an understanding that universalized vocation

(*Beruf*) among *all* baptized Christians. In Luther's view, in short, there was no difference in service to God between the baker, the labourer, the prince, and the monk: in God's eyes, each vocation was merely different in its "office."[7]

All walks of life served God and neighbour: among baptized Christians there was no hierarchy of vocations under the justification of God, for each Christian was called to serve in his or her walk or station. For Luther, the spiritual kingdom was radically equal in the eyes of God, even though there had to be offices of pastoral leadership and authority over the faithful. This spiritual equality of vocation had the effect of *elevating* political service from what Luther perceived to be its denigration by the church in the Middle Ages, thus restoring it to its proper place as a worthy calling. But this restoration of political service as divine vocation, coupled with the separation of kingdoms, had the combined effect of rendering political service, particularly princely and civic rule, as among the most important and honourable of all vocations. To be sure, Luther in no way argued that political callings were spiritually higher, as if to render them mirror images of the clerical and cloistered privileges that he so vociferously denounced; at the same time, however, he would repeatedly account for political service as a vocation unlike any other in its importance for the health and well-being of the community, both temporally and spiritually.

Consider again Luther's account of the godly ruler in his *Commentary on Psalm 82*: with responsibilities over his people that included securing the good in their persons and property against evildoers, securing the realm against outside threats, supporting good pastors, and the preaching of the Word, the good prince, Luther argued, was aptly given the ancient Roman title *pater patriae* (Father of the Fatherland), an honorific name that had been conferred by the Roman Senate on political greats such as Marcus Tullius Cicero, Julius Caesar, and Caesar Augustus. The vocation of Luther's good prince, as a *Landesvater* or *Heiland* (saviour of the country),[8] while by no means conferred with any special grace, was nevertheless elevated to a place of unequalled importance in this earthly life. Luther believed that

7 For an overall account of Luther's theology of vocation, see Wingren, *Luther on Vocation*.

8 LW 13: 58; WA 31 I: 205.

these titles were so appropriate for the godly prince that he used them in his *Sermons on the Catechism* (1528) and again in *The Large Catechism* (1529).[9]

Praise of Temporal Government

Belying a view that he was dour or quietistic about "the world," Luther's writings on temporal authority typically contained emphatic praise for what he considered to be one of God's greatest and most precious gifts. Strangely, in the history of political thought, this fact has gone largely unnoticed, despite the fact that it affords some insight into Luther's own thinking on the divine nature and origin of political government. Once again, his interpretation of the *Song of Songs* serves as a fine example of this praise. As an "encomium" of the political order, communicated through the passionate and erotic longing of the lover and the beloved, Luther argued that the poem was entirely fitting (with its earthly literal meaning) as praise of God's most precious gift to the world, temporal government. This commentary was no odd outlier to Luther's political thought, nor was it some strange attempt to interpret a strange biblical book, for such praise of government is found throughout his vast body of work. In his biblical commentaries, letters, treatises, polemics, and casual conversations (as recorded in the *Table Talk*), Luther insisted that temporal government was a most precious divine gift, worthy of honour and unyielding praise.

For Luther, this emphasis on the *praise* of government was for him an essential part of the effort to reform the church and to understand Christianity's relationship to temporal power. His boasting about *Temporal Authority* in his 1526 treatise *Whether Soldiers, Too, Can Be Saved* showed not only that he thought that the ideas about government in the work were sound, but also that he had insisted on thanksgiving and exultation for that most cherished divine gift. Luther wrote that this *praise* of government was one of his greatest contributions: "I might boast here that not since the time of the apostles have the temporal sword and temporal government been so clearly described *or so highly praised* as by me."[10] Luther's praise of

9 LW 51: 149–50; WA 30 I: 70–1; BC 406.

10 LW 46: 95. The emphasis is mine.

government was not merely rhetorical flourish but a fitting expression of the theological grounding upon which he had built his political thought.

LUTHER AND THE MODERN SECULAR STATE

Luther and the Modern State in Political Theory

What were the long-term influences and effects of Luther's political thought? A persistent argument in the study of political thought has been that Luther's thinking significantly contributed to the rise of the modern state. In his classic 1907 work, *Studies of Political Thought from Gerson to Grotius,* John Neville Figgis attempted to explain the modern state through several late medieval and early modern influences. After the papalism–conciliarism divide, but before the Huguenot and Presbyterian apologetics, the rise of the Society of Jesus, and the Dutch revolt against Spain, Figgis's Luther was a pivotal thinker in the rise of early modern absolutism. "Had there been no Luther," Figgis wrote, "there could never have been a Louis XIV."[11] "The medieval mind," he wrote, "conceived of its universal Church-State, with power ultimately fixed in the Spiritual head bounded by no territorial frontier; the Protestant mind places all ecclesiastical authority below the jurisdiction and subject to the control of the 'Godly prince,' who is omnipotent in his own dominion."[12] For Figgis, "Luther's conception of the State and of duty to one's neighbour paved the way for that of Hegel."[13] In Figgis's understanding, Luther's lasting contribution to politics was the sovereign territorial state and its denial of any extraterritorial community or authority.

Quentin Skinner's *The Foundations of Modern Political Thought* has been one of the most important and influential studies on the origins of modern political thought and the modern state. Rather than focusing on the writings of political thinkers as such, Skinner sought to present a history of political ideas in the late medieval and early modern period: "I begin in the late thirteenth century, and carry the story

11 Figgis, *Studies of Political Thought from Gerson to Grotius*, 62.
12 Ibid., 55.
13 Ibid., 62.

down to the end of the sixteenth, because it was during this period, I shall seek to show, that the main elements of a recognizably modern concept of the State were gradually acquired."[14] Skinner wished to distinguish his work from a "textualist" mode of political theory, which he faulted for not presenting genuine histories but, rather, only decontextualized interpretations of the great political texts.[15] Skinner's method aimed to more closely link political behaviour to political thought; he argued that scholars must grasp the ideological context of their authors in order to grasp what the authors were doing in writing great texts.[16] More precisely, Skinner sought to interpret important texts, survey ideological formation and change, and analyze the relation between ideology and the political action it represented.[17] Thus, Skinner's analysis of Luther placed its emphasis on the "social and intellectual matrix out of which his works arose."[18]

For Skinner, the key to understanding Luther's political thought was his insistence on the complete unworthiness of humankind.[19] By this insistence, Luther allied himself, Skinner argued, with the Augustinian world view against the Thomistic. It also led to the principle that would define Luther's reformation: justification by *sola fides*. From this overarching principle, Luther derived two revolutionary ideas: a devaluation of the church as a visible institution, and the displacement of the priesthood as an intermediary between God and humankind. Skinner argued that Luther's political ideas were implied in his theory of the church; since he deprived the church of jurisdictional powers, political powers were given much broader authority. The implication of Luther's theology, Skinner wrote, was that the "tremendous theoretical battle waged throughout the Middle Ages by the protagonists of the *regnum* and the *sacerdotium* [was]

14 Skinner, *Foundations of Modern Political Thought*, vol. 1, xi.

15 Responses to Skinner's criticism of the so-called textualists were made in the years following the book's publication; see Tarcov, "Quentin Skinner's Method and Machiavelli's *Prince*" and Zuckert, "Appropriation and Understanding in the History of Political Philosophy: On Quentin Skinner's Method."

16 Thus, his study of early modern political thought was founded on his original criticism of the conventional study of political philosophy; see Skinner, "Meaning and Understanding in the History of Ideas."

17 For a concise summary of Skinner's approach and method to the study of political philosophy, see Tully, "The Pen Is a Mighty Sword: Quentin Skinner's Analysis of Politics."

18 Skinner, *Foundations of Modern Political Thought*, vol. 1, x.

19 Ibid., vol. 2, 3.

suddenly brought to an end."[20] For Skinner, Luther's political writings embodied two principles of immense significance: the New Testament became the final authority on political and social questions (although Skinner did not explain how that worked in practice), and Christians were by Holy Writ required to submit themselves without qualification to governing authorities (although this principle itself, of course, must be carefully qualified). Skinner argued that there were many "forerunners of Lutheranism," which in part accounts for why his theological and political ideas were so influential for so long over so many countries.[21] But in Skinner's assessment Luther's contribution to the foundations of modern political thought was the encouraging and legitimizing of unified and absolutist monarchies.

Distinct from Skinner's methodology, but similar in its overarching aim to account for modern politics, Sheldon Wolin's *Politics and Vision* was written as an apology for "political philosophy in its traditional form" and a general defence of political philosophy against "those who were eager to jettison what remains of the tradition."[22] Within this project, Luther was seen as a harbinger of national particularism in his stalwart efforts to "depoliticize religion,"[23] which was particularly manifested in his campaign against the church hierarchy. Wolin argued that the Christian tradition throughout the Middle Ages, in its sacraments, systematic theology, and institutions, was infused with a subtle political language; Luther's reform, Wolin argued, sought to purge this language from the church. Wolin saw in Luther a bias against institutions, which had certain effects on both church and temporal government. In the church it had the effect of making Luther oppose monasticism and the papacy as "strictly human contrivings"; Luther's anti-institutionalism, Wolin argued, caused him to neglect the importance of religious institutions as political restraints.[24] He argued that Luther, by depoliticizing religion, deprived the political order of moral sustenance and thus furthered the political irrelevancy of any Christian ethics while at the same time

20 Ibid., 15.
21 Ibid., chap. 2, "Forerunners of Lutheranism," 20–64.
22 Wolin, *Politics and Vision*, v.
23 Ibid., 142.
24 Ibid., 159, 162.

freeing political power from restraint. Thus, Wolin agreed with Figgis that Luther contributed to political absolutism and the rise of the state, although for Wolin Luther's bias against ecclesial institutions contributed more to the rise of absolutism than any aspect of his positive political theory.

With such classic texts of political theory leading the way, Luther's political thought has since been strongly linked to the rise of the modern state and early modern absolutism in the history of political thought. But one major problem with this general view of Luther's political influence is that it fails to withstand the charge of anachronisms that distort his own foundational political ideas. The use of the word "state" is one such anachronism: to be sure, as Skinner describes, the word "state" began to be used in the sixteenth century, but there was no such use in Luther, and he was very far from employing *any* recognizable synonym for what "state" would come to mean for the political science of the twentieth and twenty-first centuries. "Religion" is also a word similarly difficult to apply to Luther: Wolin's argument, for example, on the "depoliticization" of "religion" assumes a category of "religion" and a category of "politics" that Luther would have found nearly incomprehensible: not only was his two kingdoms idea steeped in both biblical *and* political language, but he insisted that human life in either one was in the modern sense "religious," since one duly served God in *both*. Luther's own words and works defy political histories that link him too intimately with the advent of the modern state.

Complex Histories of Modernity and Secularism

The influence of Luther on the modern state is made even more suspect in light of recent historical and philosophical studies of modernity, secularism, and the Reformation. Considering the relationship between Luther's political thought and modern politics begs the question of how "modern" political thought and practice are to be defined. This is enormously difficult to answer, and there is no clear consensus among political theorists. For Leo Strauss and many of his students, modern political thought and practice began when the ancient standards of "the good" and the best life were rejected as the overarching purpose of politics in favour of an ethic of effective rule that assumes human beings to be vicious. For Strauss, the paragon of this modern shift was Machiavelli.[25] For Quentin Skinner and J.G.A. Pocock, as foremost theorists of an opposing school favouring contextual approaches to political thought, modern political thought similarly began with a turn of ideas and practice that is also strongly linked to Machiavelli and his teaching on "maintaining the state." Modernity begins, Skinner concludes in his second volume, when the foundations of the state – as an omnipotent and impersonal power – have been completed.[26] Luther, as the prominent figure in Skinner's volume on the Reformation, was part of that modern turn.

In both these historical theories, Luther's precise contributions to "modern" political thought and practice still remain very difficult to discern. On the one hand, there is a significant (and perhaps, for many, surprising) convergence between Luther's political ideas and Machiavelli's: to begin with, they share a similar "realist" emphasis on the necessity of coercive power, a similar criticism of ecclesial power, and a general agreement on the need for good laws with effective rule. On the other hand, the foundations of Luther's political thought greatly contrasted with Machiavelli's: the reformer's theological and biblical reasoning is *entirely* absent in *The Prince* or *The Discourses.* This fact is enormously significant for the interpretation of Luther in the project of modern political thought. The theological and biblical foundations of Luther's thinking preclude any simple assignment of his thought as representing either a rejection of ancient standards of "the good" (like Strauss's Machiavelli) or a proto-modern state thinker (like Skinner's Machiavelli). Luther's law and gospel theology, his insistence on salvation as *sola fides*, and his two kingdoms all point to a political order, created and sustained by God. For Luther, politics could not be seen or understood apart from the eternal governance of God. Thus, the "state" as "omnipotent" and "impersonal," or the prince needing to know how *not* to be good, could not in any way be countenanced, in Luther's thinking, through biblical revelation or natural reasoning.

In a manner closely related to his supposed influence on modern political thought, Luther has also been linked with the concomitant growth of secularism in modern politics. In this version of modern

25 Strauss, *Thoughts on Machiavelli* and "What Is Political Philosophy?"

26 Skinner, *Foundations of Modern Political Thought*, vol. 2, 358.

political history, for example Wolin's *Politics and Vision*, Luther is considered an early advocate of the separation of "church and state" and so an advocate of political thought and practice as a sphere of thought and action apart from religion. Behind this seminal role for Luther in the formation of modern political thought and practice is a history of secular progress. In its most famous Enlightenment and post-Enlightenment articulations, such as those of Auguste Comte (who welcomed it) and Max Weber (who was more ambivalent), is the idea that as civilization develops it invariably becomes secularized and accompanied by the loss of religious belief. Obviously, such an idea is a very long way from anything Luther envisioned or defended. But, apart from the anachronism with Luther's own thought, recent historians and philosophers, such as Charles Taylor in *A Secular Age*, have rather convincingly shown that the growth of secularism in the public sphere has been anything but a straight line of continual progress in Western history.[27] Secularism has by no means been an inevitable march of Enlightenment that brings the decline of religion. With the Enlightenment idea of the progress of secularism cast into doubt, and Luther's works showing abundant evidence *against* any relegation of "religion" outside the political sphere, a new account of secularity in modern political thought, and Luther's role in it, needs to be cast. Luther, who called political government a "holy order," cannot justifiably be seen as a separator of politics and religion: such an argument must be born out of ignorance of his thought, ignorance of the complexity of modern history, or both.

Luther's influence on the development of the modern secular state, a development he would have surely denounced, can perhaps be best argued as an indirect and unintentional consequence of this political thought. In a similar but much more global mode, Brad Gregory has recently argued in *The Unintended Reformation* that the sixteenth century's religious revolution, while intended to settle salvation in the afterlife and bring order to the world, brought the unintended consequences of pluralism and individual freedom.[28] If indeed Luther's political thought contributed to such an outcome, as Skinner and Wolin have argued, a new and much more complex

27 Taylor, *A Secular Age*.

28 Gregory, *The Unintended Reformation*.

history of Reformation political thought remains to be written, for the Luther of their accounts does not match the Luther we read.

This book begins this history by focusing on Luther's works and the immediate context in which he wrote, and its account of his political thought has aimed to hew as closely as possible to his own articulation. Thus, the emphasis is much more theological than previous of the history of political thought have typically been. If Luther contributed to the rise of the modern state or secular politics, this analysis ought to make that influence all the more striking, for his political thought was an extension and application of his theology and understanding of the Bible, and was not in the first order a political philosophy per se.[29] Indeed, if this argument holds true, then Luther's contributions to secular modernity were rooted first and foremost in his theology. Several significant examinations of Luther's theology and modernity have made compelling contributions to the assessment of this relationship. Joshua Mitchell's *Not by Reason Alone* examines Luther's interpretation of the Bible and his theology of human nature as a key to the changing ideas of authority in the early modern period.[30] Michael Allen Gillespie's *The Theological Origins of Modernity* emphasizes how Luther's theological focus on the Incarnation led to his new views on God's salvation, humanity, and nature, which echoed what Gillespie describes as the "nominalist revolution" in the theology and philosophy of the high middle ages.[31] These studies offer very compelling accounts of Luther's political and philosophical influence in later centuries.

But, as the scholarship of Gregory and Gillespie show, tracing and assessing the influence of certain ideas throughout the centuries is an arduous task. That task becomes even more complicated if "influence" includes rejections or inversions of the original meaning or intent of these ideas. To adequately answer how much Luther influenced political modernity – however that is defined – requires a treatment beyond the scope and purpose of this book and a deep engagement with the arguments and conclusions of the studies mentioned here. But by providing a comprehensive account of Luther's

29 This same point begins Forrester's essay, "Martin Luther and John Calvin," 318.

30 Joshua Mitchell, *Not by Reason Alone*.

31 See Gillespie, *The Theological Origins of Modernity*, 101–28.

political thought, grounded in a study of his works throughout his long career, this book has instead aimed to provide a clear and succinct account of what his political ideas were, based on a wide range of his works, and their immediate historical contexts. It has aimed to give an account that, based on all available primary sources and with appropriate criticism, is as close as possible to how Luther would have described the body of his political thought.

LUTHER AND THE "MOST PRECIOUS JEWEL" OF GOVERNMENT

Luther understood himself foremost as a preacher of the Word and a pastor of the gospel. His political thought, as we have seen, was inextricably bound to his evangelical theology and mission as a reformer of the church. As a pastor and preacher, Luther nevertheless directly confronted some of the most vexing questions of political thought, such as the legitimacy of coercion and the foundations of political authority. Luther also responded to these questions with rich, biblically based political ideas that he maintained consistently throughout his reforming career.

Luther's two kingdoms teaching grounded temporal authority as a divine gift of God to humanity for the sake of ordering worldly affairs, as distinct from the spiritual authority that communicated God's grace. Luther thereby believed that he was explaining how human beings existed as both "inner" and "outer" creatures. There was an overarching pastoral concern to this teaching, for Luther's two kingdoms, based on that theological and ontological distinction, fit well with the command of the New Testament that Christians were to be "in" the world but not "of" the world. The command of Christ to "turn the other cheek" and the teaching of Paul to obey all government were by no means, for Luther, antithetical teachings but deeply reconcilable directives to Christians that were to be at home in the created order *and* bestowed with Christ's saving grace. For Luther, not only was it possible to be saved by Christ and serve the political order; it was in fact imperative upon all faithful Christians to serve, honour, and praise temporal government, God's "most precious jewel on earth."

Bibliography

Althaus, Paul. *The Ethics of Martin Luther.* Translated by Robert Schultz. Philadelphia: Fortress Press, 1972.

Angermeier, Heinz. *Die Reichsreform 1410–1555: Die Staatsproblematik in Deutschland zwishen Mittelalter und Gegenwart.* Munich: C.H. Beck, 1984.

Arand, Charles P., Robert Kolb, and James A. Nestingen. *The Lutheran Confessions: History and Theology of the Book of Concord.* Minneapolis: Fortress Press, 2012.

Aulinger, Rosemarie, ed. *Deutsche Reichstagsakten unter Kaiser Karl V*, vol. 3. Göttingen: Vandenhoeck & Ruprecht, 1972.

Bainton, Roland. "The Bible in the Reformation." In *The Cambridge History of the Bible*, vol. 3, *The West From the Reformation to the Present Day*, edited by S.L. Greenslade, 1–37. Cambridge: Cambridge University Press, 1963.

Baker, J. Wayne. "Church Discipline or Civil Punishment: On the Origins of the Reformed Schism, 1528–1531." *Andrews University Seminary Studies* 23, no. 1 (1985): 3–18.

Banner, Helen. "Hierocratic Arguments." In *Encyclopedia of Political Theory*, edited by Mark Bevir, vol. 2, 620–8. Thousand Oaks, CA: Sage, 2010.

Barth, Hans-Martin. *The Theology of Martin Luther: A Critical Assessment.* Translated by Linda M. Maloney. Minneapolis: Fortress Press, 2013.

Barth, Karl. Review of *Religiöser Sozialismus: Grundfragen der christlichen Sozialethik*, by Paul Althaus. *Das Neue Werk* 4 (1922), 461–72.

Baylor, Michael G., ed. *The Radical Reformation.* Cambridge: Cambridge University Press, 1991.

Bellarmine, Robert. *On the Temporal Power of the Pope.* In *On Temporal and Spiritual Authority*, edited by Stefania Tutino. Indianapolis: Liberty Fund, 2012.

Benecke, Gerhard. *Maximilian I (1459–1519): An Analytical Biography*. London: Routledge and Kegan Paul, 1982.

Berman, Harold J. *Law and Revolution II: The Impact of the Protestant Reformations on the Western Legal Tradition*. Cambridge, MA: Harvard University Press, 2003.

Black, Christopher F. "Perugia and Papal Absolutism in the Sixteenth Century." *The English Historical Review* 96, no. 380 (1981): 509–39.

Blickle, Peter. *The Revolution of 1525: The German Peasants' War from a New Perspective*. Translated by Thomas A. Brady Jr. and H.C. Midelfort. Baltimore: Johns Hopkins University Press, 1985.

Bohnstedt, John W. "The Infidel Scourge of God: The Turkish Menace as Seen by German Pamphleteers of the Reformation Era." *Transactions of the American Philosophical Society* 58, no. 9 (1968): 1–58.

Brandi, Karl. *The Emperor Charles V*. London: J. Cape, 1939.

Brecht, Martin. *Martin Luther: His Road to Reformation, 1483–1521*. Translated by James A. Schaaf. Minneapolis: Fortress Press, 1985.

– *Martin Luther: Shaping and Defining the Reformation*. Translated by James L. Schaaf. Minneapolis: Fortress Press, 1990.

– *Martin Luther: The Preservation of the Church, 1532–1546*. Translated by James L. Schaaf. Minneapolis: Fortress Press, 1993.

Bubenheimer, Ulrich. "Thomas Müntzer." In *The Oxford Encyclopedia of the Reformation*, vol. 3, edited by Hans J. Hillerbrand and translated by Michael G. Baylor, 99–102. Oxford: Oxford University Press, 1996.

Burns, J.H., and Thomas M. Izbicki. *Conciliarism and Papalism*. Cambridge: Cambridge University Press, 1997.

Calvin, John. *Institutes of the Christian Religion*, 1536 edition. Translated by Ford Lewis Battles. Grand Rapids, MI: Eerdmans, 1986.

Cameron, Euan. *The European Reformation*. Oxford: Oxford University Press, 1991.

Cargill Thompson, W.D.J. "Luther and the Right of Resistance to the Emperor." *Studies in Church History* 15 (1975): 159–202.

– *The Political Thought of Martin Luther*. Sussex: Harvester Press, 1984.

– "The Two Kingdoms and the Two Regiments: Some Problems of Luther's *Zwei-Reiche-Lehre*." *The Journal of Theological Studies* 20, no. 1 (1969): 164–85.

Carty, Jarrett A. *Divine Kingdom, Holy Order: The Political Writings of Martin Luther*. St Louis, MO: Concordia Publishing House, 2012.

– "Martin Luther's Political Interpretation of the Song of Songs." *Review of Politics* 73, no. 2 (2011): 449–67.

Chastel, André. *The Sack of Rome*. Translated by Beth Archer. Princeton, NJ: Princeton University Press, 1983.

Cochlaeus, Johannes. *The Deeds of Martin Luther From the Year of the Lord 1517 to the Year 1546 Related Chronologically to all Posterity*. In *Luther's Lives*, translated by Elizabeth Vandiver, Ralph Keen, and Thomas D. Frazel. Manchester: Manchester University Press, 2002.

Creasman, Allyson F. *Censorship and Civic Order in Reformation Germany, 1517–1648*. Surrey: Ashgate, 2012.

Dante Alighieri. *Monarchy*. Edited and translated by Prue Shaw. Cambridge: Cambridge University Press, 1996.

Delumeau, Jean. "Rome: Political and Administrative Centralization in the Papal State in the Sixteenth Century." In *The Late Italian Renaissance, 1525–1630*, edited by Eric Cochrane, 1525–630. New York: Harper Torchbooks, 1970.

Ebeling, Gerhard. "Der vierfache Schriftsinn und die Unterscheidung von litera und spiritus." In *Lutherstudien I*, 51–61. Tübingen: J.C.B. Mohr, 1971.

– "On the Doctrine of the *Triplex Usus Legis* in the Theology of the Reformation." In *Word and Faith*, translated by James W. Leitch, 62–78. Philadelphia: Fortress Press, 1963.

Engelbrecht, Edward A. *Friends of the Law: Luther's Use of the Law for Christian Life*. St Louis: Concordia Publishing House, 2011.

Estes, James M. *Peace, Order, and the Glory of God: Secular Authority and the Church in the Thought of Luther and Melanchthon*. Leiden: E.J. Brill, 2005.

Figgis, John N. *Studies of Political Thought from Gerson to Grotius*. Cambridge: Cambridge University Press, 1923.

Fisher-Galati, Stephen. *Ottoman Imperialism and German Protestantism, 1521–1555*. Cambridge: Harvard University Press, 1959.

Forrester, Duncan. "Martin Luther and John Calvin." In *History of Political Philosophy*, 3rd ed., edited by Leo Strauss and Joseph Cropsey, 318–55. Chicago: University of Chicago Press, 1987.

Francisco, Adam S. *Martin Luther and Islam: A Study in Sixteenth-Century Polemics and Apologetics*. Leiden: Brill, 2007.

Frommel, Christoph L. "Papal Policy: The Planning of Rome during the Renaissance." *Journal of Interdisciplinary History* 17, no. 1 (1986): 39–65.

Furcha E.J. and H. Wayne Pipkin, eds. and trans. *Selected Writings of Huldrych Zwingli*. Eugene, OR: Wipf and Stock, 1984.

Gilbert, Felix. *The Pope, His Banker, and Venice*. Cambridge: Harvard University Press, 1980.

Gillespie, Michael Allen. *The Theological Origins of Modernity*. Chicago: University of Chicago Press, 2008.

Gregory, Brad S. *The Unintended Reformation*. Cambridge, MA: Belknap Press of Harvard University Press, 2012.

Gritcsh, Eric W. *Martin Luther's Anti-Semitism: Against His Better Judgment.* Grand Rapids, MI: Eerdmans, 2012.

– *Reformer without a Church: The Life of Thomas Muentzer.* Philadelphia: Fortress Press, 1967.

Harran, Marilyn J. *Martin Luther: Learning for Life.* St. Louis, MO: Concordia Publishing House, 1997.

Höpfl, Harro. *The Christian Polity of John Calvin.* Cambridge: Cambridge University Press, 1982.

– *Luther and Calvin on Secular Authority.* Cambridge: Cambridge University Press, 1991.

Howard, Thomas Albert. "Reformation Commemorations: Then and Now." Lecture. Gordon College, Wenham, MA, 15 November 2013.

Janz, Denis R. *The Westminster Handbook to Martin Luther.* Louisville, KY: Westminster John Knox Press, 2010.

John of Paris. *On Royal and Papal Power.* Translated by Arthur P. Monahan. New York: Columbia University Press, 1974.

Junghans, Helmar "The Augsburg Confession." In *The Oxford Encyclopedia of the Reformation,* vol. 1, edited by Hans J. Hillerbrand and translated by Robert E. Shillenn, 93–7. Oxford: Oxford University Press, 1996.

Kingdon, Robert M. "The Political Thought of Peter Martyr Vermigli." In *Peter Martyr Vermigli and Italian Reform,* edited by Joseph C. McClelland, 121–40. Waterloo, ON: Wilfrid Laurier University Press, 1981.

Kirchener, Hubert. *Luther and the Peasants' War.* Translated by Daryl Jodock. Philadelphia: Fortress Press, 1972.

Kittelson, James M. "Luther as Educational Reformer." In *Luther and Learning,* edited by Marilyn J. Harran, 95–114. London: Associated University Press, 1985.

Kolb, Robert and Charles P. Arand. *The Genius of Luther's Theology.* Grand Rapids, MI: Baker Academic, 2008.

Krieger, Karl-Friedrich. *König, Reich und Reichsreform im Spätmittelalter.* Munich: R. Oldenbourng Verlag, 1992.

Kristeller, Paul Oskar. "Humanism." In *The Cambridge History of Renaissance Philosophy,* edited by Charles B. Schmitt, 113–38. Cambridge: Cambridge University Press, 1988.

Lohse, Bernhard. *Martin Luther's Theology.* Translated by Roy A. Harrisville. Minneapolis: Fortress Press, 1999.

Luther, Martin. *Luther's Works.* American edition. Edited by Jaroslav Pelikan, Hilton C. Oswald, and Helmut T. Lehmann. 79 vols. Saint Louis,

Philadelphia, and Minneapolis: Concordia Publishing House and Fortress Press, 1955–.

– *Martin Luthers Werke: Kritische Gesamtausgabe, Briefwechsel.* 18 vols. Weimar: Böhlau, 1930–1985.

– *Martin Luthers Werke: Kritische Gesamtausgabe, Schriften.* 85 vols. Weimar: Böhlau, 1883–.

– *Martin Luthers Werke: Kritische Gesamtausgabe, Tischreden.* 6 vols. Weimar: Böhlau, 1912–21.

Machiavelli, Niccolò. *Discourses on Livy.* Translated by Harvey C. Mansfield and Nathan Tarcov. Chicago: University of Chicago Press, 1996.

Mäkinen, Virpi. *Lutheran Reformation and the Law.* Leiden: Brill, 2006.

Maritain, Jacques. *Trois Réformateurs: Luther, Descartes, Rousseau.* Paris: Plon, 1925.

Marsilius of Padua, *Defensor Pacis.* Edited and translated by Alan Gewirth. Toronto: University of Toronto Press, 1980.

Maxfield, John A. *Luther's Lectures on Genesis and the Formation of Evangelical Identity.* Kirksville, MO: Truman State University Press, 2008.

McGovern, William M. *From Luther to Hitler: The Story of Fascist-Nazi Political Philosophy.* Boston: Houghton-Mifflin, 1941.

McGrath, Alister E. *The Intellectual Origins of the European Reformation.* Oxford: Basil Blackwell, 1987.

– *Luther's Theology of the Cross: Martin Luther's Theological Breakthrough.* Oxford: Basil Blackwell, 1985.

– *Reformation Thought: An Introduction.* Oxford: Blackwell, 1999.

Melanchthon, Philip. Corpus Reformatorum. Philip Melanthonis opera qua supersunt omnia. Edited by Karl Gottlief Bretschneider and Heinrich Ernst Bindseil. 28 vols. Halle and Braunschweig: Schwetschke, 1834–60.

Miller, Gregory J. "Luther on the Turks and Islam." *Lutheran Quarterly* 14 (2000): 79–97.

Mitchell, Joshua. *Not by Reason Alone.* Chicago: University of Chicago Press, 1993.

Nischan, Bodo. "Albert of Brandenburg." In *The Oxford Encyclopedia of the Reformation,* vol. 1, edited by Hans J. Hillerbrand and translated by Robert E. Shillenn, 15–6. Oxford: Oxford University Press, 1996.

Oberman, Heiko A. *Luther: Man between God and the Devil.* Translated by Eileen Walliser-Schwarzbart. New York: Doubleday, 1990.

O'Malley, John W. *Praise and Blame in Renaissance Rome.* Durham, NC: Duke University Press, 1979.

– *Trent and All That: Renaming Catholicism in the Early Modern Era.* Cambridge, MA: Harvard University Press, 2000.

Ozment, Stephen. *The Age of Reform, 1250–1550.* New Haven, CT: Yale University Press, 1980.

Parker, Geoffrey. "The Political World of Charles V." In *Charles V, 1500–1558, and his Time,* edited by Hugo Soly, 113–226. Antwerp, Belgium: Mercatorfonds, 1999.

Partner, Peter. *The Lands of St. Peter: The Papal State in the Middle Ages and the Early Renaissance.* Berkeley: University of California Press, 1972.

– "Papal Financial Policy in the Renaissance and Counter-Reformation." *Past and Present* 88, no. 1 (1980): 17–62.

– *Renaissance Rome.* Berkeley: University of California Press, 1976.

Post, Regnerus Richardus. *The Modern Devotion: Confrontation with Reformation and Humanism.* Leiden: E.J. Brill, 1968.

Potter, G.R. *Zwingli.* Cambridge: Cambridge University Press, 1976.

Prodi, Paulo. *The Papal Prince: One Body, Two Souls; The Papal Monarchy in Europe.* Cambridge: Cambridge University Press, 1987.

Rex, Richard. "Humanism." In *The Reformation World,* edited by Andrew Pettegree, 51–70. London: Routledge, 2000.

Schramm, Brooks and Kirsi I. Stjerna, eds. *Martin Luther, the Bible, and the Jewish People: A Reader.* Minneapolis: Fortress Press, 2012.

Schwiebert, E.G. *Luther and His Times.* St Louis, MO: Concordia Publishing House, 1950.

– "The Medieval Pattern in Luther's View of the State." *Church History* 12, no. 2 (1943): 98–117.

Scott, Tom, and Robert W. Scribner, eds. *The German Peasants' War: A History in Documents.* Atlantic Highlands, NJ: Humanities Press, 1990.

Shaw, Christine. *Julius II: The Warrior Pope.* Oxford: Oxford University Press, 1993.

Shirer, William S. *The Rise and Fall of the Third Reich: A History of Nazi Germany.* New York: Simon and Schuster, 1960.

Shoenberger, Cynthia Grant. "Luther and the Justifiability of Resistance to Legitimate Authority." *Journal of the History of Ideas* 40, no. 1 (1979): 3–20.

Siemon-Netto, Uwe. *The Fabricated Luther: The Rise and Fall of William Shirer's Myth.* St Louis, MO: Concordia Publishing House, 1995.

Skinner, Quentin. *The Foundations of Modern Political Thought,* vol. 1, *The Renaissance.* Cambridge: Cambridge University Press, 1978.

– *The Foundations of Modern Political Thought,* vol. 2, *The Age of Reformation.* Cambridge: Cambridge University Press, 1978.

– "Meaning and Understanding in the History of Ideas." *History and Theory* 8, no. 1 (1969): 3–53.

Spitz, Lewis W. *Luther and German Humanism.* Brookfield, VT: Variorium, 1996.

– "Luther and Humanism." In *Luther and Learning: the Wittenberg University Luther Symposium,* edited by Marilyn J. Harran, 69–94. Selinsgrove, PA: Susquehanna University Press, 1983.

– "Luther's Ecclesiology and His Concept of the Prince as *Notbischof.*" *Church History,* 22 (1953): 113–41.

Steinmetz, David C. "Luther and the Late Medieval Augustinians: Another Look." *Concordia Theological Monthly* 44, no. 4 (1973): 245–60.

– *Luther and Staupitz: An Essay in the Intellectual Origins of the Protestant Reformation.* Durham, NC: Duke University Press, 1980.

Stinger, Charles L. *The Renaissance in Rome.* Bloomington: Indiana University Press, 1985.

Strauss, Leo. *Thoughts on Machiavelli.* Chicago: University of Chicago Press, 1958.

– "What Is Political Philosophy?" In *What Is Political Philosophy? and Other Studies.* Chicago: University of Chicago Press, 1959.

Tarcov, Nathan. "Quentin Skinner's Method and Machiavelli's *Prince.*" *Ethics* 92, no. 4 (1982): 692–709.

Taylor, Charles. *A Secular Age.* Cambridge, MA: Belknap Press of Harvard University Press, 2007.

Tully, James. "The Pen Is a Mighty Sword: Quentin Skinner's Analysis of Politics." In *Meaning and Context: Quentin Skinner and His Critics,* 7–25. Cambridge: Polity Press, 1988.

VanDrunen, David. *Living in God's Two Kingdoms: A Biblical Vision for Christianity and Culture.* Wheaton, IL: Crossway Books, 2010.

– *Natural Law and the Two Kingdoms: A Study in the Development of Reformed Social Thought.* Grand Rapids, MI: Eerdmans, 2010.

Walton, Robert C. *Zwingli's Theocracy.* Toronto: University of Toronto Press, 1967.

Wengert, Timothy J. "Philip Melanchthon and a Christian *Politics.*" *Lutheran Quarterly* 17, no. 1 (2003): 29–62.

Westfall, Carroll William. *In This Most Perfect Paradise: Alberti, Nicholas V, and the Invention of Conscious Urban Planning in Rome, 1447–1455.* University Park: Penn State University Press, 1974.

Whitford, David M. "*Cura religionis* or Two Kingdoms: The Late Luther on Religion and the State in the Lectures on Genesis." *Church History* 73, no. 1 (2004): 41–62.

– *Tyranny and Resistance: The Magdeburg Confession and the Lutheran Tradition.* St Louis, MO: Concordia Publishing House, 2001.

Wiesflecker, Hermann. *Kaiser Maximilian I: Das Reich, Österreich und Europa an der Wende zur Neuzeit.* Vienna: Oldenbourg Verlag, 1971–86.

Williams, George H. "The Radical Reformation." In *Oxford Encyclopedia of the Reformation*, vol. 3, edited by Hans J. Hillerbrand and translated by Michael G. Baylor, 375–84. Oxford: Oxford University Press, 1996.

– *The Radical Reformation*, 3rd ed. Kirksville, Missouri: Truman State University Press, 2000.

Wingren, Gustaf. *Luther on Vocation.* Translated by Carl C. Rasmussen. Eugene, OR: Wipf and Stock, 2004.

Witte Jr., John. *From Sacrament to Contract: Marriage, Religion, and Law in the Western Tradition.* Louisville, KY: Westminster John Knox Press, 2012.

– *Law and Protestantism.* Cambridge: Cambridge University Press, 2002.

– *The Reformation of Rights: Law, Religion, and Human Rights in Early Modern Calvinism.* Cambridge: Cambridge University Press, 2007.

Wolgast, Eike. "Protestation of Speyer." In *The Oxford Encyclopedia of the Reformation*, vol. 4, edited by Hans J. Hillerbrand and translated by Susan M. Sisler, 103–5. Oxford: Oxford University Press, 1996.

Wolin, Sheldon. *Politics and Vision: Continuity and Innovation in Western Political Thought.* Princeton: Princeton University Press, 2004.

Wright, William J. *Martin Luther's Understanding of God's Two Kingdoms.* Grand Rapids, MI: Baker Academic, 2010.

Zophy, Jonathan W. "Electors." In *The Oxford Encyclopedia of the Reformation*, vol. 2, edited by Hans J. Hillerbrand, 31–2. Oxford: Oxford University Press, 1996.

Zuckert, Michael. *Launching Liberalism.* Lawrence: University Press of Kansas, 2002.

Index